CHILD ABUSE AND VIOLENCE

CHILD ABUSE AND VIOLENCE

TOM I. RICHARDSON AND MARSHA V. WILLIAMS
EDITORS

Nova Biomedical Books
New York

Copyright © 2008 by Nova Science Publishers, Inc.

All rights reserved. No part of this book may be reproduced, stored in a retrieval system or transmitted in any form or by any means: electronic, electrostatic, magnetic, tape, mechanical photocopying, recording or otherwise without the written permission of the Publisher.

For permission to use material from this book please contact us:
Telephone 631-231-7269; Fax 631-231-8175
Web Site: http://www.novapublishers.com

NOTICE TO THE READER

The Publisher has taken reasonable care in the preparation of this book, but makes no expressed or implied warranty of any kind and assumes no responsibility for any errors or omissions. No liability is assumed for incidental or consequential damages in connection with or arising out of information contained in this book. The Publisher shall not be liable for any special, consequential, or exemplary damages resulting, in whole or in part, from the readers' use of, or reliance upon, this material.

Independent verification should be sought for any data, advice or recommendations contained in this book. In addition, no responsibility is assumed by the publisher for any injury and/or damage to persons or property arising from any methods, products, instructions, ideas or otherwise contained in this publication.

This publication is designed to provide accurate and authoritative information with regard to the subject matter covered herein. It is sold with the clear understanding that the Publisher is not engaged in rendering legal or any other professional services. If legal or any other expert assistance is required, the services of a competent person should be sought. FROM A DECLARATION OF PARTICIPANTS JOINTLY ADOPTED BY A COMMITTEE OF THE AMERICAN BAR ASSOCIATION AND A COMMITTEE OF PUBLISHERS.

Library of Congress Cataloging-in-Publication Data

Child abuse and violence / Tom I. Richardson and Marsha V. Williams, editors.
  p. cm.
 ISBN 978-1-60456-128-9 (hardcover)
 1. Child abuse. 2. Child welfare. 3. Children--Violence against. I. Richardson, Tom I. II. Williams, Marsha V.
 HV6626.5.C485 2007
 362.76--dc22
           2007047059

Published by Nova Science Publishers, Inc. ✤ New York

Contents

Preface   vii

Chapter I   The Need for Systematic and Intensive Training of Forensic Interviewers   1
Ann-Christin Cederborg and Michael E. Lamb

Chapter II   Physical Abuse of Children Born to Adolescent Mothers: The Continuation of the Relationship into Adult Motherhood and the Role of Identity   19
Tracie O. Afifi and Douglas A. Brownridge

Chapter III   Empirical Support for a Conceptual Model of Posttraumatic Stress Disorder among Survivors of Child Sexual Abuse   43
Oxana Gronskaya Palesh, Elizabeth Looney, Daniel Batiuchok, Cheryl Koopman, Karni Ginzburg, Mydzung Bui, Catherine C. Classen, Bruce Arnow and David Spiegel

Chapter IV   Problems with the Social Treatment of Child Abuse Cases in Japan : The Forensic Pathologist's View   59
Masataka Nagao and Yoshitaka Maeno

Chapter V   Adam Walsh Child Protection and Safety Act: A Sketch   81
Charles Doyle

Chapter VI   Internet: Status Report on Legislative Attempts to Protect Children from Unsuitable Material on the Web   89
Marcia S. Smith

Chapter VII   Intra-Familial Sexual Abuse (Incest) among Korean Adolescents   97
Kim Hyun Sil and Kim Hun Soo

Chapter VIII   Model of Abuse Prophylaxis for Academy Community   115
Elizabeth Krawczyk

Chapter IX	Outcomes of Parental Corporal Punishment: Psychological Maladjustment and Physical Abuse *Piyanjali de Zoysa, Peter A. Newcombe and Lalini Rajapakse*	**121**
Index		**163**

Preface

Child abuse and neglect is as, at a minimum any recent act or failure to act on the part of a parent or caretaker which results in death, serious physical or emotional harm, sexual abuse or exploitation; or an act or failure to act which presents an imminent risk of serious harm. Four major types of maltreatment are usually included: neglect, physical abuse, sexual abuse, and emotional abuse. Although any of the forms of child maltreatment may be found separately, they often occur in combination. This new book presents new and important research in the field.

Chapter I - This chapter emphasizes the need to further encourage and train forensic interviewers to follow expert recommendations in how to forensically interview children.

Children from about 4 years of age are able to give information in response to open ended questions and details elicited in this way are more likely to be accurate. Younger children are, however, more likely than older children to give inaccurate information in response to yes/no questions, to respond affirmatively to misleading questions about non experienced events, and to acquiesce to suggestions.

Research presented in this chapter show that forensic interviewers do not follow best practice guidelines. Altogether 20 police officers and 130 children were involved in the analysis. The police officers did not provide children of all ages with sufficient opportunities to retrieve information in response to open-ended prompts before resorting to more focused prompts, especially when invitations elicited more details than did focused prompts from children of all ages.

Previous researchers have show that, when interviewers are intensively trained over a longer period of time in courses that involve systematic, repeated practices, feed-back monitored stimulations, and systematic analysis of actual recorded forensic interviews the training can be successful. Such competence will make it easier for the children to be believed when reporting about their experiences. Considering the fact that open ended questions are more likely to be accurate, this chapter suggests that planners of interviewing courses need to focus more attention on ways to improve interviewer behaviour. Otherwise there is a continued risk that the quality of information provided by children can be called in question because interviewers lack competence.

Chapter II - Child abuse can have devastating consequences for children and families. In terms of prevention and intervention efforts, it is important to identify populations at increased risk for child abuse. It is well established in the child abuse literature that children born to adolescent mothers are at a heightened risk for the perpetration of child abuse. However, little is known about the extent to which this relationship persists among those who became mothers as adolescents but are now within adulthood. Such knowledge is important since adolescence is a relatively short period in the lifecycle, but is one that sets the stage for a lifetime of parenting, including abusive parenting. Applying Erikson's theory, it is argued that impaired identity resulting from adolescent parenthood will increase the risk of child abuse. The purpose of this study is to investigate the manner in which variables that serve as proxies for identity formation, namely education, employment, and self-esteem, are associated with child abuse among children of formerly adolescent mothers (FAMs). Using a representative sample of 4,387 Canadian mothers, both descriptive and logistic regression analyses are conducted. The results demonstrate that children of FAMs are, indeed, more likely to be abused than children of non-FAMs. With few exceptions, the identity variables operate as hypothesized. However, the multivariate analyses show that identity formation alone is an insufficient explanation for the higher likelihood of child abuse for children of FAMs. Not only do the results suggest that Erikson's theory is inadequate as an explanation of the heightened risk of child abuse of children born to FAMs', but the analyses also imply that a more holistic approach is needed to fully comprehend this phenomenon. The paper concludes with a proposed holistic framework for understanding FAMs higher likelihood of child abuse.

Chapter III - Previous research has documented many detrimental psychological and behavioral consequences of child sexual abuse. One of the long-term effects of childhood sexual abuse (CSA) is the development of posttraumatic stress disorder (PTSD) symptoms. It is important to take steps toward development and validation of a conceptual model that identifies key characteristics associated with PTSD among survivors of child sexual abuse. Such a model can be helpful in developing a more coherent understanding of problems closely associated with PTSD in this population for the purpose of improving treatment programs for CSA survivors. The conceptual model that is examined in this study focused on key aspects of the sense of self, which would appear to involve core aspects of traumatic stress associated with CSA. Specifically, this study examined several self-development characteristics that included beliefs about self worth, guilt, shame, and identity impairment in relation to PTSD symptoms in women with a history of child sexual abuse. Research participants were 139 women with a history of child sexual abuse who were considered to be at high risk for HIV infection due to abuse of drugs or alcohol, engaging in risky sex and/or having a history of sexual revictimization. Participants completed self-report measures that assessed abuse specific factors (including the duration of their child sexual abuse and the number of times that they had been sexually abused in childhood), as well as their self-development characteristics (their beliefs about self worth, abuse-related guilt and shame, and identity impairment), and their PTSD symptoms. Multiple linear regression examined whether beliefs about self worth, guilt, shame, and identity impairment accounted for a significant amount of variance in predicting PTSD symptoms. The results showed that this model accounted for 39% of the variance in PTSD symptoms ($adj\ R^2 = .35$), with PTSD symptoms found to be significantly related to longer duration of abuse, greater sense of shame, and greater identity impairment. These findings indicate that the duration of abuse and shame and identity impairment are sources of difficulty for CSA survivors and suggest that these factors may contribute to the development of PTSD symptoms. In addition, the results suggest that treatment providers need to address shame and identity issues in treating PTSD symptoms in CSA survivors.

Chapter IV - The authors present five cases of fatal child abuse and highlight the problems associated with social treatment of child abuse cases in Japan. Recently, in Japan, there have been fatal child abuse cases in which neighbors have been aware of the signs of abuse but have not notified the Child Care Authorities. Lack of concern about child welfare in the community is the greatest obstacle to protecting children at risk of abuse. The most effective means of preventing child abuse is to educate the community about how to recognize the signs of abuse and to inform the authorities. The authors emphasize that the community has an obligation to protect children against crime, including child abuse.

The role of the Social Services in preventing child abuse has been extended. Forensic pathologists are now required to play key roles in child abuse prevention, and in Japan their activity should be extended to the administrative field.

Chapter V - The Adam Walsh Child Protection and Safety Act, P.L. 109-248 (H.R. 4472), serves four purposes. It reformulates the federal standards for sex offender registration in state, territorial and tribal sexual offender registries, and does so in a manner designed to make the system more uniform, more inclusive, more informative and more readily available to the public online. It amends federal criminal law and procedure, featuring a federal procedure for the civil commitment of sex offenders, random search authority over sex offenders on probation or supervised release, a number of new federal crimes, and sentencing enhancements for existing federal offenses. It creates, amends, or revives several grant programs designed to reinforce private, state, local, tribal and territorial prevention; law enforcement; and treatment efforts in the case of crimes committed against children. It calls for a variety of administrative or regulatory initiatives in the interest of child safety, such as the creation of the National Child Abuse Registry.

This is an abridged version of CRS Report RL33967, *Adam Walsh Child Protection and Safety Act: A Legal Analysis*, by Charles Doyle, without the footnotes and citations to authority found in the longer report.

Chapter VI - Preventing children from encountering unsuitable material, such as pornography, as they use the Internet is a major congressional concern. Several laws have been passed, including the 1996 Communications Decency Act (CDA), the 1998 Child Online Protection Act (COPA), and the 2000 Children's Internet Protection Act (CIPA). Federal courts ruled, in turn, that certain sections of CDA, COPA, and CIPA were unconstitutional. All the decisions were appealed to the Supreme Court. The Supreme Court upheld the lower court decision on CDA in 1997. It has heard COPA twice, in 2002 and 2004, and each time remanded the case to a lower court; an injunction against the law's enforcement remains in place. The Supreme Court upheld CIPA on June 23, 2003. Congress also passed the "Dot Kids" Act (P.L. 107-317), which creates a kid friendly space on the Internet, and the "Amber Alert" Act (P.L. 108-21) which, inter alia, prohibits the use of misleading domain names to deceive a minor into viewing material that is harmful to minors. Congress remains concerned about these issues. This is the final edition of this report.

Chapter VII - Intra-familial childhood sexual abuse (incest) is now recognized as a major public health concern, both because of its widespread nature and because increasing evidence indicates that incest has a wide range of traumatic effects in childhood as well as serious long-term sequelae in adult life.

Despite the attention it has received in recent years, the sexual victimization of children or adolescents has not declined. However, the prevalence of intra-familial sexual abuse has proven difficult to determine. For example, the utilized methods of data collection and the reluctance or inability of children to disclose abuse have likely contributed to underestimation of the rates of intra-familial child sexual abuse. The most widely used method for determining the extent to which members of a population acknowledge being sexually abused has been self-reporting surveys; however, estimates derived from such surveys vary dramatically depending on the population sampled (e.g., college students vs. clinical or special groups such as hospitalized psychiatric patients and runaway youth). In addition, underestimation may arise from the utilized definition of incest. In many studies, incest has been defined as sexual intercourse between participants who are related by some formal or informal bond of kinship that is culturally regarded as a bar to sexual relations. In practice, incestuous experiences may include a variety of acts, such as touching or fondling of sexual body parts, masturbation, oral sex, vaginal or anal intercourse, or penetration of those orifices by objects

Far fewer studies have examined intra-familial sexual abuse in Asian populations (e.g. Koreans) than in Western populations. Although several factors may contribute to the lack of attention paid to intra-familial sexual abuse among Asian societies, one of the most important factors may be the collective worldview of Asian societies versus the individual worldview of Western societies. In societies with a collective worldview, the identities of individuals are deeply embedded in the groups to which they belong (e.g., family, school, and country) and the needs of the group often take precedence over the needs of a given individual. Within a collective orientation, therefore, individual family members may be overlooked in order to protect the family from shame when problems such as incest arise, thus contributing to low rates of disclosure, strong denial, and underreporting of intra-familial sexual abuse.

Indeed, in two representative Korean clinical cases presented below, incest was only identified following the victims' admission to psychiatric units for their mental problems and psychological turmoil.

Chapter VIII - The problem of the use of psychoactive substances has not always been considered as the main issue in Poland. It is regarded that the 90's apart from the positive changes following the transformation of the system, contributed to a considerable increase of undesirable problems. Thus, the use of drugs and abuse of alcohol became popular as a style among young people. Students established a specific community of young-adults. The problem following the use of psychoactive substances seemed not to concern them.

Even so, the real scale and range of the problem isstill obscure. The initial results of research shows that about 40 % of researched had had drug initiation, 84 % faced the problem in their environment. Special attention should be paid to unknown substances provided by legal drugs which often were used by young people. In Poland the problem of abuse of diverse drugs has been increasing. This group is treated marginally and is not included in preventive projects.

Only by monitoring a series of changes which happen during the process of studying are the authors able to define the influence of the university environment on the use of psychoactive substances. This enables us to define the frequency and changeableness of the determinant. The results of research show that students in different forms gain different experiences in the use of psychoactive substances. Current knowledge shows that particular substances and the features which lead to or prevent against destructive behavior are the main factors. The data are very essential and helpful for creating projects covering prevention.

Our model of prevention against drug addiction among young adults is based on the belief that all people have the right of choice. The only way of making the right decisions (including health) is to acquire good knowledge and to understand yourself.

Salutogenesis and the theory of coherency allow us to look at the whole problem in a different way. We have to try to understand which psychological and social factors are a predisposition to healthy or unhealthy behaviors. Some substances are "welcome" among students of each specialization. The choice of substance may depend on specific deficits in coping and conditions of study.

The model includes both forms: educational (information about drugs) and practical (strengthening resources for healthy decisions). Essential subject and reinforcement each resource depends on a specific character of specialization and what the authors have to precede by is a public opinion-pool. Prophylaxis can be effective on the condition that it is adapted to the peculiarity of the recipient.

Chapter IX - The use of corporal punishment as a disciplinary method is a much debated topic in the area of parent-child relations. Recent research has shown that such punishment is associated with adverse psychological and physical outcomes for children. This chapter will address this issue in the cultural context of Sri Lanka where specific information about the experiences of disciplining children and its outcomes is lacking. The research reported here is part of a larger study of the outcomes of child-directed violence on 12-year-old children. The study incorporated a number of measures including the Parent-Child Conflict Tactic Scale [CTSPC: Straus, Hamby, Finklehor, Moore, & Runyan, 1998] and Personality Assessment Questionnaire [PAQ: Rohner, 1999] which were translated, adapted and validated for the Sri Lankan context. A Psychosocial Questionnaire (PSQ) was also designed specifically for this study to assess selected correlates (including non-parent-to-child violence, children's attitude to corporal punishment, parent-child relationship, and children's support network) hypothesized to be associated with parental use of corporal punishment and its psychological outcomes.

The validated instruments were used in a cross-sectional study of 12-year-old Sinhala speaking government school children in the Colombo district. Participants were chosen according to a stratified random sampling technique. The final sample size was 1226 (M age = 11.83 years, SD = 0.51 years; 61% females). The children reported a high prevalence of corporal punishment and physical abuse. A predictive model examining the association between corporal punishment and psychological maladjustment was tested. It was found that not only did corporal punishment directly predict a child's maladjustment but that non-parent-to-child violence (i.e., domestic, school, peer, and community violence) significantly impacted this association. A predictive model examining the association between corporal punishment and physical abuse was also tested. The results showed that corporal punishment is moderately but significantly associated with physical abuse.

Taken together, these findings inform the authors understanding of children's perceptions of parenting behaviors and their impact on children. In particular, they highlight that, though many Sri Lankans believe in the efficacy of corporal punishment, it does appear to be associated with negative outcomes for children. It is hoped that the empirical findings from this research program can assist and support social policy-makers as they plan guiding principles for positive parenting and develop programs aimed at raising awareness among Sri Lankan parents on healthy disciplinary methods.

In: Child Abuse and Violence
Editors: T. Richardson, M. Williams, pp. 1-17

ISBN: 978-1-60456-128-9
© 2008 Nova Science Publishers, Inc.

Chapter I

The Need for Systematic and Intensive Training of Forensic Interviewers

Ann-Christin Cederborg* and Michael E. Lamb**
*Department of Behavioural Sciences and Learning
Linkoping University, Sweden
**Faculty of Social and Political Sciences,
University of Cambridge
Cambridge, United Kingdom

Abstract

This chapter emphasizes the need to further encourage and train forensic interviewers to follow expert recommendations in how to forensically interview children.

Children from about 4 years of age are able to give information in response to open ended questions and details elicited in this way are more likely to be accurate. Younger children are, however, more likely than older children to give inaccurate information in response to yes/no questions, to respond affirmatively to misleading questions about non experienced events, and to acquiesce to suggestions.

Research presented in this chapter show that forensic interviewers do not follow best practice guidelines. Altogether 20 police officers and 130 children were involved in the analysis. The police officers did not provide children of all ages with sufficient opportunities to retrieve information in response to open-ended prompts before resorting to more focused prompts, especially when invitations elicited more details than did focused prompts from children of all ages.

Previous researchers have show that, when interviewers are intensively trained over a longer period of time in courses that involve systematic, repeated practices, feed-back monitored stimulations, and systematic analysis of actual recorded forensic interviews the training can be successful. Such competence will make it easier for the children to be believed when reporting about their experiences. Considering the fact that open ended questions are more likely to be accurate, this chapter suggests that planners of interviewing courses need to focus more attention on ways to improve interviewer behaviour. Otherwise there is a continued risk that the quality of information provided by children can be called in question because interviewers lack competence.

Introduction

It is not possible to assess the true incidence of child sexual abuse because sexual abuse is a very private and easily concealed crime which typically involves only the victim and perpetrator. The victim's verbal disclosure of abuse is often not just the primary, but also the only, evidence that the abuse occurred. Because corroborative evidence is often lacking, alleged sex crimes against children are extremely difficult to investigate. In addition, the alleged victim's and the suspect's reports can provide contradictory accounts of what actually happened (Lamb, 2003). This makes it imperative that the best possible interview techniques be used to elicit information from the child that can be used in legal proceedings. The goal of this chapter is to summarize research findings about ways to elicit information of the highest quality from alleged victims of sexual abuse. The chapter starts with brief summaries of research on children's capacities and on effective interview techniques. The summaries are thereafter discussed in relation to findings from a recent study of interview practice in Sweden. The chapter concludes with an urgent appeal for policy makers and professionals to improve interviewer training so that they can do a better job eliciting information from alleged victims of abuse.

Children's Capacities to Provide Information

Valuable information can be obtained from children as young as 4 years of age but interviewing children requires careful investigative procedures. To adapt interview techniques to children's needs, police officers must be aware of the children's capacities especially when they have specific handicaps that reduce their ability to describe their experiences effectively. Such difficulties do not necessarily mean that the children are incapable of being informants.

Intrinsic factors, such as the child's developmental level, influence the amount of information reported (i.e., the amount of information provided typically increases with age; see, e.g., Goodman and Reed, 1986; Leippe, Romanczyk and Manion, 1992). Young children not only remember less than older children, but also appear to forget more rapidly (Baker-Ward, Gordon, Ornstein, Larus, and Clubb, 1993; Lamb, Sternberg, and Esplin, 2000; Ornstein, Gordon, and Larus, 1992; Schneider and Bjorklund, 1998). With increasing age, children recall more information regardless of delay (Lamb et al., 2000; Lamb, Sternberg, Orbach, and Esplin, 2003) but there are no age differences in the proportion of details elicited using invitations (Lamb et al., 2003). When the events happened, their personal significance, and whether or not they have been discussed in the interim also affect recall (Cordon, Pipe, Liat, Melinder, and Goodman, 2003). Once encoded in memory, for example, stressful and traumatic events can often be recounted in detail even after considerable delays (Fivush, McDermott Sales, Goldberg, Bahrick, and Parker, 2004; Cordon et al., 2003).

In general, the performance of children with intellectual disabilities (IDs) appears comparable to that of normally developing peers with the same mental age (Fowler, 1998; Henry and Gudjonsson, 1999; Iarocci and Burack, 1998; Michel, Gordon, Ornstein and Simpson, 2000; Zigler, 1969). How children with autistic or autistic like syndromes perform as eyewitnesses has not been investigated but they may have problems making eye contact and expressing emotions when being interviewed. Verbal autistic youngsters may also fail to understand both questions about other people's knowledge or beliefs and the gestures others use when trying to direct their attention (Trevarthen, 2000). Similarly, they may not be able to answer questions if interrupted while speaking. Thus, they may give lengthy and detailed speeches about concrete experiences yet be unable to answer simple questions about the same event (Gillberg, 1995). This suggests that interviewers may need special skills to accommodate children's unique needs and that the accuracy of children's reports is influenced by child characteristics as well as by the competence of the adult interviewers.

Recommended Interview Practices

Like adults, children can be informative witnesses, even when they have intellectual disabilities and, in general, interview techniques recommended for normally developing children are also appropriate for children with IDs (see, for example, Bull and Cullen, 1992; Clare and Gudjonsson, 1993; Henry and Gudjonsson, 1999; Milne and Bull, 1998). The quality of the questions asked decisively affects the accuracy and completeness of children's reports, and over the last two decades, researchers who study forensic interview practices have provided remarkably consistent insights into the best ways of obtaining information from children (APSAC, 1990, 2002; Bull, 1992, 1995; Fisher and Geiselman, 1992; Jones, 1992; Lamb and Brown, in press; Lamb, Sternberg, Orbach, Hershkowitz, and Esplin, 1999; Milne and Bull, 1999; Poole and Lamb, 1998; Saywitz and Goodman, 1996; Walker and Warren, 1995; Yuille, Hunter, Joffe, and Zaparniuk, 1993).

Despite differences in emphasis, professionals agree that children should be interviewed as soon as possible after the alleged offenses by interviewers who intrude as little as possible and encourage children to provide as much information as possible in the form of narratives elicited using open-ended prompts. Before substantive issues are discussed, interviewers are typically urged to explain their roles, the purpose of the interview, and the ground rules (e.g., that the children should limit themselves to descriptions of events "that really happened" and should correct the interviewer, request explanations or clarification, and acknowledge ignorance, as necessary). When focused questions are needed to elicit forensically relevant information, investigators are urged to use these prompts as sparingly as possible and as late in the interview as possible, striving to return the child to narrative responding whenever relevant information is disclosed.

Open-ended questions prompt respondents to recall information from memory and do not specify the contents of the memories that are to be retrieved. As a result, they elicit richer and more accurate reports than more focused prompts do. The latter often require that respondents recognize one of the options suggested by the interviewers and this constrains and shapes their responses, making them less accurate than responses to open-ended questions (Dale,

Loftus, and Rathbun, 1978; Dent and Stephenson, 1979; Hutcheson, Baxter, Telfer, and Warden, 1995; Lamb and Fauchier, 2001; Oates and Shrimpton, 1991; Orbach and Lamb, 2000). Responses to individual free-recall prompts are three to five times more informative than responses to more focused questions (e.g. Lamb, Hershkowitz, Sternberg, Boat, and Everson, 1996; Lamb and Fauchier, 2001; Sternberg, Lamb, Hershkowitz, Esplin, Redlich, and Sunshine, 1996; Orbach and Lamb, 2001). Younger children are especially likely to give inaccurate responses to focused questions (Brady, Poole, Warren, and Jones, 1999).

Even though some practitioners believe that young children usually fail to provide forensically valuable information when asked open-ended questions (e.g., Bourg, Broderick, Flagor, Kelly, Ervin, and Butler, 1999: Hewitt, 1999: Saywitz and Goodman, 1996) a recent study showed that child victims from 4 years of age can indeed provide substantial amounts of information in response to open-ended questions (Lamb, Sternberg, Orbach, and Esplin, 2003).

Research Findings about Interview Practices

Despite well substantiated and professionally endorsed recommendations, studies of forensic interviewing in England, Finland, Israel, Sweden, and the United States show that interviewers seldom offer children the opportunity to respond to open-ended questions. Instead they largely rely on focused questions that are more likely to elicit inaccurate information (for example Cederborg, Orbach, Sternberg, and Lamb, 2000; Craig, Scheibe, Kircher, Raskin, and Dodd, 1999; Davies, Wetscott, and Horan, 2000; Korkman, Santilla and Sandnabba, 2006; Lamb, Hershkowitz, Sternberg, Esplin, Hovav, Manor, and Yudilevich, 1996; Sternberg, Lamb, Davis and Westcott, 2001; Walker and Hunt, 1998). These results are consistent with studies showing that classroom-based training programs for investigative interviewers, however intense, may impart knowledge about desirable practices but have little if any effect on the actual behavior of forensic investigators (Aldridge and Cameron, 1999: Freeman and Morris, 1999: Lamb et al., 2002; Stevenson, Leung, and Cheung, 1992; Warren, Woodall, Thomas, Nunno, Keeney, Larson, and Stadfeld, 1999). It is, however, possible to effect improvements in the quality of forensic interviewing when interviewers follow structured interview guidelines that show them how to establish rapport and to use appropriate open-ended free recall and directive prompts. Such training increases interviewers' use of open-ended questions and reduces undesirable practices including the use of option posing and suggestive prompts (Orbach, Hershkowitz, Lamb, Sternberg, Esplin, and Horowitz, 2000; Sternberg, Lamb, Orbach, Esplin, and Mitchell, 2001).

The effectiveness of such training can be reinforced when interviewers are systematically and extensively trained to follow a very detailed, specific, and flexible interview protocol and are given continuing supervision and feedback on simulated as well as actual forensic interviews. Both the intense training and the continued 'quality control' appear necessary to maintain improvements in interviewers' behavior (Orbach et al., 2000; Sternberg, Lamb, Orbach, Esplin, and Mitchell, 2001; Lamb, Sternberg, Orbach, Hershkowitz, Horowitz, and Esplin, 2002).

The recommendations mentioned above may have been unknown for practitioners when Swedish interviews studied by Cederborg et al. (2000) were conducted. Cederborg et al. found that these forensic interviewers relied heavily on option posing and suggestive prompts which may have reduced the accuracy of the information provided by the children, inadvertently reducing the value and admissibility of the children's statements. These findings underlined the need for police investigators to adopt and maintain practices that enhance the quality of information provided by young victims.

In the present chapter, we wanted to revisit the issues illuminated by the earlier discouraging results. We wanted to know if interview quality had improved since 1995, when the interviews studied by Cederborg et al. were conducted. In addition, whereas that study involved 6 experienced but untrained police officers from a middle sized town interviewing suspected victims of child sexual abuse, the present study involved a selected group of 14 police officers in a specialized unit in Stockholm. Eight of the police officers had received no training in how to interview children beyond their regular 3-year training at the police academy but they worked alongside 6 police officers who had received specialized training after their basic training at the academy. Unfortunately, this specialized training did not involve the introduction of a structured protocol or continued supervision on real cases and 'quality control'. The 14 police officers interviewed alleged victims of both physical and sexual abuse during 2000.

The Data

Investigator Training

Altogether, 14 police officers participated in this new study. Eight (4 male; 4 female) had received no training in interview techniques after graduation from the police academy (36 cases), 4 (1 male: 3 female) had between one and five weeks of intensive training (15 cases) and two females had both received 5 weeks of intensive training and attended a university course on abused children (7 cases). The latter courses involved theoretical knowledge about abuse and its consequences as well as a brief mention of interviewing techniques, but did not provide training about or practice interviewing children. The eight police officers who had not received any specialized training worked in the same group as the trained officers. The researchers were told by the police officer who sent the transcripts that these untrained colleagues were expected to use these formally trained colleagues as resources but we do not know if that really happened, but they are described as "supervised" interviewers below. The 6 police officers who had some kind of specialized training are described as "trained" interviewers below. The interviewers in Cederborg et al.'s (2000) study are described as 'untrained' below.

Subjects

A total of 60 transcribed police interviews involving allegations of sexual and physical abuse and performed during 2000 were provided by the specialized unit in Stockholm. Two cases were excluded because they involved sexual harassment rather than sexual and physical abuse. The remaining 58 interviews involved children between 4.2 and 13.1 years of age (M = 10.3 years). Thirty-two cases involved suspicion of physical abuse, 25 involved suspicion of sexual abuse and one case involved both sexual and physical abuse. To ensure that this suspected victim cannot be recognised it was combined with the sexual abuse cases for purposes of analysis. Of the 32 physical abuse cases, 24 alleged victims were boys and eight were girls; ages ranged between 6.3 and 13.1 years (M= 11 years). The 26 sexual abuse cases involved 21 girls and 5 boys ranging in age from 4.2 to 13.3 years (M=9.7 years). The delay between the incident (or last incident in cases of multiple abuse) and the interview ranged from 0 to 1820 days (M=104 days). Information about delay was missing in 6 cases.

Fourteen of the 32 physically abused children reported in the interviews that they were attacked with an object (belt, potatoes, pot, remote-control, shoehorn, shoes, stick, or wire). In all but one case it appeared in the interviews that the children felt negative emotions (e.g., fear, disgust, annoyance, pain). Twenty one of the children reported a single incident whereas 11 reported multiple incidents. Fifteen of the incidents happened in the home of the alleged victim, and 17 happened away from the children's homes. Twenty five of the suspects were male, and five were female. In two cases, there were both female and male suspects.

The 26 allegations of sexual abuse included anal or genital penetration (N=5), fondling of sexual organs (N=6), touching of sexual organs over the clothes (N=7) and sexual exposure (N=8). In the interviews, 23 children expressed that they felt negative emotions about the act and the perpetrator. Five of the incidents happened in the home of the alleged victims and 21 happened away from the victims' homes. Eighteen of the children reported a single incident, whereas 8 reported multiple incidents. All the 26 suspects were males.

A review of the files revealed that most of the suspects (23) were familiar with the children (physical abuse N= 13; sexual abuse N=10), although 18 were unfamiliar (physical abuse N= 8; sexual abuse N=8). Sixteen of the suspects were immediate family members (physical abuse N=11; sexual abuse N= 5). One adult suspected of sexual abuse was a more distant family member.

The Cederborg et al. (2000) study involved 72 alleged victims of sexual abuse (64 females and 8 males) ranging in age from 4.2 to 13 years (M=8.85) who were interviewed in 1995. The alleged crimes included anal or genital penetration (N=17), fondling of sexual organs (N=36), touching of sexual organs over the clothes (N=5), and sexual exposure (N=14). Twenty-three of the incidents happened in the homes of the alleged victims, and 49 happened away from the victims' homes. Fifty-six of the children reported a single incident, whereas 16 reported multiple incidents. There was huge variation in the length of the gap between the incident (or last incident, in multiple incident cases) and the interview, ranging between 0 and 1689 days (4.5 years; M=184.65 days). Information about delay was missing in 6 cases.

Most of the suspects were immediate family members (N=29), 7 were other family members, and the children were familiar with 26 others. Ten suspects were not known to the child.

Method

All interviews with the children were transcribed from video recordings. One native Swedish speaker identified substantive utterances (those related to the investigated incident) and tabulated the number of new details concerning the investigated event using a technique developed by Yuille and Cutshall (1986, 1989; Cutshall and Yuille, 1990) and elaborated by Lamb and colleagues (1996). Details were defined as words or phrases identifying or describing individuals, objects, or events (including actions) related to the investigated incident. Details were only counted when they were new and added to an understanding of the target incidents and their disclosure. As a result, restatements were not counted.

The coder also reviewed the transcripts and categorized each interviewer utterance, defined by a "turn" in the discourse or conversation, using the categories developed by Lamb et al. (1996). For the purpose of these ratings, we did not distinguish between questions and statements.

Interviewer statements made during the portion of the investigative interviews concerned with substantive issues were placed in one of the following categories (Lamb et al., 1996):

1. *Invitations*. Utterances, including questions, statements, or imperatives, prompting free-recall responses from the child. Such utterances do not limit the child's focus except in a general way (for example, "Tell me everything that happened"), or use details disclosed by the child as cues (for example, "You mentioned that he touched you. Tell me everything about the touching.").
2. *Directive utterances*. These refocus the child's attention on details or aspects of the alleged incident that the child has already mentioned, providing a category for requesting additional information using "Wh-" questions (cued recall).
3. *Option-posing utterances*. These focus the child's attention on details or aspects of the alleged incident that the child has not previously mentioned, asking the child to affirm, negate, or select an investigator-given option using recognition memory processes, but do not imply that a particular response is expected.
4. *Suggestive utterances*. These are stated in such a way that the interviewer strongly communicates what response is expected (for example: "He forced you to do that, didn't he?") or they assume details that have not been revealed by the child (for example: *Child:* "We laid on the sofa." *Interviewer*: "He laid on you or you laid on him?").

The rater, who was fluent in both Swedish and English, was trained on an independent set of English transcripts until she reached 90% agreement with American raters regarding the identification of details and utterance types. This level of proficiency was reached before she began coding the Swedish transcripts included in the study. The Swedish rater remained reliable (≥ 95%) with American raters who independently coded randomly chosen transcripts of interviews in English during the period that the Swedish interviews were being coded.

Results

Investigator Behaviour

Both the trained and the supervised police officers used more utterances in the substantive portions of the interviews than the untrained interviewers in the previous study. The mean numbers of utterances by trained, supervised, and untrained interviewers were 115.15, 84.08 and 74.8, respectively. This means that the substantive parts of the interviews were longer in this new sample than in the previous one. The average number of prompts of each type did not vary significantly by age and interviewer training or by type of abuse and training. Table 1 shows the average number and proportion of utterances in relation to type of abuse and training.

Table 1. Reliance on different types of utterances by trained and supervised interviewers

Utterance Type	Sexual Abuse Trained M # (SD)	M %	Supervised M # (SD)	M %	Physical Abuse Trained M # (SD)	M %	Supervised M # (SD)	M %
Invitation	7.38 (3.66)	5.24 (1.81)	4.18 (4.11)	4.30 (3.04)	6.21 (3.70)	8.19 (5.69)	5.22 (3.07)	7.64 (3.82)
Directive	77.75 (44.80)	53.95 (17.24)	49.88 (26.90)	53.66 (9.61)	52.21 (34.06)	55.96 (14.43)	41.50 (26.18)	51.28 (9.95)
Option-Posing	57.13 (56.10)	34.27 (11.98)	31.82 (16.74)	36.35 (10.83)	28.14 (21.46)	30.53 (11.11)	26.56 (16.63)	34.07 (11.35)
Suggestive	8.63 (7.57)	6.55 (6.58)	4.94 (3.28)	5.68 (3.17)	3.71 (3.42)	5.32 (7.51)	4.44 (3.85)	7.01 (7.67)

Numbers in parentheses are standard deviations.

Both the trained and supervised interviewers relied heavily on suggestive, option-posing, and directive questions. The smallest proportions of option-posing (30.53%; SD= 11.11) and suggestive (5.32%; SD= 7.51) questions were posed by trained interviewers to alleged victims of physical abuse and the highest proportions of option-posing (36.35%; SD= 10.83) and suggestive (5.68%; SD= 3.17) questions were asked by supervised interviewers in sexual abuse cases. In all groups, between 51.28% (SD=9.95) and 55.96% (SD=14.43) of the utterances were directive. Invitations were least frequently asked except by trained interviewers investigating suspicious of physical abuse. Supervised interviewers investigating allegations of physical abuse utilized almost the same proportions of invitations and suggestive prompts as the trained (Sexual abuse: supervised 4.30% (SD= 3.04); trained 5.24% (SD=1.81): Physical abuse: supervised 7.64% (SD=3.82); trained 8.19% (SD=5.69)). The officer who interviewed the child believed to have been both physically and sexually abused was trained and she used 5.06% invitations, 62.36% directive, 29.78 % option-posing and 2.8 % suggestive prompts. As in the previous study (Cederborg et al., 2000), therefore, the 'expert' investigators we studied seldom used invitations to elicit information (see Table 2).

Table 2. Differences in the behavior of untrained, supervised and trained interviewers

Utterance Type	Untrained (N=6) M # (N=72)	M %	Supervised (N=8) M # (N=35)	M %	Trained (N=6) M # (N=23)	M %
Invitation	3.78 (3.64)	6 (6)	4.71 (3.60)	6 (3.81)	6.73 (3.59)	7 (4.73)
Directive	32.29 (24.61)	41 (13)	45.57¤ (26.48)	53 (9.72)	63.65¤ (39.76)	55 (14.86)
Option-Posing	29.26 (19.66)	39 (11)	29.11 (16.65)	35 (11)	39.30 (38.43)	32 (11)
Suggestive	9.49 (7.80)	14 (9)	4.69 (3.54)	6 (5.88)	5.47 (5.55)	6 (6.91)

Numbers in parentheses are standard deviations
¤ p< .02

A comparison among the untrained, supervised and trained interviewers showed that the proportion of open ended questions was the same (between 6% and 7%). The trained interviewers asked significantly more directive questions than the supervised interviewers (trained M=63.65 (SD= 39.77); supervised M=45.57 (SD=26.49), p<.02) but proportionally they were quite similar (trained 55% (SD=14.86); supervised 53% (SD=9.72) and both groups used more directive questions than the untrained interviewers did (41% (SD=13)). The latter interviewers were much more reliant on option-posing questions (39% (SD=11)) than the trained (32% (SD=11) and supervised (35%; SD=11) interviewers. The trained and supervised interviewers also used fewer suggestive questions (6% SD=trained 6.91; SD=5.88) than the untrained interviewers did (14%;SD=9).

Even though the trained and supervised interviewers thus employed better interview techniques than the untrained interviewers, their use of option-posing and suggestive prompts remained high. This is a problem because these types of questions are more likely to elicit inaccurate information from children. Table 3 shows how much of the information provided by the children could be called into question because of how the questions were asked.

There was little difference in the total number of details elicited by supervised or trained interviewers, both of whom elicited 9% more details than the untrained interviewers. The interviewers in this study obtained more details using directive questions (41%, SD=13.63; 46%, SD=17, for the trained and supervised interviewers, respectively) than the untrained interviewers (35% (SD=15.14) and they elicited far fewer details than the untrained interviewers did using focused prompts (supervised 41%, trained 36%, untrained 57%). Unfortunately, the average proportion of details elicited using invitations was still very small (17%).

Table 3. Number and proportion of details elicited using different utterance types in relation to level of training

Utterance Type	Untrained (N=6) M # (N=72)	M %	Supervised (N=8) M # (N=35)	M %	Trained (N=6) M # (N=23)	M %
Invitation	15.04 (27.11)	8 (11.44)	47.29 (50.62)	17 (15.68)	46.52 (46.94)	17 (14.29)
Directive	57.32 (59.63)	35 (15.14)	107.14 (85.31)	41 (13.63)	150.21 (112.61)	46 (17)
Option-Posing	58.11 (50.96)	41 (17.18)	77.89 (49.42)	33 (12.21)	88.00 (68.51)	31 (15.32)
Suggestive	20.14 (25.16)	16 (14.10)	18.57 (24.74)	8 (6.5)	14.83 (19.42)	5 (7.39)

Numbers in parentheses are standard deviations

The interviewed children provided more details in response to the few invitations asked as well as fewer details when asked option- posing and suggestive prompts than did the children in Cederborg et al.'s study, perhaps because the first substantive questions asked by the untrained interviewers (N=72) were invitations 18 times, and option-posing and suggestive 45 times, whereas the supervised and trained interviewers (N=58) used invitations 43 times and option- posing and suggestive prompts 14 times to initiate their substantive inquiry.

On average, children in all age groups provided more details in response to invitations that in response to any other type of question (see Table 4).

The younger children provided on average 3.30 details per invitation (SD= 4.80) compared to 2.62 details per option-posing prompt (SD=1.16). On average, directive questions elicited the least information (1.81; SD=0.45). The 7 to 9 year olds provided almost twice as many details when asked invitations (5.86; SD= 5.53), as opposed to option-posing (2.59; SD= 2.59) and suggestive (2.59; SD=3.81) prompts. Even in this age group, however, directive utterances elicited the fewest details (1.97; SD=1.06). Children in the oldest age group (10 to 13 years old) provided almost twice as many details in response to invitations (10.98; SD=10.92) as opposed to suggestive prompts (4.20; SD=6.77), option-posing (2.8; SD=1.32) and directive (2.52; SD= 1.47) prompts. The latter was again the question type that elicited the smallest average number of details.

There were also significant differences in the average number of details per utterance type collapsed across age groups. Invitations (M=9.17, SD= 9.97) elicited significantly more details than directives (M= 2.34, SD= 1.34; F(1,52)=5.78, p < .05) and option-posing prompts (M=2.74, SD=1.37, F(1.52)=4.47,p < .05). In addition, directives elicited significantly fewer details than option- posing prompts (F (1.52) = 6.21, p < .05).

Table 4. Mean Number of question types (MQT) in relation to mean number to details (MD) and average number (AD) of details per question type by age group

Age group	Invitation	Directive	Option-posing	Suggestive
	MQT MD AD	MQT MD AD	MQT MD AD	MQT MD AD
4-6 N=7	3.28 17 3.30 (3.04) (23.31) (4.80)	55.71 110.86 1.81 (36.71) (91.76) (.45)	24.71 62.29 2.62 (15.18) (45.83) (1.16)	3.57 6 1.91 (2.82) (4.36) (1.29)
7-9 N=10	7.20 40.8 5.86 (5.18) (36.25) (5.53)	42.90 89.40 1.97 (32.95) (81.76) (1.06)	23.20 59.20 2.59 (16.37) (56.49) (1.80)	6.30 18.90 2.59 (4.52) (32.57) (3.81)
10-13 N=41	5.49 53.61 10.98 (3.25) (52.94) (10.92)	54.63 135 2.52 (33.21) (102.88) (1.47)	37.02 90.78 2.80 (30.61) (58.17) (1.32)	4.93 18.54 4.20 (4.61) (21.61) (6.77)
Total N=58	5.52 46.98 9.17¤ (3.71) (48.78) (9.97)	52.74 124.22 2.34¤ (33.29) (98.43) (1.34)	33.16 81.90 2.74¤ (27.58) (57.40) (1.37)	5 17.09 3.65 (4.42) (22.68) (5.95)

¤ p< .05

Conclusion

Open-ended questions require multiple-word responses and allow interviewees to choose which aspects of the event to describe, even when children are asked to tell more about an incident they have already described. Open ended follow up questions focus interviewees on particular parts of the account but do not dictate what specific further information to provide. This free recall technique was effective for children of all ages. Even very young children were able to produce information when asked such questions, and children from all three age groups provided more details in response to invitations rather than other types of prompts. In addition, the interviewed children provided more details in response to the few invitations asked than in the Cederborg et al study. This can be explained by the fact that the first question asked in the substantial phase by the new interviewers tended to be open-ended invitations whereas the untrained interviewers studied by Cederborg et al tended to open with suggestive questions.

Research has shown that it is possible to improve the quality of information elicited from alleged victims of abuse when principles are not only taught but interviewers continue to receive guidance and supervision (Lamb, et al., 2002b). The trained police officers had participated in courses in which principles of effective interviewing were explained but they were not trained on real cases and continuous supervision was not offered to them. Unfortunately, this type of training is known to be less effective than courses in which intensively trained interviewers are encouraged to continue following best practice guidelines. After such training and continued guidance, investigators have been shown to elicit most information (51%) using open invitations (Lamb et al., 2003; Orbach et al., 2000; Sternberg et al., 2001) whereas the trained police officers in this study elicited only 7 % in this way.

Interviewers may use few invitations when asking young children about their experiences because they consider them incapable of providing informative responses to very general prompts (Lamb et al., 2003) but they may also mistakenly believe that they fully understand how to use these recommended questions types. Because children as young as 4 years of age can provide substantial amounts of forensically important information in response to open-ended questions, forensic interviewers need to provide children of all ages with the opportunities to recall information in response to such question types before assuming that more focused prompts are needed. This recommendation is especially important in light of several demonstrations that younger children are more likely than older children to give inaccurate information in response to yes/no (option-posing) questions (Brady et al., 1999), to respond affirmatively to misleading questions about non experienced events (Poole and Lindsay, 1998), and to acquiesce to suggestions (e.g., Cassel, Roebers, and Bjorklund, 1996; Ceci and Huffman, 1997; Ceci, Ross, and Toglia, 1987; Robinson and Briggs, 1997).

The findings suggest a misperception among the planners of interviewing courses about what makes a person an expert interviewer. The specialized training received by the interviewers we studied appeared to have little effect on the police officers' usage of open-ended questions. The study gives evidence that Swedish child abuse interviews are (still) not conducted in a way that is consistent with guidelines recommended by experts in the field. Previous research has show that, when interviewers are intensively trained over a longer period of time in courses that involve a structured protocol, repeated practice, feed-back monitored simulations, and systematic analysis of actual recorded forensic interviews, training can be very successful (Lamb et al., 2002a; Lamb, Sternberg, Orbach, Esplin and Mitchell, 2002b). Interviewers can utilize open-ended questions without a structured protocol but research shows that interviewers who use such a tool dramatically increase their use of open-ended questions, which in turn imply that children provide higher quality information (Lamb et al., 1999, 2002; Pipe et al., 2004).

Other researchers have similarly reported that intensive courses that do not involve continued supervision and quality control have little impact on interviewers' behaviour (Aldridge and Cameron, 1999; Craig et al., 1999; Davies and Wilson, 1997; Memon, Bull and Smith, 1995; Stevenson et al., 1992; Warren et al., 1999). Unfortunately, the specialized training offered to some of the participating police officers did not involve continuous training in best practice guidelines including a structured protocol that have operationalized the consensus recommendations of diverse professionals and scholars. This may explain why their interviews were very similar in many respects to those conducted by the six untrained interviewers in the previous study.

The trained and supervised interviewers used more directive questions as well as fewer focused questions than the untrained officers did, however. This clearly reflects an improvement in interviewing behaviour, although is still not big enough because such questions can diminishes the children's opportunities to increase their depiction of details. Directive questions are usually focused on specific details or concepts and can be answered in one or two words. When interviewers rely more on open-ended questions, rather than directive questions, children are thus encouraged to provide more elaborative responses (Poole and Lamb, 1998).

Considering the fact that children at all ages can provide information in response to open ended questions (e.g., Lamb et al., 2003) and that details elicited in this way are more likely to be accurate, this study suggests that planners of interviewing courses need to focus more attention on ways to improve interviewer behaviour. Otherwise there is a continued risk that the quality of information provided by children can be called in question because interviewers lack competence. There is thus a considerable need to develop training courses that include systematic, intensive training and supervision on real cases over time so interviewers can acquire and maintain the ability to obtain as much information as possible using open-ended questions.

References

Aldridge, J., and Cameron, S. (1999). Interviewing child witnesses: Questioning strategies and the effectiveness of training. *Applied Developmental Science*, 3, 136-147.

American Professional Society on the Abuse of Children. (1990). *Guidelines for psychological evaluation of suspected sexual abuse in young children.* Chicago, IL: Author.

American Professional Society on the Abuse of Children. (2002). *Guidelines for psychosocial evaluation of suspected sexual abuse in young children.*(rev.ed.). Chicago, IL:APSAC

Baker-Ward, L., Gordon, B. N., Ornstein, P. A., Larus, D. M., and Clubb, P. A. (1993). Young children's long term retention of a pediatric examination. *Child Development*, 64, 1519-1533.

Bourg,W., Broderick,R., Flagor, R., Kelly, D.M., Ervin, D. L.,and Butler, J. (1999). A *child interviewer's guidebook.* Thousand Oaks, CA: Sage.

Brady, M., Poole, D. A., Warren, A., and Jones, D. (1999). Young children's responses to yes-no questions: Patterns and problems. *Applied Developmental Science*, 3, 47-57.

Bull, R. (1992). Obtaining evidence expertly: The reliability of interviews with child witnesses. *Expert Evidence*, 5-12.

Bull, R. (1995). Innovative techniques for the questioning of child witnesses, especially those who are young and those with learning disability. In M. S. Zaragoza, J. R. Graham, G C. N. Hall, R. Hirschman. and Y S. Ben-Porath. *Memory and testimony in the child witness* (vol 1 pp, 179-194)) Thousand Oaks, CA: Sage.

Cassel, W.S., Roebers, C.E.M., and Bjorklund, D.F. (1996). Developmental patterns of eyewitness responses to repeated and increasingly suggestive questions. *Journal of Experimental Child Psychology*, 61,116-133.

Cederborg, A-C., Orbach, Y., Sternberg, K, J., and Lamb, M. E. (2000). Investigative interviews of child witnesses in Sweden. *Child Abuse and Neglect,* 24, 1355-1361.

Ceci, S.J., and Huffman, M.L.C. (1997). How suggestible are preschool children? Cognitive and social factors. *Journal of the American Academy of Child and Adolescent Psychiatry*, 36, 948-958.

Ceci, S.J., Ross, D.F., and Toglia, M.P. (1987). Age differences in suggestibility: Narrowing the uncertainties. In S.J. Ceci, M.P. Toglia and D.F. Ross (Eds.), *Children's eyewitness memory* (pp79-91). New York: Springler-Verlag.

Craig, R. A., Scheibe, R., Kircher, J., Raskin, D. C., and Dodd, D. (1999). Effects of interviewer questions on children's statements of sexual abuse. *Applied Developmental Science*, 3, 77-85.

Cordon, I. M., Pipe, M. E., Liat, S., Melinder, A., and Goodman, G. S. (2003). Memory of traumatic experiences in early childhood. *Developmental Review*.

Cutshall, J., and Yuille, J. C. (1990). Field studies of eyewitness memory of actual crimes. In D. C. Raskin. *Psychological methods in criminal investigation and evidence.* (pp 97-124). New York: Spring Publishing Company.

Dale, P. S., Loftus, E. F., and Rathbun, L. (1978). The influence of the form of the question on the eyewitness testimony of pre-school children. *Journal of Psycholinguistic Research*, 7, 269-277.

Davies, G., and Wilson, C. (1997). Implementation of the memorandum: An overview. In H. Westcott. and J. Jones. (Eds.), *Perspectives on the memorandum: Policy, practice and research in investigative interviewing.* (pp 1-12). Aldershot, UK: Arena Publishers.

Davies, G. M., Westcott, H.L., and Horan, N. (2000). The impact of questioning style of the eyewitness testimony of preschool children. Journal of Psycholinguistic Research, 74, 269-277.

Dent, H. R., and Stephenson, G. M. (1979). An experimental study of the effectiveness of different techniques of questioning child witnesses. *British Journal of Social and Clinical Psychology*, 18, 41-51.

Fisher, R., and Geiselman, R. E. (1992). *Memory-enhancing techniques for investigative interviewing: The cognitive interview.* Springfield, IL; Charles C Thomas

Fivush, R., McDermott Sales, J., Goldberg, A., Bahrick, L., and Parker, J. (2004). Weathering the storm: Children's long-term recall of Hurricane Andrew. *Memory. 12, 104-118.*

Freeman, K.A., and Morris, T.L. (1999). Investigative interviewing with children: Evaluation of the effectiveness of a training program for child protecting service workers. *Child Abuse and Neglect*, 23, 701-713.

Fowler, A. E. (1998). Language in mental retardation: Association with and dissociation from general cognition. In J. A. Burack., R. M. Hodapp. and E. Zigler (eds.), *Handbook of mental retardation and development.* (pp. 290-333). Cambridge: Cambridge University Press.

Gillberg, C. (1995). *Clinical child neuropsychiatry.* Cambridge; Cambridge University Press.

Goodman, G. S. and Reed, R. (1986). Age differences in eyewitness testimony. *Law and human behavior*, 10, 317-332.

Henry L.A., and Gudjonsson, G.H. (1999). Eyewitness memory and suggestibility in children with mental retardation. *American Journal on Mental Retardation*, 104, 491-508.

Hershkowitz, I., and Elul, A. (1999). The effects of investigative utterances on Israeli children's reports of physical abuse. *Applied Developmental Science*, 3. 1, 28-33.

Hewitt, S. D. (1999). *Assessing allegations of sexual abuse in preschool children*. Thousand Oaks, CA:Sage.

Hutcheson, G. D., Baxter, J. S., Telfer, K., and Warden, D. (1995). Child witness statement quality: Questions type and errors of omission. *Law and Human Behavior*, 19, 631-648.

Iarocci, G. and Burack, J. A. (1998). Understanding the development of attention in persons with mental retardation: Challenging the myths. In J. A. Burack., R. M. Hodapp. and E. Zigler (eds.), *Handbook of mental retardation and development.* (pp 349-381). Cambridge: Cambridge University Press.

Jones, D. (1992). *Interviewing the sexually abused child: Investigation of suspected abuse.* London: Gaskell.

Korkman, J.,Santilla, P., and Sandnabba, K. (2006). Dynamics of verbal interaction between interviewer and child in interviews with alleged victims of child sexual abuse. *Scandinavian Journal of Psychology,47,6, 561-564.*

Lamb, M. E., Hershkowitz, I., Sternberg, K. J., Esplin, P.W., Hovav, M., Manor, T., and Yudilevitch, L. (1996). Effects of investigative utterance types on Israeli children's responses. *International Journal of Behavioral Development*, 19, 627-637.

Lamb, M. E., Hershkowitz, I., Sternberg, K.J., Boat, B., and Everson, M.D. (1996). Investigative interviews of alleged sexual abuse victims with and without anatomical dolls. *Child Abuse and Neglect,* 20, 1251-1259.

Lamb, M, E., Sternberg, K. J., Orbach, Y., Hershkowitz, I., and Esplin, P. W. (1999). Forensic interviews of children. In R. Bull and A. Memon (Eds.), *The psychology of interviewing: A handbook* (pp 253-278). Chichester, England, New York: Wiley.

Lamb, M. E., Sternberg, K. J., and Esplin, P. W. (2000). Effects of age and delay on the amount of information provided by alleged sex abuse victims in investigative interviews. *Child Development,* 71, 6, 1586-1596.

Lamb, M. E., and Fauchier, A. (2001). The effects of question type on self contradiction by children in the course of forensic interviews. *Applied Cognitive Development*, 15, 483-491.

Lamb, M E., Sternberg, K J., Orbach, Y., Hershkowitz, D., Horowitz., and Esplin, P W. (2002a). The effects of intensive training and ongoing supervision on the quality of investigative interviews with alleged sex abuse victims. *Applied Developmental Science*, 6, 3, 114-125.

Lamb, E L., Sternberg, K. J., Orbach, Y., Esplin P. W., and Mitchell, S. (2002b). Is ongoing feedback necessary to maintain the quality of investigative interviews with allegedly abused children? *Applied Developmental Science*, 6,1, 35-41.

Lamb, M E., Sternberg, K J., Orbach, Y.,and Esplin, P W. (2003). Age differences in young children's responses to open-ended invitations in the course of forensic interviews. *Journal of Consulting and Clinical Psychology*, 71, 5, 926-934.

Lamb, M.E. (2003). Child development and the law. In R. M. Lerner, M. A. Easterbrooks, and J. Mistery (Eds.), *Handbook of psychology (vol. and) Developmental Psychology* (pp, 559-577). New York: Wiley, 2003.

Leippe, M., Romanczyk, A. and Manion, A. (1992). Eyewitness memory for a touching experience. *Journal of Applied Psychology*, 76, 367-379.

Memon, A., Bull, R., and Smith, M. (1995). Improving the quality of the police interview: Can training in the use of cognitive techniques help? *Policing and Society*, 5, 53-68.

Michel, M. K., Gordon, B. N., Ornstein, P, A., and Simpson, M. A. (2000). The abilities of children with mental retardation to remember personal experiences: Implications for testimony. *Journal of Clinical Child Psychology*, 29, 453-463.

Milne, R., and Bull, R. (1999). *Investigative interviewing: Psychology and Practice.* Chichester, UK: Wiley.

Oates, K., and Schrimpton, S. (1991). Children's memories for stressful and non-stressful events. *Medicine, Science and Law*, 31, 4-10.

Orbach, Y.,and Lamb, M. E.(2000). Enhancing children's narratives in investigative interviews. *Child Abuse and Neglect,* 24, 1631-1648.

Orbach, Y., and Lamb, M. E. (2001). The relationship between within-interview contradictions and eliciting interviewer utterances. *Child Abuse and Neglect*, 25, 323-333.

Orbach, Y., Hershkowitz, I., Lamb, M. E., Sternberg, K. J., Esplin, P., W., and Horowitz, D. (2000). Assessing the value of structured protocols for forensic interviews of alleged child abuse victims. *Child Abuse and Neglect*, 24, 6, 733-752.

Ornstein, P. A., Gordon, B. N., and Larus, D, M. (1992). Children's memory for a personally experienced event: Implications for testimony. *Pediatrics*, 94, 17-23.

Poole, D. A., and Lamb, M, E. (1998). *Investigative interviews of children: A guide for helping professionals.* Washington, DC: American Psychological Association.

Poole, D. A., and Lindsay, D. S. (1998). Assessing the accuracy of young children's reports: Lessons from investigation of child sexual abuse. *Applied and Preventive Psychology,* 7, 1-26.

Robinson, J., and Briggs, P.(1997). Age trends and eye witness suggestibility and compliance. *Psychology, Crime and Law*, 3, 187-202.

Saywitz, K .J., and Goodman, G. S. (1996). Interviewing children in and out of court: Current research and practice implications. In J. Briere.,L. Berliner.,J A. Bulkley., C. Jenny., and T. Reid. (Eds.), *The APSAC handbook on child maltreatment.* Thousand Oaks, CA.: Sage Publications.

Schneider, W.,and Bjorklund, D. F. (1998). Memory. In W. Damon, D. D. Kuhn, and R. S. Siegler (Eds.), *Handbook of child psychology: Vol 2, Cognition, perception, and language* (5th ed., pp. 467-521). New York: Wiley.

Sternberg, K. J., Lamb, M. E., Hershkowitz, I., Esplin, P., Redlich, A., and Sunshine, N. (1996). The relation between investigative utterance types and the informativeness of child witnesses. *Journal of Applied Developmental Psychology*, 17, 439-451.

Sternberg, K. J., Lamb, M. E., Davis, G. A. and Westcott, H. L. (2001). The memorandum of good practice: Theory versus application. *Child Abuse and Neglect,* 25, 669-681.

Sternberg, K J., Lamb, M E., Orbach, Y., Esplin, P. W., and Mitchell, S (2001). Use of a structured investigative protocol enhance young children's responses to free-recall prompts in the course of forensic interviews. *Journal of Applied Psychology*, 86,5, 997-1005.

Stevenson, K. M., Leung, P., and Cheung, K. M. (1992). Competency-based evaluation of interviewing skills in child sexual abuse cases. *Social Work Research and Abstracts, 28, 3,* 11-16.

Trevarthen, C. (2000). Autism as a neurodevelopmental disorder affecting communication and learning in early childhood: prenatal origins, post-natal course and effective educational support. *Prostaglandins, Leukotrienes and Essential Fatty Acids,* 63, 41-46.

Walker, A. G., and Warren, A. R. (1995). The language of the child abuse interview: Asking the questions, understanding the answers. In T. Ney (ed.), *True and false allegations of child sexual abuse: Assessment and case management.* New York, NY: Brunner/Mazel, Inc.

Walker, N., and Hunt, J. S. (1998). Interviewing child victims-witnesses: How you ask is what you get. In C. R. Thompson, D. Herrman, J. D. Read, D. Bruce, D. Payne., and M. P. Toglia. (Eds.), *Eyewitness memory: Theoretical and applied perspectives* (pp. 55-87). Mahwah, NJ: Erlbaum.

Warren, A. R., Woodall, C. E., Thomas, M., Nunno, M., Keeney, J., Larson, S. M., and Stadfeld, J. A. (1999). Assessing the effectiveness of a training program for interviewing child witnesses. *Applied Developmental Science,* 3, 128-135.

Yuille, J. C., and Cutshall, J, L. (1986). A case study of eyewitness memory of a crime. *Journal of Applied Psychology* 71(2): 291-301.

Yuille, J. C., and Cutshall. J. L. (1989). Analysis of the statements of victims, witnesses and suspects. In J. C. Yuille. *Credibility assessment.* 47: (pp 175-191). Dordrecht, Netherlands: Kluwer Academic Publishers.

Yuille, J. C., Hunter, R., Joffe, R., and Zaparniuk, J. (1993). Interviewing children in sexual abuse cases. In G. S. Goodman and B. L. Bottoms, *Child victims, child witnesses: Understanding and improving testimony.(pp 95-116).* New York: Guilford Press.

Zigler, E, (1969). Developmental versus difference theories of mental retardation and the problem of motivation. *American Journal of Mental Deficiency,* 73, 536-556

In: Child Abuse and Violence
Editors: T. Richardson, M. Williams, pp. 19-42
ISBN: 978-1-60456-128-9
© 2008 Nova Science Publishers, Inc.

Chapter II

Physical Abuse of Children Born to Adolescent Mothers: The Continuation of the Relationship into Adult Motherhood and the Role of Identity

Tracie O. Afifi[1]* *and Douglas A. Brownridge*[2]
[1] Department of Community Health Sciences, University of Manitoba,
Winnipeg, Canada, R3E 3N4
[2] Department of Family Social Sciences, University of Manitoba,
Winnipeg, Canada, R3T 2N2

Abstract

Child abuse can have devastating consequences for children and families. In terms of prevention and intervention efforts, it is important to identify populations at increased risk for child abuse. It is well established in the child abuse literature that children born to adolescent mothers are at a heightened risk for the perpetration of child abuse. However, little is known about the extent to which this relationship persists among those who became mothers as adolescents but are now within adulthood. Such knowledge is important since adolescence is a relatively short period in the lifecycle, but is one that sets the stage for a lifetime of parenting, including abusive parenting. Applying Erikson's theory, it is argued that impaired identity resulting from adolescent parenthood will increase the risk of child abuse. The purpose of this study is to investigate the manner in which variables that serve as proxies for identity formation, namely education, employment, and self-esteem, are associated with child abuse among children of formerly adolescent mothers (FAMs). Using a representative sample of 4,387 Canadian mothers, both descriptive and logistic regression analyses are conducted. The results demonstrate that children of FAMs are, indeed, more likely to be abused than children of

---

* Department of Community Health Sciences; PZ-430 PsycHealth Centre; 771 Bannatyne Avenue; University of Manitoba; Winnipeg, MB; Canada. R3E 3N4; Phone: (204) 787-5084; Fax: (204) 787-4972; E-mail: t_olfrey@umanitoba.ca.

non-FAMs. With few exceptions, the identity variables operate as hypothesized. However, the multivariate analyses show that identity formation alone is an insufficient explanation for the higher likelihood of child abuse for children of FAMs. Not only do the results suggest that Erikson's theory is inadequate as an explanation of the heightened risk of child abuse of children born to FAMs', but the analyses also imply that a more holistic approach is needed to fully comprehend this phenomenon. The paper concludes with a proposed holistic framework for understanding FAMs higher likelihood of child abuse.

Child abuse can have devastating consequences for children and families. In terms of prevention and intervention efforts, it is important to identify populations at increased risk for child abuse. Research has shown that adolescent mothers are at a heightened risk for child abuse (Bolton, Laner, and Kane, 1980; Connelly and Straus, 1992; De Paul and Domenech, 2000; Miller, 1984; Straus, Gelles, and Steinmetz, 1980). It has been estimated that between 36% and 51% of all reported cases of abuse in the United States are perpetrated by mothers who are currently within adolescence or who first gave birth during that period of their lives (Bolton, 1990). However, why this relationship exists and how it evolves with time is not well understood. An examination of the course of this relationship over time, indeed, is an understudied phenomenon in the research on child abuse.

The purpose of this research is to determine if the increased likelihood of child abuse that has been found for children born to adolescent mothers continues after the adolescent mother make the transition into adulthood and, if so, to contribute to an understanding of why this is the case. To investigate this question, the risk of child physical abuse for a child born during a woman's adolescence (referred to here as formerly adolescent mothers: FAMs) will be compared to the risk of child abuse for a child born within a woman's adulthood (adult mothers).

There is no single agreed-upon definition of physical abuse among researchers. Therefore, the use of the term in the present study must be clarified. The Health Canada (2001) definition will be used. It states that physical abuse is "the deliberate application of force to any part of a child's body, which results or may result in a non-accidental injury. It may involve hitting a child a single time, or it may involve a pattern of incidents" (p. 5). This definition of physical abuse includes physical punishment, reflecting the notion that physical abuse includes a continuum of acts ranging from levels of lesser to greater severity.

The majority of empirical research has demonstrated that a positive relationship between adolescent motherhood and child abuse does exist (Benedict, White, and Cornely, 1985; Bolton and Laner, 1981; Bolton et al., 1980; Chaffin, Kelleher, and Hollenberg, 1996; Connelly and Straus, 1992; Creighton, 1985; De Paul and Domenech, 2000; Haskett, Johnson, and Miller, 1994; Herrenkohl and Herrenkohl, 1979; Miller, 1984; Schloesser, Pierpont, and Poertner, 1992; Straus et al., 1980). For example, Garcia Coll, Hoffman, Van Houten, and Oh (1987) found that adolescent mothers compared to adult mothers used more physical punishment with their children. Using child abuse potential scores, DePaul and Domenech (2000) found that risk of child abuse was significantly higher in adolescent mothers compared to adult mothers.

No studies have found a negative relationship between adolescent motherhood and child abuse. However, there are a few studies that either do not find a significant relationship between adolescent motherhood and child abuse (Cadzow, Armstrong, and Fraser, 1999; Earp and Ory, 1980; Gil, 1970; Massat, 1993; Murphy, Orkow, and Nicola, 1985), or were inconclusive (Sherman, Evans, Boyle, Cuddy, and Norman, 1983). The inability to detect a relationship or inconclusive findings may be due to problems related to conceptualizing adolescent motherhood. It is possible that studies finding no relationship between adolescent motherhood and child abuse are confounded by a short phase of adolescence, ending at age 20. That is, child abuse resulting from the circumstances found among adolescent mothers may not manifest itself until the women are adults.

Very few researchers identify FAMs in adolescent motherhood and child abuse studies. However, when this group was included, Bolton et al. (1980) found that 36.5% of the sample of child abuse cases (n = 4,851) were perpetrated by mothers who gave birth within adolescence, including mothers currently within adolescence and FAMs. The data were collected in 1978, when only 14% of the general population in the United States were adolescents (Adams, Gullotta, and Markstorm-Adams, 1994). Similar findings emerged from a study conducted in the UK; at a time when adolescents accounted for approximately 10% of the general population in the United Kingdom, 35.9% of reported cases of child abuse were perpetrated by mothers currently within adolescence or had given birth during adolescence (Creighton, 1985).

Overall, the weight of scientific evidence suggests that adolescent motherhood is related to child abuse. However, confirming the existence of this relationship does not explain why it exists. The age of a woman when she becomes a mother may not be the only factor that contributes to her increased likelihood of child abuse. Many developmental challenges accompany the stage of adolescence that may contribute to the adolescent motherhood-child abuse relationship (Adams et al., 1994). As the process of moving from adolescence to adulthood is a developmental one, Erikson's psychosocial theory can provide a framework for understanding this process.

Theoretical Framework

Adolescent mothers are within adolescence for only a short period before they move into adulthood, yet they remain parents for a lifetime. Little, however, is known about the course of the relationship between adolescent motherhood and child abuse risk over time, as these mothers move into and through a new developmental stage. Therefore, a developmental approach may help to illuminate this relationship. Erikson's (1963) stage theory may be particularly helpful, as it addresses the role of developmental crises and their resolution in personality functioning and psychological well being. Erikson proposes that the inability to resolve a developmental crisis will be carried into the next life stage and hinder the completion of future developmental tasks.

The stage in Erikson's theory that corresponds to adolescence is "identity versus role confusion." According to Erikson, if the adolescent is unable to form a healthy identity during adolescence, the resolution of future developmental tasks will be impaired. Erikson

(1963) states that educational attainment, occupational goals, and beliefs about others' perceptions of oneself are fundamental for the formation of a secure identity during adolescence.

The additional task of parenting during adolescence creates role collision by forcing the development of parenting skills and responsibilities that are not typically required at this life stage. It could be argued that the untimely occurrence of motherhood within adolescence in Western industrial societies can interfere with the development of a strong identity because of the collision of roles, which, in turn, leads to role confusion. If motherhood occurs during adolescence, education and occupational goals may be interrupted and the negative perceptions of others may threaten the development of positive self-esteem. Eriksonian theory would predict that the resulting role confusion will end in crisis and create an impaired identity. This impaired identity is predicted to manifest itself in an inability to manage the demands of parenthood, hampering the mother's ability to recognize and meet the child's needs, and increasing the likelihood of child abuse.

Identity Variables

When applying Erikson's theory, education, occupational goals, and self-esteem become identity variables. It is necessary to discuss these variables in more detail to understand how they function and how they are theorized to continue to function over time.

Education

Following Erikson's theory, becoming a mother within adolescence may disrupt the attainment of educational goals and contribute to role confusion. Pregnancy during adolescence has indeed been associated with an increased likelihood of dropping out of high school (Freeman and Rickels, 1993). Freeman and Rickels (1993) compared adolescents who chose to have an abortion to adolescents who chose to continue the pregnancy. Two years later, 93% of the abortion group had completed high school compared to 69% of the delivery group.

Further, it has been found that abusing populations have lower educational attainment than non-abusing populations (Benedict et al., 1985; Cadzow et al., 1999; De Paul and Domenech, 2000; Schloesser et al., 1992). Benedict et al. (1985) found the mean completed years of education for an abusing sample to be 10.5 years. Therefore, a higher level of education is associated with a lower risk of child abuse. Education, at the very least, is hindered or delayed with the event of parenting within adolescence, thereby possibly increasing the risk of child abuse.

With respect to FAMs, the question becomes, will the risk of child abuse evolve as the adolescent mother becomes an adult mother? Erikson's theory would lead one to argue that lower educational attainment within adolescence will impair identity formation due to role confusion and will be carried into adulthood. Since adolescent motherhood has been shown to increase the likelihood of high school drop out (Freeman and Rickels, 1993), it is reasonable to assume that educational attainment for FAMs will be lower than for adult mothers. Therefore, it can be predicted that education will continue to be relatively low for

FAMs; thereby possibly increasing the risk of child abuse for children born to adolescent mothers compared to adult mothers.

Occupational Goals

Although occupation and employment choices are not settled within adolescence, it is during this period that various choices are explored. Adolescent mothers, compared to their non-parenting counterparts, may have less opportunity to investigate and pursue occupational interests due to the additional pressures and responsibilities of parenting. The inability to explore occupational options may translate into increased unemployment or decreased employability.

A longitudinal study by Furstenberg, Brooks-Gunn, and Morgan (1987) compared adolescent mothers and non-parenting classmates. The results of the study indicate that after six years those who had become parents in adolescence were less likely to be employed.

In comparison to non-abusive populations, abusive populations tend to have considerably higher rates of unemployment (Christoffersen, 2000; Creighton, 1985; Gillham et al., 1998; Kotch and Thomas, 1986). For example, Christoffersen (2000) found that lack of vocational training and long term maternal unemployment were more likely in abusive families compared to non-abusive families. Therefore, the risk of child abuse may increase with unemployment or decreased employability.

With the constrained opportunity to achieve occupational goals and explore employment choices that comes with adolescent motherhood, role confusion may develop creating an impaired identity and, thereby, increasing the risk of child abuse. On the basis of Eriksonian theory, it can be predicted that role confusion rooted in the continuing inability to explore occupational choices and form a healthy identity will continue into adulthood, along with decreased employment or employability and the continuation of heightened risk for child abuse.

Self-Esteem

According to Erikson, belief about others' perceptions of oneself influence the formation of a healthy identity. Believed perceptions of others that become internalized, labeled by C. H. Cooley as the "looking glass self" (Felson, 1993), affect our self-esteem (Bishop and Inderbitzen, 1995; Burnett, 1996; Burnett and McCrindle, 1999). Self-esteem has been defined as "the global evaluative dimension of the self" (Santrock, 1996, p. 384) and has been found to be a good indicator of identity formation (Hurlbut, McDonald Culp, Jambunathan, and Bulter, 1997).

How peers communicate their appraisals of the adolescent changes the adolescent's self-perceptions and self-esteem (Felson, 1993). Becoming a mother during adolescence may heighten a young woman's exposure and sensitivity to others' negative judgments and harm her self-esteem. The resulting negative view of herself may interfere with the development of a strong identity.

Research comparing the self-esteem of pregnant and non-pregnant adolescents has resulted in inconsistent findings. Some research has determined that there is a correlation between low self-esteem and adolescent pregnancy (Elkes and Crocitto, 1987; Held, 1981; Lineberger, 1987). The crisis of pregnancy during adolescence may lead to feeling overwhelmed, inadequate, unworthy, creating poor self-esteem (Zongher, 1977). Other research has been unable to confirm such a finding (McCullough and Scherman, 1991; Robinson and Frank, 1994).

Despite this discrepancy across studies, it has been demonstrated that adolescent females who experience many transitions, compared to those who do not experience many transitions during adolescence may develop lower self-esteem (Simmons, 1987). Motherhood during adolescence would create more transitions and place the adolescent mother at risk for lower self-esteem than non-parenting adolescents (Hurlbut et al., 1997). For example, Herrmann, Van Cleve, and Levisen (1998) found a significant drop in self-esteem for adolescent mothers between birth of the child and six months. Furthermore, low self-esteem of adolescent mothers has been found to predict an inability to understand the child's perspective, lack of empathy, unrealistic developmental expectations, and approval of corporal punishment, all of which may increase the likelihood of child abuse (Hurlbut et al., 1997).

Some empirical findings lend support to this prediction. In a representative sample of 644 families reported for child abuse, low maternal self-esteem was associated with child abuse (Brown, Cohen, Johnson, and Salzinger, 1998). Other research also confirms this relationship (Anderson and Lauderdale, 1982; Friedrich and Wheeler, 1982; Steele, 1987). It has been suggested that people who have low self-esteem may become abusive towards their children because they see the child as a reincarnation of their own "bad self" and, therefore, punishment of the child, in their eyes, becomes justified (Steele, 1997). Following Erikson, if self-esteem is low in adolescence due to an impaired identity it may continue to be low in adulthood, thereby maintaining an increased risk of child abuse among FAMs.

According to Erikson's theory, it could be predicted that the identity formation of FAMs will remain impaired and the adolescent motherhood-child abuse relationship will persist with increasing age. Children of FAMs will continue to have higher risk of child abuse than child born to adult mothers. This research will determine if FAMs and adult mothers differ on the identity variables of education, employment, and self-esteem and, therefore, determine if impaired identity due to role confusion persists into adulthood for FAMs. Also, this research will detect if the existence of impaired identity can account for the increased risk of child abuse for children of FAMs. Erikson's theory would predict that if impaired identity formation occurs for adolescent mothers and increases the likelihood of child abuse, then the continuing impaired identity formation will account for the heightened risk of child abuse for children of FAMs'.

This research contained three hypotheses. First, it was hypothesized that children of FAMs would be more likely to be abused than children of adult mothers. Second, it was hypothesized that FAMs would score lower than adult mothers on the three measures of adolescent identity: educational attainment, employment status, and self-esteem. Finally, it was hypothesized that lower levels of education, employment status, and self-esteem would increase the likelihood of the occurrence of child abuse and these identity variables would account for the higher odds of child abuse for children of FAMs.

Materials and Methods

The dataset used for this research was Statistic's Canada National Longitudinal Survey of Children and Youth (NLSCY) cycle three.[1] In 1998-99, approximately 32,000 families were contacted to answer a questionnaires providing information with regard to the family, household, and child. The sample was comprised of women who are biological mothers of children aged 10 to 15 years who responded to the self-completed questionnaire, from which the child abuse variable is drawn. Based on this selection, the sample size for this research was 4,387 including 4,250 adult mothers and 137 FAMs.

Measurement

Motherhood Status

Mothers were classified as either FAMs or adult mothers on the basis of their responses to an item, which asked for the mother's year of age at the birth of the target child (child responding to the self-completed questionnaire). All mothers nineteen years and younger at the time of the birth of the target child were considered FAMs. All mothers aged 22 or older at the time of birth of the target child were considered adult mothers. The three-year age spread between the two groups was designed to provide a clear differentiation between mothers who were adolescents when their child was born and those who had their child after they had entered adulthood.

Child Abuse

Children aged 10 to 15 years who participated in cycle three of the NLSCY were asked to answer a self-completed questionnaire in the privacy of their own homes while the interviewer waited. On this questionnaire, children were asked to state the frequency in which they are hit or threatened to be hit.[2] Frequencies were rated on a five-point scale: never, rarely, sometimes, often, and always. Children's responses to this item were collapsed to create a dichotomous variable with the categories of "yes" or "no" indicating that child abuse did or did not occur. This decision was made on the basis of a preliminary examination of the distribution of responses to this variable, which indicated that frequencies across the hitting categories were too few in number to allow reliable comparisons among these groups, particularly when they were further distributed across two categories of motherhood status.

Measures of Identity

Mothers' resolution of their adolescent identity crises (Erikson, 1963) was measured in three ways: educational attainment, employment status, and self-esteem. Maternal educational attainment is determined by mothers' responses to two questions. For descriptive

---

[1] Data used in the analysis were obtained by special agreement with Statistics Canada to access the NLSCY master file. The analyses are the sole responsibility of the authors. The opinions expressed do not represent the views of Statistics Canada.

[2] Although the threat of violence is a form of psychological abuse, it has been stated that psychological abuse is embedded in all forms of child abuse and, therefore, is appropriate to be included within this study's measure of child abuse (Garbarino, Gutterman, & Seeley, 1986; Hart, Brassard, & Karlson, 1996).

analysis, a categorical variable indicating the mother's highest educational attainment (less than high school, high school, some post secondary, and diploma or university degree) was used. For multivariate analysis, maternal educational attainment was measured in the number of years of education.

Maternal employment status was assessed using a categorical variable indicating if the mother was currently employed or unemployed.

According to Erikson (1963), what is critical to the formation of adolescent identity is other's perceptions of oneself. In the present study, maternal self-esteem was measured using an item asking, "How often have you felt or behaved this way during the past week?: I felt that people disliked me." Low self-esteem was defined as feeling disliked some or a little of the time to most of the time within the past week. High self-esteem was defined as feeling disliked rarely or none of the time within the past week. For multivariate analysis, the number of day in one week they felt disliked was used.

Control Variables

Control variables for this research were number of children and marital status. Number of children has been selected because the two comparison groups consisted of women who have children in different life stages. This means women having children in adolescence have a large window of opportunity to have more children compared to women who have children later in adulthood. More children has been associated with an increased risk of child abuse and, therefore, could contribute to increased risk of abuse for FAMs. By controlling for number of children, if FAMs have more children than adult mothers any additional risk of increased child abuse due to having more children has been adjusted for and a better test of the theory is permitted. Number of children was measured by a variable that asked for the number of children under 17 who live in the household.

Marital status was also controlled for in this research. Marital status is one way of understanding possible living environments. More support financially and within the household may be available for married or common-law mothers compared to mothers who are single, separated, divorced, or widowed. Therefore, marital status can provide a modest understanding of contributors within the household and account for possible economic and social support that is likely to decrease child abuse. Past research has found that adolescent mothers are more likely to be single (Leadbeater and Way, 2001) and that being single is associated with increased risk of child abuse (Murphey and Braner, 2000). In theory, FAMs are more likely to be single and, therefore, less supported. Controlling for marital status will account for this difference among comparison groups and allow for a more accurate test of the theory.

Marital status of the mother was measured using a dichotomous variable indicating being married or common law (including the living with partner) and single (including single never been married, widowed, separated, and divorced).

Methods of Data Analysis

The data analysis was conducted in two stages. To understand the differences between the comparison groups and to test hypothesis one and two, descriptive analysis techniques were used. The relationships between categorical variables were tested using cross-tabulations with chi square tests of significance. In addition to chi square tests of significance, Mann Whitney-U was also used to test the relationship between and ordinal and categorical variables. For multivariate analysis, multiple logistic regressions were used. This analysis was conducted in two phases. First, multiple logistic regression was conducted on FAMs and adult mothers separately to understand how the variables operate for each group of women. Second, a sequential analysis was used to determine the extent to which children of FAMs heightened risk of child abuse relative to children of adult mothers is accounted for by the identity and control variables.

Results

Descriptive Statistics

Child Abuse by Motherhood Status

The results of the cross-tabulation of the occurrence of child abuse by motherhood status in the present study are presented in Table 1. The results have shown that, while the majority of children are not abused, 33% of children of FAMs compared to 22% of children of adult mothers were abused. Hypothesis one, in which children of FAMs compared to children of adult mothers were expected to be more likely to be abused was confirmed with these results.

Table 1. Child Abuse and Motherhood Status (%)

	Adult Mothers	FAMs
Child Physical Abuse***		
Yes	22.2	32.8
No	77.8	67.2

***$p < .01$

Identity Variables by Motherhood Status

Table 2 contains results of each identity variable cross-tabulated with motherhood status. FAMs (24%) compared to adult mothers (10%) were more likely to have less than a high school education. Furthermore, FAMs (16%, 25%, and 35% respectively) compared to adult mothers (19%, 29%, and 42% respectively) were less likely to have graduated high school, have some post secondary education or trade school, and a community college diploma or university degree. These results support hypothesis two, which stated that FAMs would have less education than adult mothers.

Education is an ordinal level variable and, therefore, a Mann Whitney-U test was also used. The results indicate that the mean rank for FAMs compared to adult mothers' mean rank differed significantly ($p < .001$) and, therefore, the educational attainment level for each group of women was different. This finding was consistent with the results of the cross-tabulation of motherhood status by educational attainment and provided further support for the educational portion of hypothesis two.

With regard to employment status, FAMs (31%) compared to adult mothers (21%) were more likely to be unemployed. This finding supports hypothesis two, stating that FAMs compared to adult mothers would be more likely to be unemployed.

Also as expected, lower self-esteem was more predominate in FAMs (10%) compared to adult mothers (8%). Even though the direction of the relationship was consistent with the hypothesis, the self-esteem aspect of hypothesis two was not fully supported because the difference between the two groups was not statistically significant.

Table 2. Identity Variables by Motherhood Status (%)

	Adult Mothers	FAMs
Education***		
Less than high school	10.4	23.9
High school	18.6	15.9
Some post secondary	29.1	25.4
Degree or diploma	41.9	34.8
Employment ***		
Unemployed	21.1	31.4
Employed	78.9	68.6
Self-Esteem		
Low	7.9	9.5
High	92.1	90.5

***$p < .01$

Control Variables by Motherhood Status

Table 3 contains the results of the control variables cross-tabulated with motherhood status. The number of children of FAMs and adult mother were similar. According to this cross-tabulation, FAMs were not statistically more likely to have more children compared to adult mothers.

Table 3. Control Variables by Motherhood Status (%)

	Adult Mothers	FAMs
Number of children		
1 child	19.5	19.9
2 children	47.3	44.1
3 children	24.6	27.2
4 or more children	8.5	8.8
Marital Status***		
Single	15.1	29.9
Not Single	84.9	70.1

***$p < .01$

In terms of marital status, FAMs (30%) compared to adult mothers (15%) were twice as likely to be single.

Multiple Logistic Regression Analysis

Separate Logistic Regressions for FAMs and Adult Mothers

Table 4 provides the logistic regression results for child abuse of children of FAMs and children of adult mothers run separately. The results indicated that when adjusting for all other variables in the model, as hypothesized education was negatively associated with abuse of children of FAMs. As the level of education increased the odds of child abuse decreased. For every additional year of maternal education, the odds of abuse for a child of FAMs' were reduced by 18%. For each additional year of maternal education for adult mothers, odds of child abuse for these children were reduced by only 4%, but did not reach statistical significance. Therefore, the level of mother's education had a larger impact on the odds of child abuse for children of FAMs, but not for children of adult mothers.

Table 4. Results of Logistic Regression of Child Abuse and Motherhood Status

Variables	Adult Mothers n = 4204 Odds Ratio	FAMs n = 137 Odds Ratio
Education	0.958	0.821*
Unemployed	1.039	0.692
Self-Esteem	1.111**	1.196
Number of Children	1.035	1.521**
Marital Status Single	1.336***	1.876*
Constant	0.414**	1.426
-2 log-likelihood	4377	234
X^2	19	17

*$p < .10$; **$p < .05$; ***$p < .01$

With regard to employment, the relationship between employment and child abuse was not statistically significant for FAMs or adult mothers. The hypothesis that low self-esteem would increase the risk of child abuse was partially supported. Low self-esteem increased the risk of child abuse by 20% for FAMs (but did not reach statistical significance likely due to a small n) and by 11% for adult mothers. It must be stated, however, that the impact of low self-esteem for FAMs compared to adult mothers was almost twice as high, suggesting that self-esteem does play a more important role in child abuse for children of FAMs.

Having more children in the family increased the odds of child abuse for children of FAMs only. For each additional child, the odds of child abuse increased by 52% for children of FAMs. Single marital status also increased the odds of child abuse for children for both

FAMs and adult mothers. Being single created 88% increased odds of child abuse for children of FAMs and a 34% increase for children of adult mothers.

Logistic Regression for FAMs and Adult Mothers Combined

To understand the extent to which identity variables account for the relationship between child abuse of children of FAMs and adult mothers, sequential logistic regressions were run. To do this, the variables were divided into two blocks, one for identity variables and one for control variables.

Table 5 contains the results of the sequential logistic regressions. The first model in table 5 provides the motherhood status variable without any controls. Consistent with the descriptive analysis, the odds of child abuse were significantly higher for children of FAMs compared to children of adult mothers. Children of FAMs have 71% higher odds of being abused than children of adult mothers.

Table 5. Results of Sequential Logistic Regression on Child Abuse

Variables	FAMs/ Adult mothers n =4387 Odds Ratio	Identity Variables n =4341 Odds Ratio	Control Variables n =4387 Odds Ratio	Full Model n =4341 Odds Ratio
Motherhood Status				
FAMs	1.713***	1.614**	1.624***	1.550**
Adults	1.000	1.000	1.000	1.000
		BLOCK 1		BLOCK 1
			BLOCK 2	BLOCK 2
Constant	0.286***	0.586	0.236***	0.461**
-2 log-likelihood	4677	4620	4663	4610
X^2	8	21	22	31

**p < .05; ***p < .01

The difference in odds ratios of these two groups of women was statistically significant ($p < .01$). The second model controls for identity variables. When controlling for identity variables, the odds of child abuse for children of FAMs compared to children of adult mothers were reduced by 10%, but remained statistically significant ($p < .05$). The third model includes only the control variables.. When controlling for marital status and number of children, the odds of child abuse for children of FAMs compared to adult mothers decreased by 9% and remained statistically significant ($p < .01$). The final model adjusted for all independent variables in the study. When all the variables in the model are controlled, the odds of child abuse for children of FAMs compared to children of adult mothers were reduced by 16%. In other words, controlling for all variables in the model, children of FAMs still had a 55% higher odds of child abuse compared to children of adult mothers. The results from the logistic regression determine that hypothesis three was only partially supported. While taken separately, the identity variables and control variables were important for explaining some of the variance in the increased odds of child abuse among children of

FAMs. Although neither the identity nor the control variables fully account for this relationship.

Discussion

Child abuse is a public health problem. It is important to identify at-risk populations to inform prevention and intervention efforts. Past research has demonstrated that adolescent mothers are at increased risk of abusing their children (Benedict et al., 1985; Chaffin et al., 1996; Creighton, 1985). The present study extents this area of research with the findings that this relationship continues even when the adolescent mother is an adult. The continuation of this relationship into adulthood highlights the importance of identifying FAMs in research.

In short, this research determines that children born to adolescent mothers continue to be at a greater odds for child abuse compared to children born to adult mothers. According to Erikson's theory, this increased risk may be attributable to poor identity formation, as reflected in mothers' levels of education, employment status, and self-esteem.

Identity Variables and Motherhood Status

Educational Attainment

Based of previous research on adolescent parenting populations (De Paul and Domenech, 2000; Freeman and Rickels, 1993), it was hypothesized that educational attainment would be lower among FAMs than among adult mothers. The present findings support this hypothesis. Even though women can continue their education after having a child within adolescence, their rate of progress or achievement may be lower compared to women without such a disruption. The present findings suggest that completing high school may be likely for individuals who have the responsibility of childrearing.

Erikson's theory predicts that lower levels of education will interfere with the formation of a secure identity. It was hypothesized that low educational attainment would increase the likelihood of child abuse (Benedict et al., 1985; Cadzow et al., 1999; Schloesser et al., 1992). Lower levels of educational attainment did not have a large impact on the odds of child abuse for adult mothers. Yet, the impact of lower education on the risk of child abuse was considerably greater for children of FAMs. Each additional year of maternal education reduced of the odds of the occurrence of child abuse by 18% for children of FAMs. A possible explanation as to why education impacted the odds of child abuse for children of FAMs but not for children of adult mothers may be found within the framework of Erikson's theory. According to this theory, education may be especially important for FAMs because, according to Erikson's theory, it helps to form a secure identity and it is the ill formed identity that increases the risk of child abuse. Adult mothers' education during adolescence is not interrupted by motherhood and, consequently, the formation of a secure identity is more likely. Additional years of education for FAMs may help to increase the likely of forming a secure identity and, therefore, have a greater impact on decreasing the odds of child abuse for children born to these women.

The results of this research indicate that education accounts for some of the increased likelihood of child abuse for children of FAMs. The impact of education is great for FAMs and, therefore, it should be included in future research on FAMs and child abuse.

Employment Status

Previous research conducted in the United States has determined that adolescent mothers have high rates of unemployment (Leadbeater and Way, 2001). It was predicted that FAMs would have higher rates of unemployment than adult mothers. The present findings demonstrate that the rate of unemployment continues to be higher for FAMs than for adult mothers, supporting this hypothesis. Higher rates of unemployment for FAMs may be based on lower levels of education, inability to explore employment options, and/or decreased employability because of additional responsibilities of childrearing commencing in adolescence. It is possible that FAMs are more likely than adult mothers to decide to be stay-at-home mothers, rather than hold low quality employment positions.

Self-Esteem

It was predicted that FAMs would have lower self-esteem than adult mothers. According to the present findings, this does not appear to be the case. No statistically significant differences were found for FAMs and adults mothers with regard to self-esteem. Past research on self-esteem and adolescent parenting has resulted in inconsistent findings and difficulty in understanding how self-esteem may function. Part of reason for inconsistent findings may be due to the difficult and differences in measuring self-esteem.

Alternatively, it may be the case that, with time, the FAM will adjust to her role as mother and low self-esteem will increase to normative levels. Time and the acceptance of a mothering role will not increase levels of educational attainment or increase employability, but may have a positive impact on self-esteem. As a result, self-esteem may function differently than the other identity variables.

The present research demonstrates that low self-esteem is associated with child abuse. This finding is in accordance with previous research (Brown et al., 1998). Individuals with low self-esteem may create internal working models of the self as being unworthy, inadequate, and incompetent (Harter, 1998). When these feelings occur in conjunction with childrearing challenges, such as irritable children, difficult child behaviours, or simply parent-child conflict, the mother with low self-esteem may feel she is not equipped to deal with the problem. Consequently, the mother may resort to aggressive disciplinary techniques such as hitting the child, to terminate the immediate difficult childrearing situation; potentially creating a pattern of child abuse.

Interestingly, the increased odds of child abuse for children of FAMs with low self-esteem are almost two times that for children of adult mothers with low self-esteem (although statistical significance was not reached likely due to a small n). While FAMs are not more likely to have low self-esteem than adult mothers, the fact that low self-esteem may have a larger impact for FAMs suggests that different mechanisms are functioning in the two groups of women. In other words, it may be that the root or cause of low self-esteem is different for the two groups of women. For example, FAMs' low self-esteem may be directly related to their mothering role because of exposure to negative judgments of their early parenthood.

Therefore, FAMs may associate poor feelings of themselves with parenting and, more specifically, their children, contributing to an increased risk of abusive parenting behaviour. It may be that adult mothers are able to separate their feelings about themselves from their feelings about their children because adult mothers' low self-esteem may be unrelated to their parenting role. Therefore, the adult mother's ability to cognitively separate her low self-esteem from parenting may be a preventative factor for this group.

To summarize the discussion of identity variables, this research demonstrates that FAMs differ from adult mothers on most identity variables. Therefore, the fundamental aspects required to form a healthy identity may be impaired for FAMs. In other words, it seems that the collision of adolescent and adult roles may result in confusion, which, in turn, precipitates impaired identity for FAMs.

Control Variables and Motherhood Status

Number of Children

The present research demonstrates that, in Canada, FAMs do not have more children than adult mothers. This result contradicts past research from the United States that finds women who give birth in adolescence have more children than women who give birth in adulthood (Connelly and Straus, 1992). This finding may suggest that it is not the number of children that differs between FAMs and adult mothers, but rather, when the children are conceived. It has been found that repeat pregnancies soon after the first birth are very high for adolescent mothers (Leadbeater and Way, 2001). Therefore, it may be that adolescent mothers have children close together in adolescence, but do not continue to give birth at this rate in adulthood. Consequently, when comparing these women later in life, FAMs and adult mothers will not differ in family size, but rather, the life stage in which they gave birth.

In this study, it was found that the number of children increases the odds of child abuse for children of FAMs. This finding partially supports previous research on child abuse and family size (Straus et al., 1980).[3] More children have been noted to increase the stress in the household and, therefore, represent a risk marker for child abuse (Kotch et al., 1995). As the number of members of the family increases, generally the resources become limited, creating a stressful environment conducive to child abuse.

Children of FAMs were at a 52% increased likelihood of child abuse for each additional child in the family. Since the increased odds of child abuse for children of adult mothers was very low and statistically insignificant ($p = .385$), family size did not have an impact on the risk of child abuse for these families; suggesting that adult mothers may be better equipped than FAMs to manage the demands of more children. More children in the household inevitability increases stress by requiring emotional and financial contributions for the fulfillment of the children's needs, which may be more challenging for FAMs. FAMs may have fewer effective resources to handle complex parenting circumstances created by the

---

[3] Straus (1980) suggests that the risk of child abuse increases with increasing number of children in the family up to five and then families with more that five are at a decreased level of risk. Since few families in Canada have five children or more (Statistics Canada, 1996), the focus of this discussion will be restricted to families with up to five children.

presence of increased numbers of children. Indeed, past research has shown that adolescent mothers are more reliant than adult mothers on physical means of discipline (Garcia Coll, Hoffman, Van Houten, and Oh, 1987; Stevens-Simon and Nelligan, 1998). Clearly, since the number of children in the household impacts FAMs, this variable is important for understanding the abuse of children of FAMs.

Marital Status

The present findings confirmed that, in Canada, FAMs are more likely than adult mothers to be single and supports previous research conducted in the United States demonstrating that adolescent mothers are less likely to be married (Leadbeater and Way, 2001). Adolescent women who become pregnant are less likely now than in previous decades to marry the father of the unborn child simply because of the pregnancy (Leadbeater and Way, 2001). In the United States in 1955, 85% of teenage women who became pregnant married the father, compared to 28% in 1992 (Moore, Miller, Glei, and Morrison, 1995). Nevertheless, a FAM who does not marry the father may have a difficult time finding an alternate partner to marry because of the challenges of developing a serious relationship while raising children, such as limited time and opportunities to meet a compatible mate willing to take on the responsibility of her children. These challenges may increase the likelihood that many FAMs will remain single.

Being single increases the odds of child abuse for children of both FAMs and adult mothers. Therefore, children of a single mother, regardless of her age, may be more likely to be abused because of the stress of being a single mother and surviving on one income compared to two parent families. Having less income and less support may increase the odds of child abuse. However, the increased odds of child abuse were considerably higher for children of single FAMs than for children of single adult mothers. This finding may reflect a qualitative difference in single status between these two groups of women. In the present study, single status included those who were single (never married), widowed, divorced, and separated. It may be the case that adult women tend to become single mothers due to divorce or separation while FAMs may be more likely to have never been married. If this is the case, single adult mothers may be more likely to have financial contributions from their former partners. If the FAMs are divorced or separated, they also may receive financial compensation from their former husbands. However, these husbands are likely to be formerly adolescent fathers and, therefore, financial contributions are likely to be lower compared to those from adult fathers. It is also more likely that single adult mothers are more emotionally prepared for childrearing compared to single adolescents who are likely to become pregnant by accident and are dependent on others to support their child. Therefore, a qualitative difference in single status between these two groups of women may contribute to the difference in odds of child abuse.

The Odds of Child Abuse for FAMs Relative to Adult Mothers

Results of the sequential regressions provide an understanding of the impact of each group of variables on the higher odds of child abuse for children of FAMs. Not surprisingly, the risk of child abuse for children of FAMs is the strongest when no variables are controlled. When identity variables are controlled, the risk of child abuse is reduced by a small margin. When only the control variables are controlled, the higher risk of child abuse for children of FAMs is again reduced by a small margin, but to a slightly lesser extent in comparison to the identity variables. It is when both identity and control variables are added to the model that the odds of child abuse are reduced to the greatest extent. However, even when all variables in the model are included, the odds of child abuse for children of FAMs relative to adult mothers are still substantial.

Drawing from Erikson's theory, identity variables should, for the most part, account for the increased likelihood of child abuse for children of FAMs; impaired identity formation due to role confusion should largely explain children of FAMs' heightened risk of child abuse. Controlling the identity variables does reduce the odds of child abuse for children of FAMs. The greater impact of the identity variables on the likelihood of child abuse for children of FAMs clearly demonstrates the validity of their inclusion in an explanation of the relationship between FAMs and child abuse, yet the explanatory value of these variables is very limited. The identity variables certainly do not fully account for the increased likelihood of child abuse for children of FAMs. Therefore, even though impaired identity formation appears to be greater among FAMs than adult mothers, it does not completely explain why children of FAMs are more likely to be abused. Erikson's theory offers only limited explanatory value for understanding the FAM-child abuse relationship.

The findings of the present study, therefore, suggest that Erikson's theory is inadequate as a stand-alone explanation of why children of FAMs are more likely to be abused than children of adult mothers. In a very modest capacity, identity variables aid understanding of child abuse if they are among other variables within a larger framework. The present findings suggest that a more holistic approach needs to be used to fully understand this relationship.

Implications

This research confirms that difficulties of adolescent motherhood continue into adulthood for FAMs and designates these women as an at-risk population. It should be clarified that being within an at-risk population does not indicate that all members of the group will fall victim to the at-risk behaviour. Therefore, being an adolescent or FAM does not inevitability mean that she will be a "bad" mother. Instead, membership to an at-risk population can help society understand who is more vulnerable and, therefore, who requires attention. This implies that FAMs comprise a special group of women requiring a special response to their needs as mothers. The ultimate goal is to supply these mothers with appropriate supports so that they will be able to provide a thriving environment for their children without exposing them to abuse.

To begin with, education is undoubtedly an important factor in the reduction of the risk of child abuse for children of FAMs. This research implies that keeping adolescent mothers in school will help to reduce their odds of child abuse later in adulthood. Therefore, programs need to be developed and maintained to enable these women to complete high school and provide them with an opportunity to continue a post secondary education. Adolescent parenting programs in Canada do exist but are not well developed or widely available.

The findings on employment have uncertain implications. This research is only able to speculate and not accurately understand and confirm why children of employed FAMs were more likely to be abused and, thus, detailed suggestions for improvement cannot be made at this time. It is likely however, that if children of FAMs experience greater odds of child abuse because of the quality of the mothers' employment, then an investment in the skills of these women needs to be made to increase their ability to find jobs that they find satisfying. Without further research on employment and child abuse for children of FAMs compared to children of adult mothers, such changes can only be viewed as suggestions in preliminary stages of development.

The implications of the findings on self-esteem were also difficult to interpret.

Recall that there is little difference between FAMs and adult mothers levels of self-esteem. Based on the possibility that this finding could be due to a poor measure of self-esteem, as a cautionary step, this variable should still be included in future investigations of the relationship between FAMs and child abuse. Moreover, this research demonstrates that low self-esteem increased the odds of child abuse. Increasing levels of self-esteem and positive feelings of self-worth may reduce the risk of child abuse. A program that encourages the development of parenting skills, coping strategies, creates a support network, and validates the importance of their parenting role may contribute to the increase of self-esteem and, consequently, have positive ramifications on the reduction of child abuse.

The control variables in this research also contribute to our understanding of child abuse for children of FAMs and have implications. Even though FAMs according to this research were not more likely to have more children than adult mothers, they seem to be less well equipped to handle more children. The implication of this finding is that FAMs need to be taught more effective parenting skills and coping strategies to handle the complexity of raising more than one child. Also, as a preventative measure, adolescent mothers should be informed of the stressors of having additional children.

Single marital status increased the odds of child abuse significantly more for children of FAMs compared to children of adult mothers. Therefore, efforts need to be made to equip FAMs with the means of more effective parenting skills to increase their ability to raise children in the absence of a partner.

Viewing these implications collectively provides an initial sketch of some elements that need to be included in a proactive program focused on the prevention of child abuse by FAMs in Canada. It is very apparent, however, that more research is needed to determine what accounts for the remaining unexplained risk of child abuse for children of FAMs relative to children of adult mothers. Such research needs to include a more holistic framework for analysis that can encompass the variables identified in this research, yet include other variables that will account for more of the risk of child abuse for children of FAMs.

A Proposed Holistic Approach

The contexts of the ecological model include the broader context, immediate interaction context, and developmental-psychological context (Belsky, 1993). It is argued that the variables within all contexts of the ecological model and the interactions of these variables can predict child abuse. The benefit of the multiple domains of the model is that they can incorporate and become adapted to many living circumstances. The ecological model can be applied to FAMs illuminating the sociocultural context to which these families belong.

Based on gains from the present research, education, employment, self-esteem, number of children, and marital status should be included in the ecological framework, as well as the inclusion of other variables. Variables can be organized into each context of the ecological model creating a framework to study FAMs and child abuse. The variables discussed in the holistic approach is not an exhaustive list of all the important variables to consider, but provides future direction for research on FAMs and child abuse from an ecological perspective.

Within the broader context are demographic variables as well as variables incorporating aspects of society, culture, and ethnicity. Based on the present research, number of children or family size should be included in this context. In addition to these variables, past research has identified income as an important component for understanding the heightened risk of child abuse for FAMs. Many studies have determined that low-income families have higher rates of child abuse (Brown et al., 1998; Gelles, 1989). Adolescent mothers tend to have very low income because of limited education and employment (Cadzow et al., 1999; De Paul and Domenech, 2000) and, therefore, income may be a useful variable in FAM-child abuse research.

Another variable that may be useful in future research on adolescent motherhood and child abuse is ethnicity. In Canada, the rate of adolescent pregnancy is four times higher among Aboriginal teens compared to non-Aboriginal teens (Health Canada, 1999). Similarly, in the United States, African Americans teens give birth four times the rate of Caucasian teens (National Center for Health Statistics (NCHS), 1993). As well, childrearing practices can be influenced by ethnic beliefs and, therefore, the inclusion of this variable in future research may contribute to our understanding of why some women abuse and others do not.

Within the immediate context is marital status, which in this research is a loose measure of social support. Even though these variables may be related, ideally they should be studied separately. This research has found that marital status has some explanatory power for understanding the increased risk of child abuse for children of FAMs and, therefore, should be included in future models. In addition to the support of a partner and other support networks should also be investigated. Past research has found that low perception of social support has placed young adolescents at risk for child abuse (Haskett et al., 1994). Support networks may function differently for adolescent and adult mothers and, therefore, should be included in future models. Along with marital status and social support is parenting style. Parenting behaviours associated with increased risk of child abuse are commonly found to be typical of adolescent mothers (Baranowski, Schilmoeller, and Higgins, 1990; Garcia Coll et al., 1987; Luster and Rhoades, 1989; Stevens-Simon and Nelligan, 1998).

The developmental-psychological context includes education, employment, and self-esteem, which to contribute to some degree to the understanding of the increased likelihood of child abuse for FAMs. As well as the aforementioned identity variables, maternal health and psychopathology could also be added to the variables within the developmental-psychological context. Past research has demonstrated that health problems are associated with child abuse (Lahey, Conger, Atkeson, and Treiber, 1984). Adolescent mothers may be at a greater risk for health problems due to the competing nutritional needs of the still growing mother and fetus, resulting in birth complications for the child and stunted growth for the adolescent (Hechtman, 1989). If maternal health problems persist for FAMs this variable may contribute to the increased risk of child abuse. Previous research has determined that alcohol abuse may contribute to increased likelihood of child abuse (Tarter, Hegedus, Winsten, and Alterman, 1984). Since this variable has been useful in the prediction of child abuse it may also be useful in determining if alcohol consumption is different for FAMs and adult mothers and, as a consequence, increases the risk of child abuse.

In conclusion, this research has identified a new perspective on the study of adolescent motherhood and child abuse. The risk of child abuse does continue into adulthood for women who give birth during adolescence. Ideally, the present research will stimulate others to see the importance of the issue of FAMs and child abuse. Giving birth within adolescence does not inevitably create unfit mothers or the occurrence of child abuse. However, children born to these women have a greater risk of being abused and, therefore, it is our hope that this research will contribute to the knowledge base needed to support these women so they are able to raise their children in a thriving environment.

Prevention of Child Abuse

Child abuse results in many harmful consequences for children, which can continue into adulthood. Research investigation a whole population approach to preventing child abuse needs to be supported. Additionally, research that can better identify those at-risk for child abuse may help with intervention efforts. Early intervention is important not only to terminate abuse, but also to help the child recover from its impact. Although the current research is not able to inform specific prevention efforts it does help to identify an at-risk group of women that may otherwise be forgotten once the adolescent mother enters adulthood. The increased risk of child abuse does continue as the adolescent mother enters adulthood. Therefore, even though the FAM has gotten older, the difficulties and challenges of having children during adolescence may not disappear. Therefore, the needs of these families need to be recognized and supported to prevent the incidence of child abuse.

References

[1] Adams, G. R., Gullotta, T. P., and Markstorm-Adams, C. (1994). *Adolescent life experiences* (third ed.). Pacific Grove, CA: Brooks/Cole Publishing Company.

[2] Anderson, S. C., and Lauderdale, M. L. (1982). Characteristics of abusive parents: A look at self-esteem. *Child Abuse and Neglect, 6,* 285-293.

[3] Baranowski, M. D., Schilmoeller, G. L., and Higgins, B. S. (1990). Parenting attitudes of adolescent and older mothers. *Adolescence, 25* (100), 781-790.

[4] Belsky, J. (1993). Etiology of child maltreatment: A developmental-ecological analysis. *Psychological Bulletin, 114*(3), 413-434.

[5] Benedict, M. I., White, R. B., and Cornely, D. A. (1985). Maternal perinatal risk factors and child abuse. *Child Abuse and Neglect, 9,* 217-224.

[6] Bishop, J. A., and Inderbitzen, H. M. (1995). Peer acceptance and friendship: An investigation of their relation to self-esteem. *Journal of Early Adolescence, 15* (4), 476-490.

[7] Bolton, F. G. (1990). The risk of child maltreatment in adolescent parenting. *Advances in Adolescent Mental Health, 4,* 223-237.

[8] Bolton, F. G., and Laner, R. H. (1981). Maternal maturity and maltreatment. *Journal of Family Issues, 2* (4), 485-508.

[9] Bolton, F. G., Laner, R. H., and Kane, S. P. (1980). Child maltreatment risk among adolescent mothers: A study of reported cases. *American Journal of Orthopsychiatry, 50* (3), 489-504.

[10] Brown, J., Cohen, P., Johnson, J. G., and Salzinger, S. (1998). A longitudinal analysis of risk factors for child maltreatment: Findings of a 17-year prospective study of officially recorded and self-reported child abuse and neglect. *Child Abuse and Neglect, 22* (11), 1065-1078.

[11] Burnett, P. C. (1996). Children's self-talk and significant others' positive and negative statements. *Educational Psychology, 16,* 57-67.

[12] Burnett, P. C., and McCrindle, A. R. (1999). The relationship between significant others' positive and negative statements, self-talk, and self-esteem. *Child Study Journal, 29* (1), 39-49.

[13] Cadzow, S. P., Armstrong, K. L., and Fraser, J. A. (1999). Stressed parents with infants: Reassessing physical abuse risk factors. *Child Abuse and Neglect, 23* (9), 845-853.

[14] Chaffin, M., Kelleher, K., and Hollenberg, J. (1996). Onset of physical abuse and neglect: Psychiatric, substance abuse, and social risk factors from prospective community data. *Child Abuse and Neglect, 20* (3), 191-203.

[15] Christoffersen, M. N. (2000). Growing up with unemployment: A study of parental unemployment and children's risk of abuse and neglect based on national longitudinal 1973 birth cohorts in Denmark. *Childhood: A Global Journal of Child Research, 7* (4), 421-438.

[16] Connelly, C. D., and Straus, M. A. (1992). Mother's age and risk for physical abuse. *Child Abuse and Neglect, 16,* 709-718.

[17] Creighton, S. J. (1985). An epidemiological study of abused children and their families in the United Kingdom between 1977 and 1982. *Child Abuse and Neglect, 9,* 441-448.

[18] De Paul, J., and Domenech, L. (2000). Childhood history of abuse and child abuse potential in adolescent mothers: A longitudinal study. *Child Abuse and Neglect, 24* (5), 701-713.

[19] Earp, J. A., and Ory, M., G. (1980). The influence of early parenting on child maltreatment. *Child Abuse and Neglect, 4,* 237-245.

[20] Elkes, B. H., and Crocitto, J. A. (1987). Self-concept of pregnant adolescents: A case study. *Journal of Humanistic Education and Development, 25,* 122-135.

[21] Erikson, E. H. (1963). *Childhood and Society* (second ed.). New York, NY: W. W. Norton and Company, Inc.

[22] Felson, R. B. (1993). The (somewhat) social self: A developmental affect self-appraisals. In J. Suls (Ed.), *Psychological perspectives on the self* (Vol. 4, pp. 1-26). Hillsdale, NJ: Erlbaum.

[23] Freeman, E. W., and Rickels, K. (1993). *Early Childbearing.* Newbury Park, CA: Sage Publications.

[24] Friedrich, W. N., and Wheeler, K. K. (1982). The abusing parent revisited: A decade of psychological research. *Journal of Nervous and Mental Disease, 10,* 577-587.

[25] Furstenberg, F. F., Brooks-Gunn, J., and Morgan, P. S. (1987). *Adolescent mothers in later life.* New York, NY: Cambridge University Press.

[26] Garbarino, J., Gutterman, E., and Seeley, J. (1986). *The psychologically battered child.* San Francisco, CA: Jossey-Bass.

[27] Garcia Coll, C. T., Hoffman, J., Van Houten, L. J., and Oh, W. (1987). The social context of teenage childbearing: Effects on the infant's care-giving environment. *Journal of Youth and Adolescence, 16* (4), 345-360.

[28] Gelles, R. J. (1989). Child abuse and violence in single-parent families: Parent absence and economic deprivation. *American Journal of Orthopsychiatry, 46,* 492-501.

[29] Gil, D. G. (1970). *Violence against children: physical child abuse in the United States.* Cambridge, MA: Harvard University Press.

[30] Gillham, B., Tanner, G., Cheyne, B., Freeman, I., Rooney, M., and Lambie, A. (1998). Unemployment rates, single parent density, and indices of child poverty: Their relationships to different categories of child abuse and neglect. *Child Abuse and Neglect, 22* (2), 79-90.

[31] Hart, S. N., Brassard, M. R., and Karlson, H. C. (1996). Psychological maltreatment. In L. Briere, J. Berliner, J. A. Bulkley, C. Jenny, and T. Reid (Eds.), *The APSAC handbook on child maltreatment* (pp. 72-89). Thousand Oaks, CA: Sage Publications.

[32] Harter, S. (1998). The development of self-representations. In W. Damon, I. E. Sigel, and K. A. Renniger (Eds.), *Handbook of child psychology* (5th ed., Vol. 4, pp. 553-617). New York, NY: Wiley.

[33] Haskett, M., E., Johnson, C., A., and Miller, J., W. (1994). Individual differences in risk of child abuse by adolescent mothers: Assessment in the perinatal period. *Journal of Child Psychology, 35* (3), 461-476.

[34] Health Canada. (1999). *A second diagnostic on the health of First Nations and Inuit people in Canada.* Ottawa, ON.

[35] Health Canada. (2001). A conceptual and epidemiological framework for child maltreatment surveillance, *Child Maltreatment Section* (pp. 79). Ottawa, ON.

[36] Hechtman, L. (1989). Teenage mothers and their children: risks and problems: A review. *Canadian Journal of Psychiatry, 34,* 569-575.

[37] Held, L. (1981). Self-esteem and social network of the young pregnant teenager. *Adolescence, 16*, 905-912.

[38] Herrenkohl, E. C., and Herrenkohl, R. C. (1979). A comparison of abused children and their nonabused siblings. *Journal of American Academy of Child and Adolescent Psychiatry, 18*, 260-296.

[39] Herrmann, M. M., Van Cleve, L., and Levisen, L. (1998). Parenting competence, social support, and self-esteem in teen mothers case managed by public health nurses. *Public Health Nursing, 15* (6), 432-439.

[40] Hurlbut, N. L., McDonald Culp, A., Jambunathan, S., and Bulter, P. (1997). Adolescent mothers' self-esteem and role identity and their relationship to parenting skills knowledge. *Adolescence, 32* (127), 639-654.

[41] Kotch, J. B., Browne, D. C., Ringwalt, C. L., Stewart, P. W., Ruina, E., Holt, K., Lowman, B., and Jung, J. W. (1995). Risk of child abuse or neglect in a cohort of low-income children. *Child Abuse and Neglect, 19*, 1115-1128.

[42] Kotch, J. B., and Thomas, L. P. (1986). Family and social factors associated with substantiation of child abuse and neglect reports. *Journal of Family Violence, 1* (2), 167-179.

[43] Lahey, B. B., Conger, R. D., Atkeson, B. M., and Treiber, F. A. (1984). Parenting behaviors and emotional status of physically abusive mothers. *Journal of Consulting and Clinical Psychology, 52*, 1062-1071.

[44] Leadbeater, B. J. R., and Way, N. (2001). *Growing up fast.* Mahwah, NJ: Lawrence Erlbaum Associates, Inc., Publishers.

[45] Lineberger, M. R. (1987). Pregnant adolescents attending prenatal parent education classes: Self-concept, anxiety, and depression levels. *Adolescence, 22*, 179-193.

[46] Luster, T., and Rhoades, K. (1989). The relation between child-rearing beliefs and the home environment in a sample of adolescent mothers. *Family Relations, 38*, 317-322.

[47] Massat, C. R. (1993). Is older better? Adolescent parenthood and maltreatment. *Child Welfare, 74*(2), 325-336.

[48] McCullough, M., and Scherman, A. (1991). Adolescent pregnancy: Contributing factors and strategies for prevention. *Adolescence, 26*, 809-816.

[49] Miller, S. H. (1984). The relationship between adolescent childbearing and child maltreatment. *Child Welfare, 63* (6), 553-557.

[50] Moore, K. A., Miller, B. C., Glei, D., and Morrison, D. R. (1995). *Adolescent sex, contraception, and childbearing: A review of recent research.* Washington, DC: Child Trends.

[51] Murphey, D. A., and Braner, M. (2000). Linking child maltreatment retrospectively to birth and home visit records: An initial examination. *Child Welfare, 79* (6), 711-729.

[52] Murphy, S., Orkow, B., and Nicola, R. M. (1985). Prenatal prediction of child abuse and neglect: a prospective study. *Child Abuse and Neglect, 9*, 225-235.

[53] National Center for Health Statistics (NCHS). (1993). Advance report on final natality statistics. *Supplement to the Monthly Vital Statistics Report, 41* (9).

[54] Robinson, R. B., and Frank, D. I. (1994). The relation between self-esteem, sexual activity, and pregnancy. *Adolescence, 29*, 27-36.

[55] Santrock, J. W. (1996). *Child Development* (second ed.). Dubuque, IA: Brown and Brenchmark Publishers.
[56] Schloesser, P., Pierpont, J., and Poertner, J. (1992). Active surveillance of child abuse fatalities. *Child Abuse and Neglect, 16,* 3-10.
[57] Sherman, J. K., Evans, E., Boyle, M. H., Cuddy, L. J., and Norman, G. R. (1983). Maternal and infant characteristics in abuse: A case control study. *The Journal of Family Practice, 16* (2), 289-293.
[58] Simmons, R. G. (1987). Self-esteem in adolescence. In T. Honess and K. Yardley (Eds.), *Self and identity: Perspectives across the lifespan* (pp. 172-192). New York, NY: Routledge and Kegan Paul.
[59] Statistics Canada. (1996)_*Census families in private households by number of persons, 1971-1996 censuses, Canada.* Retrieved August 27, 2002, from Statistics Canada web site: http://www.statcan.ca/english/pgdb/people/families/famil50a.html.
[60] Steele, B. F. (1987). Psychodynamic factors in child abuse. In R. E. Helfer and C. H. Kempe (Eds.), *The battered child* (fourth ed., pp. 81-117). Chicago, IL: University of Chicago Press.
[61] Steele, B. F. (1997). Psychodynamic and biological factors in child maltreatment. In M. E. Helfer and R. S. Kempe, and R. D. Krugman (Eds.), *The battered child* (pp. 73-103). Chicago, IL: The University of Chicago Press.
[62] Stevens-Simon, C., and Nelligan, D. (1998). Strategies for identifying and treating adolescents at risk for maltreating their children. *Aggression and Violent Behavior, 3* (2), 197-217.
[63] Straus, M. A., Gelles, R. J., and Steinmetz, S. K. (1980). *Behind closed doors: Violence in the American family* (1st -- ed.). Garden City, NY: Anchor Press/Doubleday.
[64] Tarter, R. E., Hegedus, A. M., Winsten, N. E., and Alterman, A. I. (1984). Neuropsychological, personality, and familial characteristics of physically abused delinquents. *American Academy of Child Psychiatry,* 668-674.
Zongher, C. E. (1977). The self concept of pregnant adolescent girls. *Adolescence, 12,* 477-488.

In: Child Abuse and Violence
Editors: T. Richardson, M. Williams, pp. 43-57

ISBN: 978-1-60456-128-9
© 2008 Nova Science Publishers, Inc.

Chapter III

Empirical Support for a Conceptual Model of Posttraumatic Stress Disorder among Survivors of Child Sexual Abuse

Oxana Gronskaya Palesh[1], Elizabeth Looney[2], Daniel Batiuchok[2], Cheryl Koopman[1], Karni Ginzburg[3], Mydzung Bui[2], Catherine C. Classen[4], Bruce Arnow[1] and David Spiegel[1]

[1]Stanford University School of Medicine, [2]Pacific Graduate School of Psychology
[3]Tel Aviv University, [4]University of Toronto, Cnanda

Abstract

Previous research has documented many detrimental psychological and behavioral consequences of child sexual abuse. One of the long-term effects of childhood sexual abuse (CSA) is the development of posttraumatic stress disorder (PTSD) symptoms. It is important to take steps toward development and validation of a conceptual model that identifies key characteristics associated with PTSD among survivors of child sexual abuse. Such a model can be helpful in developing a more coherent understanding of problems closely associated with PTSD in this population for the purpose of improving treatment programs for CSA survivors. The conceptual model that is examined in this study focused on key aspects of the sense of self, which would appear to involve core aspects of traumatic stress associated with CSA. Specifically, this study examined several self-development characteristics that included beliefs about self worth, guilt, shame, and identity impairment in relation to PTSD symptoms in women with a history of child sexual abuse. Research participants were 139 women with a history of child sexual abuse who were considered to be at high risk for HIV infection due to abuse of drugs or alcohol, engaging in risky sex and/or having a history of sexual revictimization. Participants completed self-report measures that assessed abuse specific factors (including the duration of their child sexual abuse and the number of times that they had been sexually abused in childhood), as well as their self-development characteristics (their beliefs about self worth, abuse-related guilt and shame, and identity impairment), and their PTSD symptoms. Multiple linear regression examined whether beliefs about self worth, guilt, shame, and identity impairment accounted for a significant amount of variance in predicting PTSD symptoms. The results showed that this model accounted for 39% of the variance in PTSD symptoms ($adj\ R^2=.35$), with PTSD symptoms found to be significantly related to longer duration of abuse, greater sense of shame, and greater identity impairment. These findings indicate that the duration of abuse and shame and identity impairment are sources of difficulty for CSA survivors and suggest that these factors may contribute to the development of PTSD symptoms. In addition, the results suggest that treatment providers need to address shame and identity issues in treating PTSD symptoms in CSA survivors.

Introduction

Child sexual abuse occurs at a time when an individual is in the formative stages of developing beliefs about himself or herself in relationship to other persons. Many negative consequences have been found to be associated with child sexual abuse, including an impaired sense of self and high levels of anxiety, depression, intrusive symptoms, dissociation, and sexual concerns (Banyard, Williams, and Siegel, 2002). Yet not all survivors of child sexual abuse develop significant negative consequences (Barker-Collo and Read, 2003). Research suggests that while no single variable accounts for the range of symptom development across individuals, a complex interaction among abuse-specific factors, interactions with others, and individual factors, such as attributions about the abuse, impact both symptom development and maintenance (Barker-Collo and Read, 2003). This chapter describes and tests a conceptual model that identifies key characteristics associated with PTSD among survivors of child sexual abuse. It is hoped that such a model can be helpful in guiding the design and improvement of treatment programs for CSA survivors. This model is placed within the larger context of reviewing a variety of factors that appear to be associated with PTSD for CSA. This literature is briefly summarized here with special attention given to several factors associated with the development of a sense of self that would be expected to be particularly relevant to PTSD for CSA.

Factors associated with resilience to CSA include beliefs that are modifiable, such as positive reframing, and those that are not, such as objective characteristics of the abuse. Identifying potentially modifiable variables can improve the design and possibly the efficacy of treatment programs. The following potentially modifiable variables have been shown to be positively related to resilience with adult survivors of CSA: internal locus of control (Valentine and Feinauer, 1993), social support (Dufour, Nadeau, and Bertrand, 2000), minimization (Himelein, 1996), positive reframing (Dufour et al., 2000; Himelein, 1996), refusing to dwell on the experience (Himelein, 1996), not blaming either self or fate (Feinauer, Hilton and Callahan, 2003; Feinauer and Stuart, 1996), spirituality(Valentine and Feinauer, 1993), and self regard (Valentine and Feinauer, 1993). Protective factors, such as having an internal locus of control and strong attachment relationships to parents and family, have been shown to be particularly helpful for persons with a history of CSA compared to others (Lam and Grossman, 1997). An external attribution of blame has been found to be associated with resilience in adult CSA survivors (Feinauer and Stuart, 1996).

Abuse-Specific Factors

An individual's CSA history has numerous abuse-specific characteristics, including the age at which the abuse began, the duration and frequency of the abuse, the severity of abuse, the number of different perpetrators, and the use or absence of force. Several studies have shown that abuse-specific factors correspond to the expression of psychological distress in adults with a CSA history (Bennett, Hughes, and Luke, 2000; Heath, Bean, and Feinauer, 1996; Johnson, Pike, and Chard., 2001; Steel, Sanna, and Hammond, 2004). While abuse-specific factors cannot be altered for those who are no longer being abused, early detection and intervention could potentially shorten the duration of the abuse and, in some cases, prevent the frequency and severity from increasing. The conceptual model for this study incorporates two of these abuse-specific factors--the duration and frequency of abuse. It also incorporates several characteristics of self-development described below that include beliefs about the self, guilt and shame, and identity impairment.

Trauma Reactive and Resilient Beliefs about Self-Worth

Child sexual abuse affects survivors' sense of self in many ways. Terr (1991) points out that the meaning that the victim gives to the abuse experience plays an important role in the development of sense of self. Trauma affects child's developing sense of the world and violates the basic sense of trust and safety in the world (Terr, 1991). Children who have been sexually abused tend to develop a negative attributional style and describe the world as dangerous and uncontrollable and adults as being untrustworthy (Wolfe, Gentile, and Wolfe, 1989). A negative attributional style consists of three aspects: blaming the self for the abuse (internal), considering the abuse to occur across situations (global), and to viewing it as occurring across time (stable) (Steel et al, 2004). Research shows that PTSD symptoms are strongly associated with dysfunctional beliefs and a negative attributional style in adult CSA survivors (Wenninger and Ehlers, 1998). Negative internal attributions by adult CSA survivors have been shown to predict poor psychological adjustment (Wyatt and Newcomb, 1990) and higher scores on scales that measure self-worth and beliefs (e.g. The Personal Beliefs and Actions Scale and the Worthiness of Self scale on the World Assumptions Scale (WAS)) have been associated with greater severity of PTSD symptoms in CSA survivors (Owens, 2001). This suggests that negative beliefs about self might be associated with the development of PTSD symptoms.

Guilt and Shame

Since many CSA survivors make internal attributions about the experience (Wyatt, Newcomb, and Notgrass, 1991), guilt and shame are prevalent reactions. The offender's instillation of blame, the pressure for secrecy, an awareness of social attitudes, and the reactions of others to disclosure may intensify these self-stigmatization cognitions that become incorporated into the survivor's self identity (Finkelhor and Browne, 1985).

Abuse-related guilt and shame have been shown to be related with PTSD severity among children (Feiring, Taska, and Chen, 2002; Wolfe, Sas and Wekerle, 1994) and adolescents (Feiring and Taska, 2005) victims of CSA. Among adult survivors of CSA, these self stigmatization cognitions have been shown to have long term effects and are implicated in depression (Peters and Range, 1996), suicidality (Peters and Range, 1996), trauma symptoms (Barker-Collo, 2001), dissociation (Lange et al., 1999), and psychiatric symptomatology (Coffey, Leitenberg, Henning, Turner, and Bennett 1996).

Identity Impairment

Abuse can also influence the development of self at a structural level, particularly fragmentation of a sense of self in CSA survivors. This shattering of the self has been described by several authors (Rieker and Carmen, 1986; Roth, 1993; Ulman and Brothers, 1988). However, just as not all survivors of traumatic events will develop PTSD, there is also a range in the influence of traumatic events on the development of the sense of self.

As noted by Putnam (1990), many of the problems observed in survivors of child sexual abuse arise from disturbances in self. Research suggests that a more integrated sense of self for survivors is associated with less depression, anxiety and trauma symptomatology (Classen, Field, Atkinson, and Spiegel, 1998). A greater use of image-distorting defenses has been found among persons with a CSA history than those who were not sexually abused (Callahan and Hilsenroth, 2005).

Hypotheses

This study sought to evaluate both abuse-specific and modifiable factors in predicting the development of PTSD. Specifically we hypothesized that PTSD symptoms among female CSA survivors would be greater among those who had certain abuse-specific factors (greater length of abuse and more instances of abuse) and also problems in the post-abuse, potentially modifiable factors pertaining to the sense of self (greater trauma reactive beliefs about self-worth, more abuse related guilt and shame, and greater identity impairment.

Method

Research Participants

Methods of participant recruitment included advertising through newspapers, distributing flyers, and advertising in free community advertising spaces. Respondents were initially screened on the phone followed by a face-to-face interview with a research assistant. From the 370 women who completed the screening assessment, 171 met eligibility criteria. Thirty two participants had incomplete data on the primary variables of interest and were excluded from this study, resulting in 139 participants. Participants were paid a nominal fee of $25 for the baseline assessment (and $50 for each follow-up assessment, although this study focuses on the data collected at baseline). In accordance with the policies to protect human subjects of the appropriate institutional review board, participants signed an informed consent at screening and a second informed consent once accepted into the study.

Each participant was required to meet *all* of the following inclusion criteria: a) female, b) 18 years of age or older, c) speaks and understands English, d) reports an explicit memory of sexual abuse involving genital or anal contact, e) has experienced one or more instances of sexual abuse between 4-15 years of age, f) was abused by a perpetrator who was at least 5 years older, h) gave informed consent, and i) reported at least one of three HIV risk factors within the previous year: was sexual revictimized, engaged in risky sexual behavior, or demonstrates substance abuse or dependence as delineated by the DSM-IV. Potential participants were excluded if they met *any* of the following criteria: a) was diagnosed with schizophrenia and other psychotic disorders, dementia and delirium and amnesic or other cognitive disorders, b) reported ritual abuse, c) was currently receiving psychotherapy, d) was actively suicidal within one month prior to the screening interview, or e) was determined to be unable to benefit from or be inappropriate for receiving group therapy.

One hundred and thirty nine women participated in this study. The mean age for women in the study was 36.08 (SD = 10.18, range 19 to 58). The majority of women in this sample (59%) had a Bachelor's degree or had completed at least some college, and reported their ethnic background as White/European American (66.2%). About a third of the women (37.4%) were single, and 30.9% were either married or in a relationship similar to marriage. Half of the women (51.1%) had a household income less than $39,999. See Table 1 for additional demographic information.

Measures

Sexual Abuse Specific Factors

Participants answered questions about the duration of their child sexual abuse and the number of times that they had been sexually abused.

Trauma Reactive and Resilient Beliefs about Self-Worth

Self–Worth was measured by using the Self-Worth subscale from the *World Assumptions Scale (WAS)* (Janoff-Bulman, 1989). The WAS is composed of 32 items that are scored on a Likert-type scale ranging from 1 (*strongly disagree*) to 6 (*strongly agree*), and it assesses one's basic assumptions about the world and self. Self-Worth is one of eight subscales and is comprised of 4 items 3 of which are reverse scored: "I often think I am no good at all," "I have a low opinion of myself," "I am very satisfied with the kind of person I am," and "I have reason to be ashamed of my personal character".

Shame and Guilt

These contracts were measured by the Abuse-Related Beliefs Questionnaire (ARBQ) (Ginzburg et al., in press). This scale examines guilt, shame, and resilience. In this study we used two of the ARBQ subscales: Guilt and Shame. These subscales were composed of 14 items that are scored on a five-point Likert-type scale ranging from 1 ("Strongly agree") to 5 ("Do not agree at all"). Psychometric properties of the ARBQ were examined in two CSA samples: the present study sample and a sample of women who referred to a medical clinic for medical treatment (Ginzburg et al., in press). These examinations indicated satisfactory internal consistency (for Guilt, Cronbach's alpha = .71; for Shame, Cronbach's alpha = .77) and also showed very good test-retest reliability at 12 months (r = .60 - .64).

Table 1. Descriptive Statistics for Demographic Characteristics (N = 139)

Demographics	Frequency or Mean	Percent or SD
Education		
Less than high school	9	6.5
Graduated from high school	13	9.4
Completed trade school	6	4.3
Some college	49	35.3
Bachelor's degree	33	23.7
Some graduate school	10	7.2
Master's degree	12	8.6
Ph.D., M. D., and/or J.D.	7	5.0
Racial/Ethnic background		
Black or African-American	12	8.6
Asian or Asian-American	8	5.8
Mexican American/Chicano	4	2.9
Other Latino/Hispanic	8	5.8
Native American	3	2.2
White/European American	92	66.2
Other	12	8.6
Relationship status		
Never married	52	37.4
Married/Living as married	43	30.9
Separated	10	7.2
Divorced	22	15.8
Widowed	2	1.4
Other	10	7.2
Total household income		
Less than $ 20,000	39	28.1
$20,000-39,999	32	23.0
$40,000-$59,999	27	19.4
$60,000-$79,999	7	5.0
$80,000-$99,999	15	10.8
$100,000 or above	12	8.6
Don't know/Refuse to answer	7	5.0

Identity Impairment

Identity Impairment was measured by the Inventory of Altered Self-Capacities (IASC) (Briere, 1998). The IASC is a standardized measure examining a person's sense of self, affect regulation, and relationship with others within the last six months. This self-report inventory contains 63 items and is rated on a Likert-type scale ranging from 1 (never happened) to 5 (happened very often). Identity Impairment is one of seven clinical scales and it consists of 9 items (e.g. 'Losing your identity when in relationships", "Getting confused about what you want when you are with other people", and " Wishing you understood yourself better") (Briere, 1998). : For example, psychometric properties of the IASC were examined across a normative sample and two validation samples (clinical and university) yielding good internal consistency, reliability, and validity (Briere and Runtz, 2002).

PTSD Symptoms

PTSD symptoms were assessed using the PTSD Checklist (PCL) (Blanchard, Jones-Alexander, Buckley, and Forneris, 1996). The PCL is a self-report inventory consisting of 17 items that are aligned with diagnostic criteria for PTSD, as depicted in the DSM-IV. Informants endorse distress level over the last month on a Likert-type scale from 1 (not at all) to 5 (extremely). The criterion validity of the PCL is supported by a strong correlation (r = .93) with the Clinician Administered PTSD Scale (CAPS) (Blanchard et al., 1996). Evidence also supports the test-retest reliability, convergent validity, and discriminant validity of the PCL(Blanchard et al., 1996). Excellent internal consistency has been demonstrated in previous research for the overall PCL (Cronbach's alpha = .94) as well as for the items comprising the three symptom clusters (Blanchard et al., 1996). In this study sample, the PCL also showed very good overall internal consistency (Cronbach's alpha = .89).

Results

Descriptive Statistics

Table 2 presents the means and standard deviations for PTSD symptom scores as well as for the measures assessing independent variables in this study. Fifty four percent of women scored at a cut-off score of 44 and above, which previous research with the Posttraumatic Stress Checklist has determined (Blanchard et al., 1996; Lang, Laffaye, Satz, Dresselhaus, and Stein, 2003) to indicate likely PTSD. Table 2 also presents the bivariate correlations among these variables. As can be determined from an examination of this table, none of the bivariate correlations among the independent variables in this study were so strong as to require omitting any of the potential independent variables from the multiple regression analysis testing the study hypotheses. The correlations of these independent variables with PTSD symptom scores are discussed below.

Although women's risk behaviors were not the focus of this study, the descriptive statistics on these behaviors are reported to further characterize this study's participants. Women reported that on average they were abused four times ($SD = 1.33$, Range 1 to 6). The mean duration for sexual abuse was 7.74 years ($SD = 6.59$, Range 0 to 39). The average age for nonconsensual vaginal sex was 12.31 years ($SD = 6.90$, Range 0 to 32), the average age for nonconsensual oral sex was 11.24 years ($SD = 6.71$, Range 2 to 34) and the average age for nonconsensual anal sex was slightly older 18. 72 years ($SD = 10.76$, Range 0 to 47).

Table 2. Bivariate Correlations, Means, and Standard Deviations for Age, Abuse-Related and Self-Development Variables, and PTSD Symptoms

	1	2	3	4	5	6	7	8
1. Age	—	.22*	-.08	-.04	.004	.09	-.08	.08
2. Duration of Abuse	—	—	.22**	-.08	.01	.03	-.09	.18*
3. Times Sexually Abused	—	—	—	-.09	.28**	.05	-.03	.12
4. Self-Worth	—	—	—	—	-.44**	-.48**	-.38**	-.27**
5. Guilt	—	—	—	—	—	.62**	.30**	.20**
6. Shame	—	—	—	—	—	—	.39**	.36**
7. Identity Impairment	—	—	—	—	—	—	—	.50**
8. PTSD Symptoms	—	—	—	—	—	—	—	—
Mean	36.08	7.74	7.67	14.68	2.86	3.68	25.01	46.32
(SD)	(10.18)	(6.59)	(6.61)	(5.22)	(1.06)	(3.83)	(9.08)	(13.61)

Note: ARBQ - Abuse-Related Beliefs Questionnaire, IASC-Inventory of Altered Self-Capacities, PCL –PTSD checklist; *p≤.05; *p<.05; **p<.01.

Results of Linear Regression

The results of the multiple regression analysis are shown in Table 3. The hierarchical regressions were conducted in 2 blocks. Age and descriptors of abuse (duration and number of times being abused) were entered in the first block simultaneously and accounted for 3% of the variance (adj. $R^2 = -.002$) in predicting PTSD. The reminder of the variables were entered in the second step and helped to account for a large amount of variance 39% (adj. $R^2 = .35$) in predicting PTSD symptoms, $F(7, 103) = 9.52$, $p<.001$. Duration of abuse, shame and identity impairment were significantly and positively associated with having PTSD symptoms.

Bivariate Correlations

Examination of zero order correlations in Table 2 showed that the level of PTSD symptoms was positively related to duration of abuse (p = .02), negatively to self-worth (p = .001), and positively to guilt (p = .01), shame (p < .001) and identity impairment (p < .001). There was no significant relationships between age or number of times respondents had been sexually abused in childhood with their PTSD symptom scores.

Table 3. Final Results of Multiple Regression Analysis of Age and Abuse-Related and Self-Development Variables on PTSD Symptom Scores

Variable	B	SE B	β
Age	.08	.11	.05
Duration of abuse	.37	.17	.18*
Number of times sexually abused	.54	.87	.05
Self-Worth	.05	.24	.02
Guilt	-1.78	1.36	-.14
Shame	4.06	1.60	.26*
Identity Impairment	.80	.13	.53**
Constant	7.92	10.02	

*p≤.05; **p<.001

Note. Age and duration of abuse and number of abuse events were entered in the first block and accounted for 3% of the variance (*adj. R^2*= -.002) in predicting PTSD. This table presents the final regression model that also includes the second block of variables.

Discussion

The results of this study indicate that PTSD symptoms in adult female CSA survivors are significantly associated with the duration of their childhood sexual abuse and their shame and identity impairment. Such findings support the hypothesis that PTSD symptoms among female CSA survivors would be associated with abuse specific characteristics, shame and identity impairment. In addition to these relationships that were found to be statistically significant in the context of the overall model, when the bivariate relationships were independently assessed using the correlational analysis, additional self-development variables were found to be associated with PTSD. Specifically, greater PTSD symptoms were found to be related to guilt and lack of self worth, as well as to shame, identity impairment, and to the duration of abuse. . These findings are consistent with a study conducted by Classen, Field, Atkinson, and Spiegel (Classen et al., 1998) which concluded that discrepancies between current self and ideal self were positively correlated with trauma-related symptomatology among female CSA survivors. Additionally, these findings add further support to previous literature as well as the presence of an internal, stable, and global attributional style among adult CSA survivors (Wenninger and Ehlers, 1998). To date, we are not aware of any other research that has investigated the relationships of these variables to PTSD within a single study. Therefore, these positive findings support the importance of incorporating self-development variables within a conceptual model for understanding PTSD

Our findings are in agreement with those of previous research (Bennett, et al., 2000; Heath et al., 1996; Johnson et al., 2001; Steel et al., 2004) that found that abuse-specific characteristics contribute to the development of psychological distress in childhood sexual survivors. While the number of times of being sexually abused did not have a significant association with PTSD symptoms, duration of abuse contributed uniquely to the presence of PTSD symptoms in adult CSA survivors, providing evidence that possibly chronicity plays a role in the development of PTSD for CSA.

We found that shame contributed uniquely and significantly to the presence of PTSD symptoms. This is consistent with the possibility that shame may have a pathogenic effect on PTSD, although we cannot determine from this cross sectional study design the causal relationships between the self-development variables and PTSD symptoms. A pathogenic role of shame may be explained by both intra- and interpersonal mechanisms. According to Feiring (2005), motivated to regulate shame, individuals tend to invest efforts in avoiding thinking about their experiences and avoiding disclosing their abuse to others. Indeed, Gibson and Leitenberg (2001) found that self-stigmatized individuals, characterized by high levels of guilt and shame following sexual assault, tend to rely on disengagement strategies that include problem avoidance, wishful thinking, social withdrawal, and self-criticism. Thus, shame could contribute to the development and maintenance of PTSD by disturbing the cognitive processing that is needed to integrate the trauma memories into the individual's autobiographical memories, thus preventing the successful completion of the working through, which may lead to chronic PTSD (Brewin, Dalgleish and Joseph, 1996; Ehlers and Clark, 2000). It may also lead to social isolation, thereby preventing the use of social support resources which have been shown to buffer the development of PTSD among CSA survivors (Hayman, Gold and Cott, 2003).

Although guilt and shame are highly related in CSA survivors (Ginzburg et al., in press), shame was significantly associated with severity of PTSD, but guilt did not make a unique contribution in the context of including the other independent variables in the model.. This finding is consistent with others that suggest that shame is a more powerful mediator of the negative effects of sexual abuse than self blame (Coffey et al., 1996; Ginzburg et al., in press). This pattern of results also may be interpreted with consideration of the findings from Feiring et al's (2002) study, which indicated that shame mediates the association between abuse-related internal attribution and PTSD symptoms among child victims of sexual abuse. While both shame and guilt arise in the face of violated morale standards, guilt involves a focus on specific behaviors, and shame refers to the entire self (Feiring, 2005). These finding stress the significance of self identity in the development of PTSD.

Our findings indicate that self-perception plays an integral role in the manifestation of PTSD symptoms in adult female survivors of PTSD. Specifically, our results show that identity impairment accounted for a large percentage of the variance in PTSD symptoms. According to Cole and Putnam (1992), childhood exposure to trauma, including early and repeated sexual abuse, may impair a child's ability to develop a sense of self. Such alterations in self-perception may compromise one's ability to effectively self-sooth or self-comfort, which may subsequently lead to a heightened reaction to stress (Briere and Elliot, 1994). Furthermore, Putnam's (1990) conceptual model of symptoms manifested by victims' of CSA suggests that one of the most salient negative effects of such abuse involves damaged self-image. Specifically, children often experience feelings of self-deprecation and guilt following CSA. Such feelings are frequently the result of guilt about the sexual encounter as well as the combination of pressures to remain silent and deceit from the perpetrator(s). Relative to our findings, the damaged self-image that children experience following sexual abuse may translate to distorted self-perceptions in adulthood.

Clinical Implications

Based on their literature review of PTSD in child CSA survivors, Rowan and Foy (1993) concluded that the PTSD model (proposing that the diagnosis of Post Traumatic Stress Disorder fits the symptoms associated with CSA consequences), as applied to CSA survivors, is beneficial to survivors because it displaces the burden of blame from characterlogical deficiencies of the victim to the traumatic nature of the abuse. Our findings provide further clarification regarding the interaction between self-development issues that presumably stem from the traumatic events of CSA and their associations with PTSD. Based on these findings, several clinical implications are drawn regarding the etiology and treatment of PTSD within this population. Specifically, the results provide insight regarding the diversity of factors that contribute to the development and maintenance of PTSD symptoms in female CSA survivors. To effectively treat traumatic stress in this population, it is important to attend to each of these factors. In regards to addressing patients' maladaptive self-perceptions, a possible clinical approach could involve helping the patient to develop a positive reframe of her trauma reactive beliefs about her and the world. Specifically, reframing such beliefs to external, empowering attributions instead of maintaining internal, disempowering attributions may help to alleviate the patient's burden of guilt (Feinauer and Stuart, 1996).

In addition to reframing a patient's attribution factors from internal to external, the results of this study also highlight the importance of promoting accurate self-perception, which is often fragmented in victims of abuse (Briere and Elliott, 1994). As such, clinical interventions designed to restructure self-perceptions may help victims to develop a more accurate perception of the self. Additionally, treatment modalities designed to decrease self-stigmatizations help to reduce PTSD symptoms. Incorporating problem-solving coping skills could strengthen a victim's sense of agency and bolster their confidence and ability to perform actions designed to reduce their symptoms (Diehl and Prout, 2002). Future research should examine the effects of such interventions on PTSD while examining the self-development variables of self worth, guilt, shame, and identity impairment as potential mediators of treatment effects.

Study Limitations

A potential limitation to this study involves the lack of a non-CSA and a non-HIV risk-factor control group. Consequently, the results of this study cannot determine whether or not self-perception issues are present among females who do not have a history of CSA or who are not at risk for HIV. Another limitation of this study involves the homogeneity of the participants. Although the sample is ethnically diverse, the subjects have a disproportionately high level of education, and therefore we cannot generalize the findings to all female CSA survivors diagnosed with PTSD. Also, as previously mentioned, the cross-sectional study design also presents potential limitations. As such, it is not possible to determine the existence of a causal relationship that may link self-perception factors with the expression of PTSD symptoms. However, this study also has strengths that help to balance these limitations, including clear inclusion and exclusion criteria for defining the population, use of well-validated and reliable measures, and the use of multiple regression analysis which minimizes the possibility of Type I error when examining a number of independent variables in relation to PTSD symptoms.

Conclusion

The results of this study provide support for including shame and identity impairment as core factors associated with PTSD symptoms in female CSA survivors. As such, these factors may help to provide a conceptual model of PTSD in this population which could help to guide clinical interventions. Furthermore, this study also provides correlational findings, which although not significant in the overall regression model, suggest that guilt and beliefs about self-worth may be additional factors worth considering in such a model emphasizing deficiencies and distortions in self-development among women with PTSD for CSA.

Further research is needed to replicate and further refine a conceptual model of how self-development factors are associated with PTSD. It is hoped that such research will help clinicians to further optimize clinical interventions to more effectively reduce PTSD symptoms in women with a history of child sexual abuse.

Acknowledgement

This research was funded by grant MH60556 from the National Institute of Mental Health to David Spiegel, Principal Investigator. The authors wish to acknowledge the contributions of Rashi Aggrawal, Helen Marlo, Elisabeth Thurston, Lori Peterson, Renee Schneider, Nadia Yousef, Ruth Nevo, Vicci Smith, the interviewers, therapists and supervisors, as well as Stephanie Brown and Mary Koss for their consultation, along with all of the women who participated in this research.

References

Banyard, V., Williams, L. M., and Siegel, J. (2002). Child sexual abuse in the lives of Black women: Risk and resilience in a longitudinal study. *Women and Therapy, 25*(3-4), 45-58.

Barker-Collo, S., and Read, J. (2003). Models of response to childhood sexual abuse: Their implications for treatment. *Trauma Violence and Abuse, 4*(2), 95-111.

Bennett, S. E., Hughes, H. M., and Luke, D. A. (2000). Heterogeneity in patterns of child sexual abuse, family functioning and long-term adjustment. *Journal of Interpersonal Violence, 15*(2): 134-157.

Blanchard, E. B., Jones-Alexander, J., Buckley, T. C., and Forneris, C. A. (1996). Psychometric properties of the PTSD Checklist (PCL). *Behavior Research and Therapy, 34*, 669-673.

Brewin, C. R., Dalgleish, T., and Joseph, S. (1996). A dual representation theory of posttraumatic stress disorder. *Psychological Review, 103*, 670-686.

Briere, J. (1998). Inventory of altered self-capacities (IASC): Professional manual. In. Odessa: Psychological Assessment Resources.

Briere, J., and Runtz, M. (2002). The Inventory of Altered Self-Capacities (IASC): A standardized measure of identity, affect regulation, and relationship disturbance. *Assessment, 9*(3), 230-239.

Briere, J. N., and Elliott, D. M. (1994). Immediate and long-term impacts of child sexual abuse. *The Future of Children, 4*, 54-69.

Callahan, K., and Hilsenroth, M. (2005). Childhood sexual abuse and adult defensive functioning. *Journal of Nervous and Mental Disease, 193*(7), 473-479.

Classen, C., Field, N., Atkinson, A., and Spiegel, D. (1998). Representations of self in women sexually abused in childhood. *Child Abuse and Neglect, 22*(10), 997-1004.

Coffey, P., Leitenberg., Henning, K., Turner, T., and Bennett, R.T. (1996). Mediators of the long-term impact of child sexual abuse: Perceived stigma, betrayal, powerlessness, and self blame. *Child Abuse and Neglect, 20*, 447-455.

Cole, P. M., and Putnam, F. W. (1992). Effect of incest on self and social functioning: A developmental psychopathology perspective. *Journal of Consulting and Clinical Psychology, 60*, 174-184.

Diehl, A., and Prout, M. (2002). Effects of Posttraumatic stress disorder and child sexual abuse on self-efficacy development. *American Journal of Orthopsychiatry, 72*(2), 262-265.

Dufour, M., Nadeau, L., and Bertrand, K. (2000). Factors in the resilience of victims of sexual abuse: An update. *Child Abuse and Neglect, 24*, 781-797.

Ehlers, A., and Clark, D. M. (2000). A cognitive model of posttraumatic stress disorder. *Behavior Research and Therapy, 38*, 319-345.

Feinauer, L., Hilton, H. G., and Callahan, E. H. (2003). Hardiness as a moderator of shame associated with childhood sexual abuse. *American Journal of Family Therapy, 31* (2), 65-78

Feinauer, L. L., and Stuart, D. A. (1996). Blame and resilience in women sexually abused as children. *American Journal of Family Therapy, 24*, 31-40.

Feiring, C. (2005). Emotional development, shame, and adaptation to child maltreatment. *Child Maltreatment, 10*, 307-310.

Feiring, C., and Taska, L S. (2005). The persistence of shame following sexual abuse: A longitudinal look at risk and recovery. *Child Maltreatment, 10*, 337-349.

Feiring, C., Taska, L., and Chen, K. (2002). Trying to understand why horrible things happen: Attribution, shame, and symptom development following sexual abuse. *Child Maltreatment, 7*, 26-41.

Finkelhor, D., and Browne, A. (1985). The traumatic impact of child sexual abuse: a conceptualization. *American Journal of Orthopsychiatry, 55*(4), 530-541.

Gibson, L.E., and Leitenberg, H. (2001). The impact of child sexual abuse and stigma on methods of coping with sexual assault among undergraduate women. *Child Abuse and Neglect, 25*, 1343-1361.

Ginzburg, K., Arnow, B., Hart, S., Gardner, W., Koopman, C., Classen, C., Giese-Davis, J., and Spiegel, D. (in press). The Abuse-Related Beliefs Questionnaire for survivors of childhood sexual abuse. *Child Abuse and Neglect.*

Hayman, S.M., Gold, S.N., and Cott, M.A. (2003). Forms of social support that moderate PTSD in childhood sexual abuse survivors. *Journal of Family Violence, 18,* 295-300.

Heath, V. R. Bean, and Feinauer, L. (1996). Severity of childhood sexual abuse: Symptom differences between men and women. *American Journal of Family Therapy 24*(4): 305-314.

Himelein, M. (1996). Resilient child sexual abuse survivors: Cognitive coping and illusion. *Child Abuse and Neglect, 20*(8), 747-758.

Janoff-Bulman, R. (1989). Assumptive worlds and the stress of traumatic events: Applications of the schema construct. *Social Cognition. Special Issue: Stress, coping, and social cognition, 7*(2), 113-136.

Johnson, D. M., Pike, J. L., and Chard, K. M. (2001). Factors predicting PTSD, depression, and dissociative severity in female treatment-seeking childhood sexual abuse survivors. *Child Abuse and Neglect, 25*(1): 179-198.

Lam, J., and Grossman, F. (1997). Resiliency and adult adaptation in women with and without self-reported histories of childhood sexual abuse. *Journal of Traumatic Stress, 10*(2), 175-196.

Lang, A. J., Laffaye, C., Satz, L. E., Dresselhaus, T. R., and Stein, M. B. (2003). Sensitivity and specificity of the PTSD checklist in detecting PTSD in female veterans in primary care. *Journal of Traumatic Stress, 16*(3), 257-264.

Lange, A., De Beeurs, E., Dolan, C., Lachnit, T., Sjollema, S., and Hanewald, G. (1999). Long-term effects of childhood sexual abuse: Objective and subjective characteristics of the abuse and psychopathology in later life. *Journal of Nervous and Mental Disease, 187,* 150-158.

Neumann, D. (1996). The long term sequelae of childhood sexual abuse: A meta-analytic review. *Child Maltreatment, 1*(1), 6-16.

Owens, G. (2001). Cognitive distortions among women reporting childhood sexual abuse. *Journal of Interpersonal Violence, 16*(2), 178-191.

Peters, D. K., and Range, L. M. (1996). Self-blame and self-destruction in women sexually abused as children. *Journal of Child Sexual Abuse, 5,* 19-33.

Putnam, F. W. (1990). Disturbances of "self" in victims of childhood sexual abuse. In R. Kluft (Ed). *Incest-related syndromes of adult psychopathology.* (pp. 113-131). Washington, DC, US: American Psychiatric Association.

Rieker, P., and Carmen, E. (1986). The victim-to-patient process: the disconfirmation and transformation of abuse. *American Journal of Orthopsychiatry, 56,* 360-370.

Roth, N. (1993). *Integrating the shattered self: Psychotherapy with adult incest survivors.* Northdale, NJ: Jason Aronson, Inc.

Rowan, A. B., and Foy, D. W. (1993). Post-traumatic stress disorder in child sexual abuse survivors: a literature review. *Journal of Traumatic Stress, 6*(1), 3-20.

Steel, J., Sanna, L., and Hammond, B. (2004). Psychological sequelae of childhood sexual abuse: Abuse-related characteristics, coping strategies, and attributional style. *Child Abuse and Neglect, 28*(7), 785-801.

Terr, L. C. (1991). Childhood traumas: an outline and overview. *American Journal of Psychiatry, 148*(1), 10-20.

Ulman, R., and Brothers, D. (1988). *The shattered self: A psychoanalytic study of trauma.* Hillsdale, NJ: The Analytic Press.

Valentine, L., and Feinauer, L. (1993). Resilience factors associated with female survivors of childhood sexual abuse. *American Journal of Family Therapy, 21*(3), 216-225.

Wenninger, K., and Ehlers, A. (1998). Dysfunctional cognitions and adult psychological functioning in child sexual abuse survivors. *Journal of Traumatic Stress, 11*(2), 281-300.

Wolfe, V., Gentile, C., and Wolfe, D. (1989). The impact of sexual abuse on children: A PTSD formulation. *Behavior Therapy, 20,* 215-228.

Wolfe, D. A., Sas, L, and Wekerle, C. (1994). Factors associated with the development of posttraumatic stress disorder among child victims of sexual abuse. *Child Abuse and Neglect, 18,* 37-50.

Wyatt, G., and Newcomb, M. (1990). Internal and external mediators of women's sexual abuse in childhood. *Journal of Consulting and Clinical Psychology, 58*(6), 758-767.

Wyatt, G. E., Newcomb, M., and Notgrass, S. M. (1991). Internal and external mediators of women's rape experiences. In A. Wolpert Burgess (ed). *Rape and Sexual Assault* (pp 32-43), New York: Garland.

In: Child Abuse and Violence
Editors: T. Richardson, M. Williams, pp. 59-79

ISBN: 978-1-60456-128-9
© 2008 Nova Science Publishers, Inc.

Chapter IV

Problems with the Social Treatment of Child Abuse Cases in Japan: The Forensic Pathologist's View

Masataka Nagao and Yoshitaka Maeno
Department of Forensic Medical Science, Nagoya City University, Graduate School of Medical Sciences, Nagoya 467-8601, Japan

Abstract

We present five cases of fatal child abuse and highlight the problems associated with social treatment of child abuse cases in Japan. Recently, in Japan, there have been fatal child abuse cases in which neighbors have been aware of the signs of abuse but have not notified the Child Care Authorities. Lack of concern about child welfare in the community is the greatest obstacle to protecting children at risk of abuse. The most effective means of preventing child abuse is to educate the community about how to recognize the signs of abuse and to inform the authorities. We emphasize that the community has an obligation to protect children against crime, including child abuse.

The role of the Social Services in preventing child abuse has been extended. Forensic pathologists are now required to play key roles in child abuse prevention, and in Japan their activity should be extended to the administrative field.

Keywords: *Child abuse; Neglect; Child welfare; Social Service; Education.*

1. Introduction

Child abuse has been recognized as a widespread social problem since the early 1960s [1]. It can include physical and sexual violence, neglect, or mental abuse, and has reached epidemic proportions in some industrialized countries [2]. It is a problem of great public concern, and has gained wide attention among pediatricians, psychiatrists, social workers, forensic pathologists, and workers in other fields. In Japan, a new anti-child abuse law came into effect in 2000, giving the government legal powers to challenge the custody rights of abusive parents. This law obliges doctors, nurses, teachers and welfare officials to be on the lookout for early signs of child abuse and to report it to the authorities. Even so, many children still die as a result of abuse. We previously reported a case of severe neglect in a girl aged 3 years and 20 days, who died of starvation [3]. Although several doctors, health visitors, public health practitioners, and welfare workers had expressed concern about this case, they were unable to save the child. Such workers should be recognized as playing key roles in the protection and care of children. Another major problem is failure by the public to notify the Child Care Authorities about child abuse, even when it is recognized.

We present here one case of severe neglect [3]; the fatal physical abuse of a 7-year-old girl who was confined to her home by her mother and stepfather [4]; two fatal cases of child abuse in which neighbors were unaware of the victims' disappearance for long periods [5]; and one fatal case, involving a 4-year-old boy, in which the neighbors had recognized the signs of child abuse [4]. These cases highlight the problems associated with social attitudes toward child abuse in Japan.

2. Case Report

Case 1 [3]

Case Profile
A girl aged 3 years and 20 days girl was living with her 21-year-old natural parents and her brother, aged 1 year and 6 months. The parents had not cared for the victim, had not fed her sufficiently, and had finally put her in an open packing case. One day in winter they went out with their son leaving the victim alone at home. When they returned home that night, they found her dead in the packing case.

Autopsy Findings
Autopsy revealed an emaciated girl 89 cm tall and weighing 5 kg. She had well-demarcated ribs and a concave abdomen (Figure1A). Decubitus ulcers were present on the left temporal and left occipital areas of the head and on the left of the back and pelvis (Figure 2). Bilateral contracture of the knee joints and bilateral edema of the feet were observed (Figure 1A). Dried feces and urine adhered to the waist, hip, anus, vulva and the backs of both thighs (Figure 1B). Recent subcutaneous hemorrhages were observed on the right temporal area and the face, and a few scars were present on the forehead (Figure 3). The muscles of the head, face, trunk, and lower and upper extremities were flaccid. There was no subcutaneous or omental fat (Figure 1B,C). The orbital adipose tissue was spent and the eyes were open. Because of drying of the eyes, the choroid could be seen through the dried sclera. The stomach and small intestine were contracted and empty, and the large bowel contained hard pellets of fecal material. The weights of most of the victim's organs were markedly less than the normal averages (Table 1). The thymus was extremely atrophic (1.7 g). In addition,

there was almost no glycogen in the liver on PAS (para-amino salicylic acid) staining (Figure 4).

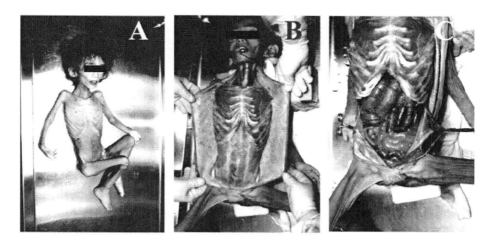

Figure 1. Case 1: A. View of the victim in the supine position. Bilateral contracture of the knee joints and bilateral edema of the feet can be seen. B. Complete lack of subcutaneous fat. C. Complete lack of omental fat.

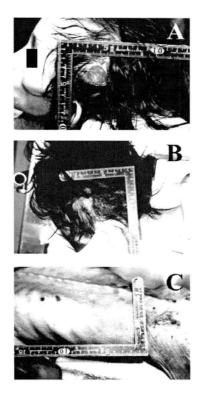

Figure 2. Case 1: Decubitus ulcers found on victim. A. Left temporal area. B. Left occipital area. C. Left side of the back and pelvis.

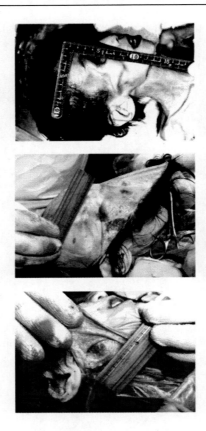

Figure 3. Case 1: Recent subcutaneous hemorrhages on the right temporal area and the right side of the face.

Table 1. Weights of organs of Case 1 at autopsy, in comparison with the mean weights in 2-year-old and 3-year-old Japanese girls

Organ	Victim (g)	Average±S.D.[*] 2 y.o.	Average±S.D.[*] 3 y.o.
Brain	980	1180 ± 96	1234 ± 110
Heart	40	62 ± 8.1	72 ± 10.2
Left lung	35	95 ± 26.6	114 ± 23.8
Right lung	40	106 ± 30.2	133 ± 33.2
Liver	210	440 ± 85	475 ± 72
Pancreas	6.8	23 ± 6.1	30 ± 9.3
Spleen	10	41 ± 14.1	45 ± 8.8
Left kidney	20	40 ± 6.5	43 ± 6.6
Right kidney	25	37 ± 5.6	42 ± 7.3
Left adrenal gland	1.7	2.2 ± 0.95	2.4 ± 0.87
Right adrenal gland	1.4	1.9 ± 0.89	2.2 ± 0.72
Thymus	1.7	25.1 ± 10.2	30.9 ± 10.9

[*]Jpn J Legal Med 1992; 46(3): 225-235.

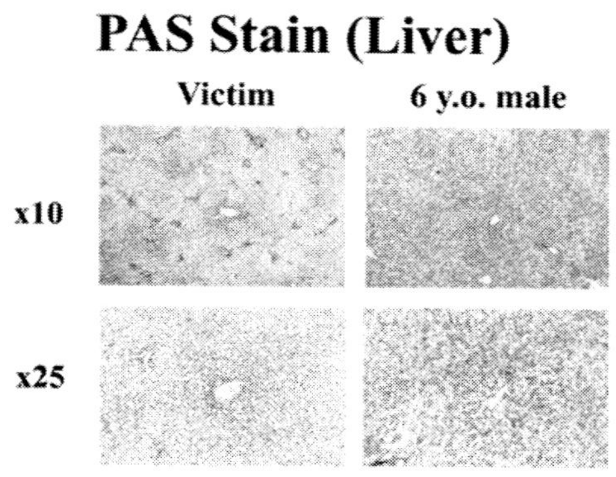

PAS Stain (Liver)

Figure 4. Case 1: PAS staining of the victim's liver. Corresponding specimens from a 6-year-old boy are included for comparison.

Background

When the victim was 2 years and 8 months old, her mother had taken her to the hospital. At that time, her body weight was 9 kg and the pediatrician diagnosed her as being malnourished. The pediatrician pressed the mother to have the girl admitted, but the mother rejected this recommendation and took her back home. Six days later the mother brought the victim back to the same hospital. Her body weight had increased to 11 kg (Figure 5), so the doctor's worries about possible child abuse were negated.

When the victim was 2 years and 9 months old, she entered the care of her grandmother. Her body weight was 10 kg and she could not stand alone. The grandmother cared for her adequately but wondered why her grandchild ate so hungrily. At 2 years, 10 months, and 11 days old, the girl was returned to her parents. Her body weight by this time was 12 kg.

The parents confessed that they kept the victim in a small room for about 30 days, and then in a packing case. The amount of food served to her decreased with time (Figure 6). When she was 3 years and 20 days old, she was found dead in the packing case. Her body weight was 5 kg at the time of death, having decreased by 7 kg (58.3% of her previous body weight) in 70 days.

Calculation of Caloric Deficit

The Recommended Dietary Allowance for Japanese, 6th edition (Public Health Council, Ministry of Health and Welfare, Japan), indicates that the requirement for basal metabolism in a 2-year-old Japanese girl is 700 kcal/day [6]. Activity factors are given as 1.3 for low physical activity (I), 1.5 for moderate activity (II), 1.7 for light-heavy activity (III) and 1.9 for heavy activity (IV). Therefore, the daily recommended dietary allowance for a 2-year-old Japanese girl is 700 kcal/day × the appropriate factor for physical activity, plus 16 kcal/day, which is the number of calories needed for weight gain. Because this child had been neglected, and had not been fed enough food, we omitted the caloric allowance for weight gain, as described below.

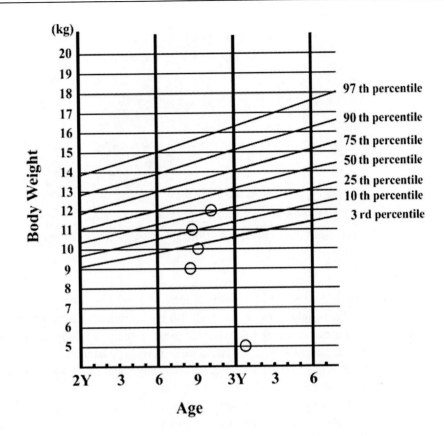

Figure 5. Case 1: Changes in the victim's body weight (open circles) on a standard growth curve for Japanese girls.

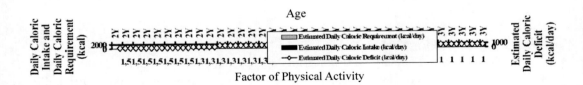

Figure 6. Case 1: Changes in the estimated daily caloric requirement, intake, and deficit of the victim.

From statements by the parents, we calculated the daily caloric requirement of the victim as 700 kcal/day (basal metabolism), multiplied by a factor for physical activity (Figure 6). The victim had stayed inside her house for the first 2 weeks, without playing outside. The parents then locked her in a small room for approximately the next 2 weeks. From this information, we estimated the factors for physical activity as 1.5 and 1.3, respectively. After that, she lay in a packing case until death. The activity factor in this period was taken as 1.0. The daily caloric deficit was calculated from the difference between the calculated daily caloric intake and the estimated daily caloric requirement, based on the estimated activity factor for the victim. The range of percentage body fat at age 1 year is 28%–30%, and that at ages 4–6 years is 22% [7]. We assumed the range at ages 2–3 years to be 24%–26%. As the victim was a thin girl, her percentage body fat was assumed to be 20%, leading to a calculated fat content of 2.4 kg (12kg × 0.2). The internal autopsy findings revealed that the victim had no subcutaneous or omental fat. Therefore, assuming that 2.4 kg of the weight deficit was attributable to loss of fat and the rest to loss of protein, we calculated the caloric deficit. Fat reserves of 2.4 kg would be sufficient to compensate for a caloric deficit of 2,400 g × 7.2 kcal/g body fat [8]. We assumed that, after the fat reserves had been exhausted, protein would have been used to compensate for the caloric deficit (4 kcal/g protein) until death. On the basis of these assumptions, the calculated body weight at the time of death was 4.988 kg (Figure 7). When we assumed the percentage body fat to be 25%, the calculated body weight was 5.468 kg.

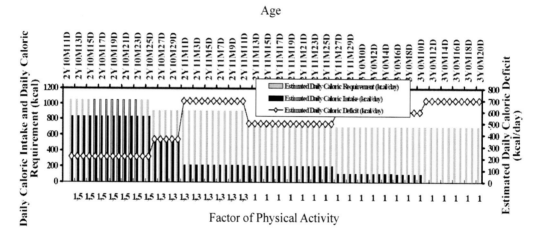

Figure 7. Case 1: Changes in the calculated body weight of the victim and the estimated caloric deficit.

Case 2. [4]

A 7-year-old girl living with her mother and stepfather was confined to the house and prevented from going to school in the end of May. One month after the girl first been been prevented from attending school, her teacher visited her house, but the parents prohibited the teacher from meeting her. After the teacher's visit, the intensity of physical abuse increased for about 3 weeks. One day in July the stepfather repeatedly lifted and droped her body several times and then found that she was not breathing. The parents called the ambulance immediately, and as soon as the emergency medical technicians arrived they performed emergency treatment for cardiac arrest, then transferred the girl to hospital. Although the doctors attempt resuscitation, they could not save the patient. Because of the presence of bilateral massive swelling and subcutaneous hemorrhage on the face (Figure 8), as well as many round skin lesions, which were initially suspected of being cigarette burns, on her legs (Figure 9), a judicial autopsy was performed.

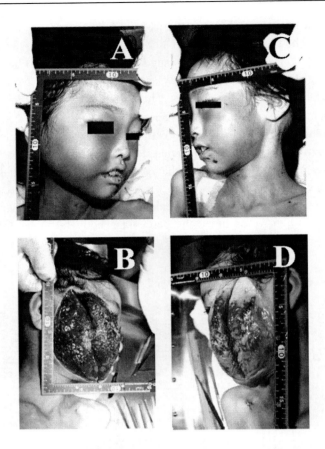

Figure 8 [4]. Case 2: A 7-year-old girl. Death from traumatic shock. Bilateral massive swelling and subcutaneous hemorrhage of the face can be seen. A. Right lateral view of the face. B. Massive subcutaneous hemorrhage on the right side of the face. C. Left lateral view of the face of Case 2. D. Massive subcutaneous hemorrhage on the left side of the face.

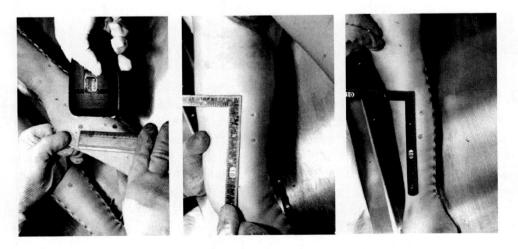

Figure 9 [4]. Case 2: The distance between the paired skin lesions found on the leg were found to match the distance between the electrodes of the stun gun.

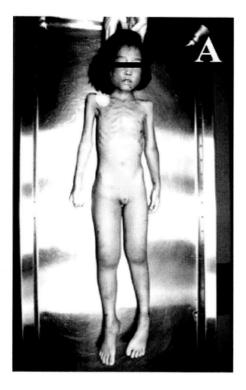 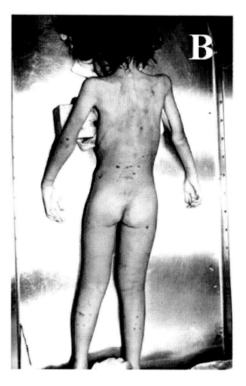

Figure 10 [4]. Case 2: A. View of the victim in the supine position. The right leg was thicker than the left leg. B. View of the victim in the prone position. Many excoriations and bruises were present on the back.

Scars from wearing handcuffs were observed on the girl's wrists and ankles, and cigarette lighter burn was present on the right thumb. The right leg was thicker than the left leg, and double linear marks were observed on the lateral side of the right thigh. The distance between the pairs of skin lesions on the leg was found to match that between the electrodes of a stun gun (4–5 cm). Many excoriations, bruises, and massive subcutaneous hemorrhages were found on the body (Figure 10). The weights of most of the victim's organs were less than the normal averages (Table 2). The thymus was extremely atrophic (5.8 g).

Table 2. Weights of organs of Case 2 at autopsy, compared with the mean weights in 7-year-old Japanese girls

Organ	Victim (g)	Average ± S.D.[*]
		7 y.o.
Brain	1,235	1,290 ± 91
Heart	90	112 ± 18.2
Left lung	110	182 ± 65.2
Right lung	110	218 ± 65.6

Table 2. Continued.

Organ	Victim (g)	Average ± S.D.*
Liver	500	648 ± 101
Pancreas	30	41 ± 8.2
Spleen	40	54 ± 10.9
Left kidney	70	63 ± 9.2
Right kidney	60	62 ± 10.3
Left adrenal gland	3	2.5 ± 0.99
Right adrenal gland	2.3	2.4 ± 0.66
Thymus	5.8	28.2 ± 14.4

*Jpn J Legal Med 1992; 46(3): 225-235.

Examination of the victim's laboratory data on admission (Table 3) revealed a low red blood cells (RBC) count and a high level of creatine kinase (CK), which was present in myocytes in the victim's blood. These findings suggest that the girl had suffered chronic anemia and massive muscular damage from repeated violence. From these findings, we diagnosed the cause of death as traumatic shock.

Case 3. [5]

A boy aged 1 year and 6 months was punched by his father because he had consumed snacks and juice without permission. His mother found him dead in bed the following morning. The father did not call the ambulance or the police, and to delay putrefaction, he placed a pile of ice on each side of the victim. One and a half months later, the father committed suicide by hanging.

Table 3. Laboratory Data for Case 2 [4]

Item	Volume on admission	Normal range
BUN (mg/dL)	18	7.7 – 19.6
Creatinine (mg/dL)	0.5	0.4 – 0.8
Na (mEq/L)	138	139.9 – 144.7
K (mEq/L)	8.2	4.26 – 5.14
CL (mEq/L)	104	103.1 – 106.7
CRP (mg/dL)	0.78	0.044 – 1.070

Item	Volume on admission	Normal range
Blood FDP (μg/mL)	400 <	5.6 – 8.0
RBC ($\times 10^4/\mu L$)	117	400 - 520
Hb (g/dL)	3.7	11.5 – 15.5
Ht (%)	12.1	35 – 45
Plts. ($\times 10^4/\mu L$)	7.8	15.0 – 35.0
WBC (/μL)	8,400	5.5 – 15.5
AST(GOT)	313	15 – 37
ALT(GPT)	119	4 – 24
LDH (U/L)	1873	280 – 588
ChE (U/L)	92	249 – 493
Amylase (U/L)	47	62 – 218
CK (U/L)	957	52 – 249
t-Bil (mg/dL)	1.5	0.45 – 0.99
d-Bil (mg/dL)	0.5	0.27 – 0.73
t-Protein (g/dL)	5.1	6.4 – 8.1

This case surfaced only after the father's death, and we performed a judicial autopsy on the dead child. Old subcutaneous hemorrhages were observed on the trunk, thighs, and chin, and bilaterally in the mandibular and occipital areas (Figure 11). The left cerebral hemisphere was light reddish, suggesting that the cause of death might have been subdural hemorrhage (Figure 12).

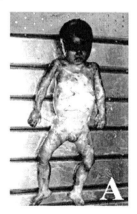  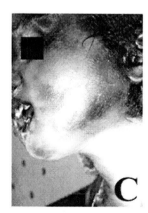

Figure 11. Case 3: A. View of the victim in the supine position. B. View of the victim in the prone position. C. Bruising is evident on the chin and the left mandibular area.

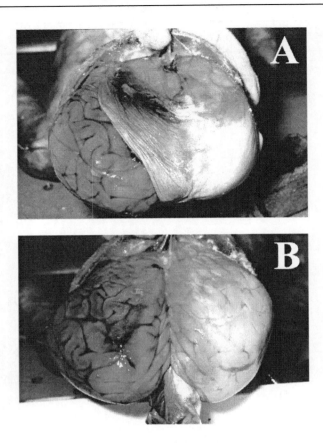

Figure 12. Case 3: A. Localized hemoglobin in the dura mater. B. Hemoglobin infiltration on the surface of the left cerebral hemisphere.

Case 4. [5]

A girl aged 3 years and 5 months who had been living with her parents, four brothers, and six sisters was reported to have been missing for more than one year. The police interrogated her mother, and in accordance with the mother's statements the victim was found in a coolerbox on the veranda. About 1 year previously, the mother had found the victim lying dead on the floor, and had wrapped her in a blanket and a plastic bag and hidden the body in a closet. The following summer, in response to complaints from a neighbor about the stench, the victim's body had been transferred to the coolerbox. The body was badly decomposed and adipoceratous (Figure 13A, B), and the stomach was ruptured (Figure 13C). These findings suggested that the victim had suffered blunt force to the abdomen. However, because of the severe postmortem changes, the cause of death could not be determined with certainty.

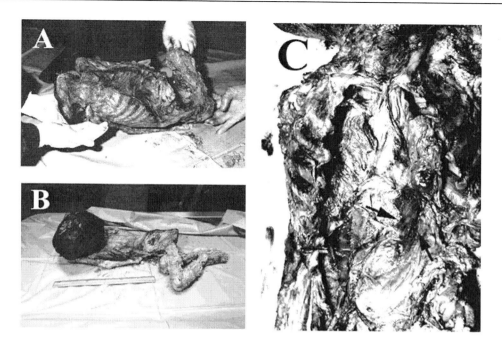

Figure 13. Case 4: A. View of the victim in the supine position. B. View of the victim in the prone position. C. Internal appearance of the abdominal organs. The stomach is ruptured along the lesser curvature (arrows).

Case 5.[4]

A 4-year-old boy living with his mother andstepfather had broken his left tibia, and his left leg was then placed in a plaster cast (Figure 14). At mid-night, he had a scratch on his left ankle. Then the father-in-law had the victim's hands tied behind the back, and he had cried bitterly. The father-in law put a face towel into his mouth and gagged him with gauze. When the the victim had stopped roaring, they found him dead.

Several brownish round bruises about 1 cm in diameter on both sides of the mandibular area (Figure 15) and a spiral fracture of the left tibia (Figure 16) were observed. Hematomas were present along the fracture lines on the left tibia. Excoriation and hemorrhage were not observed on the surface or in the subcutaneous tissues of the left tibia. These findings suggested that the victim had suffered recurrent physical abuse.

Grooves were observed around both wrists (Figure 17A). Stomach contents (Figure 17B) were present in the respiratory tract, and both lungs were congested and edematous (Figure 17C). Petechial hemorrhages were observed in the eyelids bilaterally and in the palpebral and bulbar conjunctivae (Figure 18). From these findings, we diagnosed the cause of death as asphyxia by aspiration of the stomach contents.

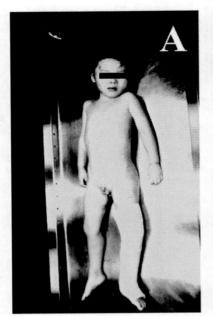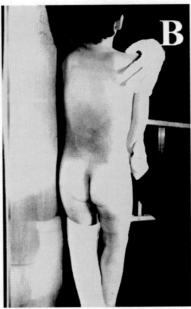

Figure 14. Case 5: A 4 year-old boy. Death from asphyxia by aspiration of stomach contents. A. View of the victim in the supine position. B. View of the victim in the prone position.

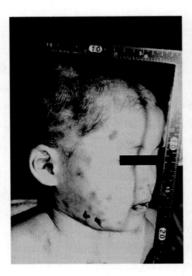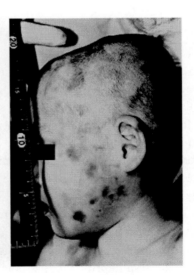

Figure 15 [4]. Case 5. Several bruises can be seen on the face.

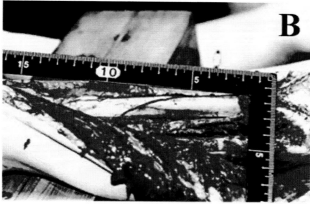

Figure 16 [4]. Case 5: A. Spiral fracture of the left tibia. B. The fracture was enlarged by supination of the knee joint and pronation of the ankle joint.

3. Discussion

In Case 1 there was no evidence that the girl's filthy diaper had been changed. The autopsy findings of the victim revealed that muscle and organ proteins had been consumed and the stores of glycogen in the liver had been burned up. These findings suggest that the malnutrition was due to marasmus (the lack of both calories and protein), not kwashiorkor (dietary protein deficiency with a still substantial intake of energy) [9]. The victim had gained 2 kg in 6 days at the age of 2 years and 6 months (Figure 5). These facts indicate that she had not suffered from an intestinal absorption disorder, but instead had been maltreated by her parents.

Figure 17. Case 5: A. Grooves around both wrists of the victim. B. Stomach contents. C. Stomach contents present in the bronchus.

The presence of decubitus ulcers on the victim's left side, contracture of both knee joints, and edema of both feet indicates that the victim had been lying on her left side for a long time. Conversely, recent subcutaneous hemorrhages on the right side of her face indicated that her parents had hit her on the head and face several days before her death. Scars on the forehead suggested that the victim had suffered recurrent physical abuse.

Abused or neglected children suffer serious stress. Stressors trigger physiological responses, including activation of the hypothalamic-pituitary-adrenal axis, which releases glucocorticoids. An increase in endogenous glucocorticoid levels induces apoptosis of the thymocytes in the cortex of the thymus, resulting in thymic involution [10,11]. Thymic involution is an important factor in determining child abuse, and has been reported to be an important parameter for estimating the degree and duration of child abuse [12]. The victim's thymus was severely affected, showing that she had been suffering serious stress and severe malnutrition for a long time.

To verify that the parents had maltreated the victim, from the parents' statement we developed a theoretical calculation model of her caloric deficit. Although the victim had no access to water, the parents gave her 100 to 150 mL milk once every few days. The degree of dehydration was unclear. One previous study [13] classified dehydration as mild (5%), moderate (10%), or severe (15%). Thus, we extrapolated the hydrated death weights to be 5.263 kg (5 kg÷0.95) to 5.882 kg (5 kg÷0.85). The model assumed a body fat content of 20% or 25%. It also assumed that protein would be used for energy only after the fat reserves had been exhausted. In reality, both fat and protein are broken down at the same time. However, in this case, almost all the body fat was spent on compensating for the caloric deficit. The calculated body weight of 4.988-5.468kg at death was close to the hydrated actual weight. Therefore, this theoretical model verified the parents' statements.

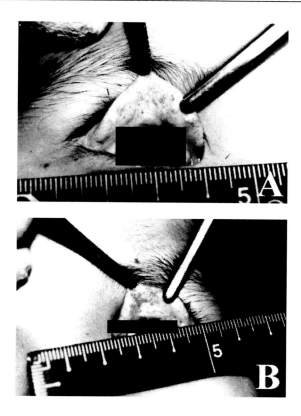

Figure 18. Case 5: Petechial hemorrhages in the bilateral eyelids and in the palpebral and bulbar conjunctivae in the victim. A. Right. B. Left.

Madea and Brissie, in reporting on the starvation of a 6-week-old baby, calculated the number of days of total food and liquid deprivation [13]. The rate of daily physical activity is stable in a 6-week-old baby, and the daily caloric requirement can be calculated reliably. However, the daily physical activity of young children varies, so estimating caloric deficit is more difficult in starved young children than in starved infants. Our calculation method is more applicable to cases of nutritional neglect than that described in the previous report [13]. To verify the reliability of the statements of perpetrators, it might be useful to calculate the caloric deficit on the basis of their statements, as described here.

About 4 months before the death of Case 1, her mother had taken her to a hospital. At that time, her body weight was 9 kg and the pediatrician diagnosed her as being malnourished. The pediatrician pressed the mother to have the victim admitted, but the mother rejected this recommendation and took the girl back home. Six days later, the mother brought the victim back to the same hospital. At this time, her body weight had increased to 11 kg, and the doctor's doubts about possible child abuse were negated.

A crucial factor in this case was the inability of the pediatrician to recognize the case as one of child neglect, because of the 2-kg weight gain shown by the victim in 6 days. Although awareness of, and attention to, child abuse has recently improved among Japanese clinicians, it is still inadequate compared with that in the United States. Japanese medical school courses offer only a few hours of lectures on child abuse. To protect Japanese children against abuse, it is important that medical students and interns are educated adequately about child abuse during their undergraduate and postgraduate training. The main aim of receiving training should be to acquire the ability to recognize the signs and symptoms of physical abuse, neglect, and sexual abuse. Physical indicators of child abuse include bruises on uncommonly injured body surfaces; marks made by blunt instruments, burns, human hands or bite; evidence of poor care or failure to thrive; scalds; and unexplained retinal hemorrhages. Injuries of the genitourinary tract, perineal pain, and sexually transmitted diseases are indicative of sexual abuse. Knowledge of child abuse should be shared among medical practitioners, public health practitioners, and welfare workers [14].

The crucial problem for treatment in Case 2 was that the teacher had not been able to meet with the victim and confirm her safety. The anti-child abuse law in Japan defines child abuse as physical abuse, neglect, sexual abuse, or emotional maltreatment. This girl was confined to her home by her parents, who had prevented her from coming to school. Truancy, which is not defined as child abuse by the law, was the result of the parents' locking the girl in the house, and we should therefore recognize this case as one of neglect and therefore child abuse as defined by the law. If the parents of truanting pupils prohibit teachers from visiting them at home, then schools should recognize these cases as child abuse and cooperate with the Child Abuse Authorities in taking action. However, in Case 2, the school was unable to recognize the signs of abuse and did not move to save the victim. Moreover, two severe abuse cases of confined schoolchildren to their home by their parents, similar to Case 2, have occurred in Japan after 1 year and 2.5 years in Japan [15,16]. These results indicate that educators in Japan have not yet learned their lesson from Case 2. To prevent abuse of schoolchildren, teachers should, at the very least, acquire knowledge of child abuse, as described above.

On the other hand, there have also been some recent fatal cases of child abuse in which neighbors failed to notify the Child Care Authorities, even though they had recognized the signs of abuse [4]. In Case 5, the neighbors recognized bruises on the face of the victim and his crying at midnight 2 weeks before his death. They notified the caretaker of the apartment where the boy lived, but not the Child Care Authorities. In Cases 3 and 4, the victims' disappearance was not been noticed by neighbors for a long period. The victim in Case 1 might have suffered recurrent physical abuse. Lack of concern about child welfare in the community is the greatest obstacle to protecting children at risk of abuse. The most effective means of preventing child abuse is to educate the community about how to recognize the signs of child abuse and to report it to the authorities. We emphasize that the community has an obligation to protect children from crime, including child abuse.

According to one report of forensic autopsies on battered children in Japan (1990–1999), public support for child welfare could prevent more than 100 murder cases over a 10-year period [17]. Kitamura et al. reported that some negative life events experienced during childhood were correlated with poorer quality of life measures in some subgroups [18]. The roles of the Social Services in preventing child abuse have been extended [19]. Aichi Prefectural Child Welfare Centers (Figure 19), which deal with child abuse cases occurring in Aichi Prefecture (with the exception Nagoya City), commissioned MN to be their medico-legal adviser in 2002. The duty of the medico-legal adviser is to differentiate injuries on a child's body due to abuse from those due to genuine accidents, and to educate child welfare and health care workers about child abuse [20–22]. As shown in Table 4, MN consulted on 44 cases over a period of 3 years and 5 months, and in almost of these cases the children were successfully separated from their parents. On the basis of forensic pathological evidence, the Centers have been able to separate children from abusive parents with certainty. Welfare and health care workers who attend the lectures are gradually becoming aware that they, themselves, play key roles in the protection and care of children, particularly in respect of the identification and detection of child abuse. To obtain Family Court orders for removal of parental power, expert opinions are exhibited in court, and no fatalities have yet been reported in child abuse cases in which the Centers have been involved. Forensic pathologists are also required to play key roles in the prevention of child abuse [20, 22]. The activities of forensic pathologists in Japan should be extended to the administrative field.

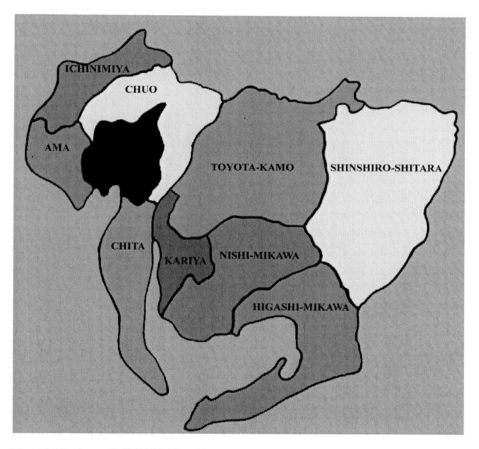

Figure 19. Aichi Prefectural Child Welfare Centers.

Table.4 Activities of MN as a Medico-legal Adviser for the Aichi Prefectural Child Welfare Centers (April 2002 to August 2005)

Kind of consultation	Number
Consultation on suspected child abuse cases	44
Expert opinion	3
Lecture	8
Total	55

References

[1] Kempe H, Silverman FN, Steele BF, Droegemueller W, Silver HK. The battered child syndrome. *JAMA* 1962; 181:17-24.

[2] Kobayashi M, Naya Y, Suzuki A, Kato Y, Hirata Y, Gough D. Child abuse viewed through the hot-line in Osaka, Japan. *Acta Pediatr. Jpn.* 1995; 37: 272-8.

[3] Nagao M, Maeno Y, Koyama H, Seko-Nakamura Y, Monma-Ohtaki J, Iwasa M, Li XZ, Kawashima N, Yano T. Estimation of caloric deficit in a fatal case of starvation resulting from child abuse. *J. Forensic. Sci.* 2004; 49(5): 1073-6.

[4] Nagao M. Problems of social treatment for child abuse cases as viewed by a forensic pathologist. *Pediatr. Jpn.* 2004; 45(12): 2213-9. (in Japanese)

[5] Nagao M, Koyama H, Maeno Y, Iwasa M, Kato H, Seko-Nakamura Y, Monma-Ohtaki J, Li XZ, Tsuchimochi T. Two fatal cases of child abuse in which neighbors were unaware of the victims' disappearance for a long period. *Legal Med.* (in press)

[6] Society of informatics for health and nutrition. Recommended dietary allowance. Dietary reference intakes.[in Japanese] Tokyo: Dai-Ichi Shuppan Publishing Co. Ltd.,1999.

[7] Nakamura H, editor. Growth disorders and nutrition of children. [in Japanese] Osaka: Nagai Shoten Co., Ltd., 1998.

[8] Iwamatsu S, Haccho Y, editors. Nutrition education. 3rd ed. Rev. [in Japanese] Tokyo: Ishiyaku Publishers, Inc., 1995.

[9] Graham GG. Starvation in the modern world. *N. Engl. J. Med.* 1993; 328: 1058-1061.

[10] Gruber J, Sgonc R, Hu YH, Beug H, Wick G. Thymocyte apoptosis inducing by elevated endogeneous corticosterone levels. *Eur. J. Immunol.* 1994; 24: 1115-1121.

[11] Tarcic N, Ovadia H, Weiss DW, Weidenfeld J. Restraint stress-induced thymic involution. and cell apoptosis are dependent on endogenous glucocorticoids. *J. Neuroimmunol.* 1998; 82: 40-46.

[12] Fukunaga T, Mizoi Y, Yamashita A, Yamada M, Yamamoto Y, Tatsuno Y, Nishi K. Thymus of abused/neglected children. *Forensic. Sci. Int.* 1992; 53: 69-79.

[13] Meade JL, Brissie M. Infanticide by starvation: calculation of caloric deficit to determine degree of deprivation. *J. Forensic. Sci.* 1985; 30: 1263-1268.

[14] Henry BM, Ueda R, Shinjo M, Yoshikawa C. Health education for nurses in Japan to combat child abuse. *Nurs. Health Sci.* 2003; 5: 199-206.
[15] Mainichi Shimbun. 2004. 4. 16.
[16] Yomiuri Shimbun. 2004. 1. 26.
[17] Planning and Development Committee of Japanese Society of Legal Medicine. Forensic autopsy cases of battered children in Japan (1990-1999). Nippon Hoigakkai Zasshi 2002; 56(2/3): 276-86. (in Japanese)
[18] Kitamura T, Kawakami N, Sakamoto S, Tanigawa T, Ono Y, Fujihara S. Quality of life and its correlates in a community population in a Japanese rural area. *Pshychiatry Clin. Neurosci.* 2002; 56: 431-41.
[19] Sakai S, Okuyama M, Inoue N, editors. Medical Diagnosis and Management of Child Abuse and Neglect. Tokyo: Nanzando, 2005, (in Japanese)
[20] Tokyo Shimbun. 2005. 2. 28.
[21] Shikoku Shimbun. 2005. 4. 11.
[22] Chunichi Shimbun. 2005. 7. 31.

In: Child Abuse and Violence
Editors: T. Richardson, M. Williams, pp. 81-87

ISBN: 978-1-60456-128-9
© 2008 Nova Science Publishers, Inc.

Chapter V

Adam Walsh Child Protection and Safety Act: A Sketch[*]

Charles Doyle

Abstract

The Adam Walsh Child Protection and Safety Act, P.L. 109-248 (H.R. 4472), serves four purposes. It reformulates the federal standards for sex offender registration in state, territorial and tribal sexual offender registries, and does so in a manner designed to make the system more uniform, more inclusive, more informative and more readily available to the public online. It amends federal criminal law and procedure, featuring a federal procedure for the civil commitment of sex offenders, random search authority over sex offenders on probation or supervised release, a number of new federal crimes, and sentencing enhancements for existing federal offenses. It creates, amends, or revives several grant programs designed to reinforce private, state, local, tribal and territorial prevention; law enforcement; and treatment efforts in the case of crimes committed against children. It calls for a variety of administrative or regulatory initiatives in the interest of child safety, such as the creation of the National Child Abuse Registry.

Sex Offender Registration

Earlier federal law, the Jacob Wetterling Act, encouraged the states to establish and maintain a registration system. Each of them has done so. The Walsh Act preserves the basis structure of the earlier law, expands upon it, and makes more specific matters that were previously left to individual choice. For purposes of compliance by the states and other jurisdictions the prior law remains in effect until the later of three years after enactment or one year after the necessary software for the new uniform, online system has become available. For registrants, however, the new requirements became effective upon enactment.

---

[*] Excerpted from CRS Report RS22646 dared 4-17-07

Who Must Register

The class of offenders required to register has been expanded under the act. The group includes anyone found in the United States and previously convicted of a federal, state, local, tribal, military, or foreign qualifying offense, although strictly speaking violations of the laws of the District of Columbia or U.S. territories are not specifically mentioned as qualifying offenses. Offenders must register in each state or territory in which they live, work, or attend school. There are five classes of qualifying offenses: crimes identified as one of the specific offenses against a minor; crimes in which some sexual act or sexual conduct is an element; designated federal sex offenses; specified military offenses; and attempts or conspiracy to commit any offense in the other four classes of qualifying offenses. The inventory of qualifying offenses is subject to exception. Conviction for an otherwise qualifying foreign offense does not necessitate registration if it was not secured in a manner which satisfies minimal due process requirements under guidelines or regulations promulgated by the Attorney General. Nor does conviction of a consensual sex offense require registration if the victim is an adult not in the custody of the offender, or if the victim is 13 years of age or older and the offender no more than four years older. Finally, juvenile delinquency adjudications do not constitute qualifying convictions unless the offender is 14 years of age or older at the time of the misconduct and the misconduct adjudicated is comparable to, or more severe than, aggravated sexual assault or attempt or conspiracy to commit such an offense. There are no specific limitations on registration based on convictions that have been overturned, sealed or expunged under state or foreign law or on convictions for which the offender has been pardoned. There are no specific limitations on requirements that flow from past convictions regardless of their vintage. Instead, the Attorney General is authorized to promulgate rules of applicability.

Registration Retirements

Those required to register must provide their name, social security number, the name and address of their employers, the name and address of places where they attend school, and the license plate numbers and descriptions of vehicles they own or operate. The jurisdiction of registration must also include a physical description and current photograph of the registrant and a copy of his driver's license or government issued identification card; a set of fingerprints, palm prints, and a DNA sample; the text of the law under which he was convicted; a criminal record that includes the dates of any arrests and convictions, any outstanding warrants, as well as parole, probation, supervisory release, and registration status; and any other information required by the Attorney General. The regularity with which registrants must appear for new photographs and to verify their registration information depends upon their status. It is at least every three months for Tier III offenders. Tier II offenders must reappear no less frequently than every six months. Tier I offenders must reappear for new photographs and verification at least once a year. Tier I offenders must maintain their registration for 15 years, which can be reduced to 10 years. Tier II offenders must maintain their registration for 25 years. Tier III offenders must maintain their registration for life, which can be reduced to 25 years.

Failure To Comply

Jurisdictions that fail to comply after the act becomes fully effective run the risk of having their Byrne program funds reduced by 10%. The act makes failure to register a federal crime for offenders convicted of a federal qualifying offense, or who travel in interstate commerce, or who travel in Indian country, or who live in Indian country. Violations are punishable by imprisonment for not more than 10 years and by an additional penalty to be served consecutively, of not less than five, nor more than 30 years, if the offender commits a crime of violence. Moreover, violation exposes an offender's to term of supervised release for any term of years not less than five years or for life. If the offender is a foreign national ("an alien"), he becomes deportable upon conviction.

Adjustments in Federal Criminal Law

The Adam Walsh Child Protection and Safety Act is focused, as its name implies, upon child protection and safety. Its efforts involve the creation of new federal crimes, the enhancement of the penalties for preexisting federal crimes, and the amendment of federal criminal procedure, among other things. Many of these efforts are child-specific; some are more general. The new federal crimes include the following.

- Murder in the course of a wider range of federal sex offenses.
- Internet date rape drug trafficking.
- Kidnaping that involves the use of interstate facilities.
- Child abuse in Indian country.
- Production of obscene material.
- Obscenity or pornography in Internet source codes.
- Child exploitation enterprises.

The amendments to federal criminal procedure are a bit more numerous and somewhat more likely to implicate crimes in addition to those committed against children. Among their number are:

- Random searches of sex offender registrants as a condition of probation or supervised release.
- Expanded DNA collection from those facing federal charges or convicted of any federal offense.
- Elimination of the statute of limitations for various sexual crimes or crimes committed against a child.
- Participation of state crime victims in federal habeas proceedings.

- Study of the elimination of marital privileges in abuse cases.
- Preventive detention in cases involving a minor victim or a firearm.
- Compensation for guardians ad litem.
- Government control of evidence in pornography cases.
- ! Forfeiture procedures in obscenity, exploitation and pornography cases.
- Murder during course of various sex offenses as a felony murder predicate.
- Civil commitment procedure for federal sex offenders.

The act's penalty enhancements are the most extensive of its amendments to federal criminal law and procedure. It establishes new sentencing ranges for the federal crimes of murder, kidnaping, maiming, or aggravated assault when the victim is a child. In the case of murder, the penalty is imprisonment for any term of years not less than 30 years, imprisonment for life, or death; in the case of kidnaping or maiming, imprisonment for life or any term of years not less than 25 years; and in the case of aggravated assault, imprisonment for life or any term of years not less than 10 years. While the new minimums terms of imprisonment must yield to any otherwise applicable higher mandatory minimum, the new maximum penalties trump any otherwise applicable maximum. The provision has the effect of making capital offenses out of several federal murder statutes that heretofore were punishable only by a term of imprisonment when the victim is a child and when the misconduct involves the intentional killing of the victim or a reckless, fatal act of violence. The act increases penalties for several other child offenses including:

Crime	Imprisonment: Prior	Imprisonment: New
Use of mail/interstate commerce facilities to coerce or entice a child to engage in sexual activities, 18 U.S.C.2422(b)	Not less than five years/not more than 30 years	Not less than 10 years/not more than life, *§203*
Transporting a child in interstate commerce for sexual activity, 18 U.S.C. 2423(a)	Not less than five years/not more than 30 years	Not less than 10 years/not more than life, *§204*
Sexual abuse in a federal prison or enclave, 18 U.S.C. 2242(a)	Not more than 20 years	Any term of years or for life, *§205*
Aggravated sexual abuse of a child, 18 U.S.C. 2241(c)	Any term of years or for life	Not less than 30 years or for life, *§206(a)(1)*

Crime	Imprisonment: Prior	Imprisonment: New
Abusive sexual contact with a child, 18 U.S.C. 2244(a)(1)	Not more than 10 years	Any term of years or for life (18 U.S.C. 2244(a) (5)), §206(2)
Sexual exploitation of a child by an offender with a prior federal conviction for sex trafficking or a state conviction for sexual abuse, sexual contact of a ward, or child pornography, 18 U.S.C. 2251(e)	Not less than 15 years/not more than 30 years	Not less than 30 years or for life, §206(b)(1)(A), (B)
Sexual exploitation of a child resulting in death, 18 U.S.C. 2251(e)	Death or imprisonment for any term of years or for life	Death or imprisonment for not less than 30 years or for life, §206(b)(1)(C)
Traffic in child sexually exploitive material by an offender with a prior state or federal conviction for sex trafficking in children, 18 U.S.C. 2252(b)	Not less than five years/not more than 20 years	Not less than 15 years/not more than 40 years, §206(b)(2)
Traffic in child pornography by an offender with a prior state or federal conviction for sex trafficking in children, 18 U.S.C. 2252A(b)	Not less than five years/not more than 20 years	Not less than 15 years/not more than 40 years, §206(b)(3)
Use of a misleading Internet domain name to induce a child to view harmful material, 18 U.S.C. 2252B	Not more than four years	Not more than 10 years, §206(b)(4)
Overseas production of child sexually exploitive material for export to the U.S., 18 U.S.C. 2260 (a),(c)	Not more than 10 years; not more than 20 years for recidivists	Not less than 15 years/ not more than 30 years; not less than 25 years/ not more than 50 years for 2d offenders; not less than 35 years nor more than life for offenders with 2 or more prior convictions; death or not less than 30 years or for life if death results, §206 (b)(5)

Crime	Imprisonment: Prior	Imprisonment: New
Overseas production of child pornography material for export to the U.S., 18 U.S.C. 2260(b), (c)	Not more than 10 years/ not more than 20 years for recidivists	Not less than five years/ not more than 20 years; not less than 15 years/ not more than 40 years for recidivists, §206 (b)(5)
A. Sex trafficking in children by a recidivist, 18 U.S.C. 1591 B. Commission of certain federal sex crimes by an offender with a prior federal sex crime conviction (18 U.S.C. 1591 not a predicate), 18 U.S.C. 3559(e)	A. Not more than 40 years (if the victim is 14 to 18 years old); any term of years or life (if the victim is under 14) B. life imprisonment	A/B. life imprisonment (18 U.S.C. 1591 becomes a predicate for section 3559(e) purposes), §206 (c)
Sexual abuse of a ward in a federal prison or enclave, 18 U.S.C. 2243 (b)	Not more than five years	Not more than 15 years, §207
Sex trafficking in children by a recidivist, 18 U.S.C. 1591	Not more than 40 years (if the victim is 14 to 18 years old); any term of years or life (if the victim is under 14)	Not less that 10 years or for life (if the victim is 14 to 18); any term of years not less than 15 years or life (if the victim is under 14), §208
False statements relating to an offense under 18 U.S.C. 1591, 2250, chs.109A, 110, or 117, 18 U.S.C. 1001	Not more than five years	Not more than eight years, §141(c)

Grant Programs

The act establishes, reinforces, and revives several grant programs devoted to child and community safety, including the following.

- Big Brothers Big Sisters of America (authorizing appropriations totaling $58.5 million through FY2011). ! National Police Athletic League (authorizing appropriations totaling $64 million through FY2010).
- State, local and tribal governments in order to outfit sex offenders with electronic monitoring devices (authorizing appropriations totaling $15 million through FY2009).
- Public and private entities that assist in treatment of juvenile sex offenders or that assist the states in their enforcement of sex offender registration requirements (authorizing appropriations totaling $30 million through FY2009).

- Facilitating the prosecution of cases cleared as a consequence of the DNA backlog elimination (authorizing necessary appropriations through FY2011).
- Law enforcement agencies to combat sexual abuse of children (authorizing necessary appropriations through FY2009).
- A private nonprofit entity for a program of crime prevention media campaign (authorizing appropriations totaling $34 million through FY2010).
- State, local and tribal government programs for the voluntary fingerprinting of children (authorizing appropriations totaling $20 million through FY2011).
- The Rape, Abuse and Incest National Network (RAINN) to operate a sexual assault hotline, conduct media campaigns, and provide technical assistance for law enforcement (authorizing appropriations totaling $12 million through FY2010).
- To enable state, local and tribal entities to verify the addresses of registered sex offenders (authorizing necessary appropriations through FY2009).

Other Child Safety Initiatives

The act includes a wide assortment of other provisions designed to prevent, prosecute or punish the victimization of children. Among them are sections that broaden access to federal criminal records information systems, create a national child abuse registry, expand recordkeeping requirements for those in the business of producing sexually explicit material, immunize officials from civil liability for activities involving sexual offender registration, and authorize and direct the Department of Justice to establish and maintain a number of child protective activities.

In: Child Abuse and Violence
Editors: T. Richardson, M. Williams, pp. 89-95

ISBN: 978-1-60456-128-9
© 2008 Nova Science Publishers, Inc.

Chapter VI

Internet: Status Report on Legislative Attempts to Protect Children from Unsuitable Material on the Web[*]

Marcia S. Smith

Abstract

Preventing children from encountering unsuitable material, such as pornography, as they use the Internet is a major congressional concern. Several laws have been passed, including the 1996 Communications Decency Act (CDA), the 1998 Child Online Protection Act (COPA), and the 2000 Children's Internet Protection Act (CIPA). Federal courts ruled, in turn, that certain sections of CDA, COPA, and CIPA were unconstitutional. All the decisions were appealed to the Supreme Court. The Supreme Court upheld the lower court decision on CDA in 1997. It has heard COPA twice, in 2002 and 2004, and each time remanded the case to a lower court; an injunction against the law's enforcement remains in place. The Supreme Court upheld CIPA on June 23, 2003. Congress also passed the "Dot Kids" Act (P.L. 107-317), which creates a kid friendly space on the Internet, and the "Amber Alert" Act (P.L. 108-21) which, inter alia, prohibits the use of misleading domain names to deceive a minor into viewing material that is harmful to minors. Congress remains concerned about these issues.

Background

The Internet has become a pervasive tool used by children to research school projects, look for entertainment, or chat with friends. Parents and policy makers are concerned that children are encountering unsuitable material — such as pornography —while they use the Internet. Most agree that protecting children requires a multi-faceted approach, with parental

---

[*] Excerpted from CRS Report RS21328 dated January 30, 2006

or other adult supervision as a key ingredient. Many also believe that legislation is needed. Several federal laws have been enacted, including the 1996 Communications Decency Act (CDA), the 1998 Children's Online Protection Act (COPA), and the 2000 Children's Internet Protection Act (CIPA).

Such legislation has proved difficult to draft in a manner that does not violate rights guaranteed by the Constitution, particularly the First Amendment. One difficulty is that there can be considerable disagreement as to what is "unsuitable," "inappropriate," or "harmful," just as what constitutes pornography can be debated. Even the definition of "children" can be problematical, since some material may be inappropriate for a pre-teen, but not for a senior in high school. (Sexually explicit e-mail was addressed in the CAN-SPAM Act. See CRS Report RL31953.)

1996 Communications Decency Act (CDA)

Congress passed the Communications Decency Act (CDA) as Title V of the 1996 Telecommunications Act (P.L. 104-104), on February 8, 1996. That day, the American Civil Liberties Union (ACLU) filed suit against portions of the CDA; the American Library Association (ALA) and others filed suit later. They challenged two sections of the law — 47 U.S.C. § 223(d) and 47 U.S.C. § 223(a)(1)(B) — that made it a crime to engage in "indecent" or "patently offensive" speech on computer networks if the speech could be viewed by a minor (defined as under 18). The plaintiffs argued that the provisions were unconstitutional because they prohibited speech protected by the First Amendment, and the terms indecent and patently offensive were overbroad and vague. In June 1996, a special three-judge panel of the U.S. District Court in Philadelphia, established under procedures set forth in the CDA, agreed. It issued a preliminary injunction barring enforcement of those provisions. Under the CDA, the government could appeal the case directly to the Supreme Court, which it did. (For more information, see CRS Report 97-660). In *Reno v. American Civil Liberties Union*, 521 U.S. 844 (1997), the Supreme Court upheld the lower court's ruling that the provisions were unconstitutional. Specifically, it found that, with regard to the use of the term "indecent," the CDA "is a blanket restriction on speech" and could be found to be constitutional only if it "serves to promote a compelling interest" and is the "least restrictive means to further the articulated interest."[1] The Court did not find that it met those tests.

In 2003, Congress passed the PROTECT Act (P.L. 108-21), which amended CDA by substituting "child pornography" for "indecent." Thus, it now bans obscenity and child pornography, neither of which is protected by the First Amendment. Therefore the act no longer raises the constitutional issues that formed the basis of that Supreme Court ruling (see CRS Report 95-804 for more information).

A suit was filed in December 2001 by Barbara Nitke, the National Coalition for Sexual Freedom ([http://www.ncsfreedom.org/] and others to overturn section 223(a)(1)(B) as it relates to obscenity (Nitke v. Ashcroft, 253 F. SUPP. 2D 587 (S.D.N.Y. 2003). A special three-judge panel of the U.S. District Court for the Southern District of New York rejected the arguments in July 2005.[2]

1998 Child Online Protection Act (COPA)

Congress next passed the Child Online Protection Act (COPA), as Title XIV of the FY1999 Omnibus Appropriations Act (P.L. 105-277), signed into law October 21, 1998. COPA prohibits communication of material that is "harmful to minors" on a website that seeks to earn a profit. COPA defines minor as under the age of 17, instead of 18 as in CDA. The term "material that is harmful to minors" is defined as "any communication, picture, image, graphic image file, article, recording, writing, or other matter of any kind that is obscene or that (A) the average person, applying contemporary community standards, would find, taking the material as a whole and with respect to minors, is designed to appeal to, or is designed to pander to, the prurient interest; (B) depicts, describes, or represents in a manner patently offensive with respect to minors an actual or simulated sexual act or sexual contact, actual or simulated normal or perverted sexual act, or a lewd exhibition of the genitals or post-pubescent female breast; and (C) taken as a whole, lacks serious literary, artistic, political or scientific value for minors."

Congress reportedly was optimistic that COPA would survive constitutional challenges because of the stated exceptions for communications that had literary, artistic, political or scientific value, its application only to commercial sites, and use of "harmful to minors" rather than "indecent." The definition of "harmful to minors" was based on the obscenity test created in *Miller v. California*, thereby requiring jurors to apply "contemporary community standards" when assessing material. The ACLU filed suit challenging the constitutionality of COPA, arguing that it violated the First Amendment rights of adults, and did not use the least restrictive means to advance a compelling government interest. A preliminary injunction was issued against enforcement on the act in February 1999, which was upheld by the Third Circuit Court of Appeals in June 2000. The Third Circuit ruled that the act was unconstitutional because its use of "community standards" resulted in material available to a nationwide audience being judged by the standards of the community most likely to be offended, since one cannot make material on the Internet available in some communities but not in others.

The Department of Justice appealed the Third Circuit's decision to the Supreme Court. In May 2002, the Supreme Court held that COPA's use of the term "community standards" alone did not make the statute unconstitutional and vacated the Third Circuit's decision. However, the Court expressed no view as to whether COPA was unconstitutional for other reasons, remanded the case to the Third Circuit, and allowed the preliminary injunction to remain in effect. The Third Circuit again ruled in March 2003 that the law was unconstitutional. That decision was also appealed to the Supreme Court. On June 29, 2004, the Court affirmed the Third Circuit's preliminary injunction, but did not rule on whether the act is unconstitutional, instead remanding the case to the Third Circuit for trial. The Court concluded that the government did not demonstrate that COPA was the least restrictive means of achieving the goal; that, for example, the use of filters may be more effective. (See CRS Report 95-804.) In January 2006, it became publicly known that the Justice Department was seeking data from major search engine companies (e.g., Yahoo!, MSN, America Online, and Google) on search terms employed by users, reportedly as part of an effort to demonstrate that filters are insufficient to protect children, and therefore COPA is needed. Google officials are resisting the subpoena (see CRS Report RL31408 for more information).

COPA also created a Child Online Protection Commission to study methods to help reduce access by minors to material that is harmful to minors. The COPA Commission released its report in October 2000 [http://www.copacommission.org/report/], concluding that a combination of public education, consumer empowerment technologies and methods, increased enforcement of existing laws, and industry action was needed. Also in 1998, Congress directed (in P.L. 105-314, the Sexual Predators Act) the National Research Council (NRC) to conduct a study on how to limit the availability of pornography on the Internet. The 2002 NRC report, *Youth, Pornography, and the Internet*, similarly concluded that a multifaceted approach was needed.

2000 Children's Internet Protection Act (CIPA)

Congress next passed the Children's Internet Protection Act (CIPA) as Title XVII of the FY2001 Consolidated Appropriations Act (P.L. 106-554), signed into law on December 21, 2000. The law requires schools and libraries that receive federal funding to use filtering technologies to block from minors Web pages that contain material that is obscene, child pornography, or harmful to minors.[3] CIPA also requires libraries receiving federal funds to block websites containing obscene material or child pornography from access by adults. Minors are defined as persons under 17. The term "harmful to minors" is somewhat different than in COPA. In CIPA, it is any "picture, image, graphic image file, or other visual depiction that (A) taken as a whole and with respect to minors, appeals to a prurient interest in nudity, sex, or excretion; (B) depicts, describes, or represents in a patently offensive way with respect to what is suitable for minors, an actual or simulated sexual act or sexual contact, actual or simulated normal or perverted sexual act, or a lewd exhibition of the genitals; and (C) taken as a whole, lacks serious literary, artistic, political or scientific value as to minors." An exception allows blocking features to be disabled by an adult to allow access for "bona fide research or other lawful purposes." For more detail on CIPA, see CRS Report 95-804.

The ALA and ACLU challenged sections 1712(a)(2) and 1721(b) as they apply to public libraries only. Opponents of the law say the software required to block the material cannot determine which material is protected by free speech. They also say that the law is unenforceable, censors speech to adults as well as children, is overbroad and vague, and denies those without home computers the same access to information. In May 2002, a three-judge federal district court in Philadelphia established under the terms of CIPA ruled that "it is currently impossible ... to develop a filter that neither underblocks nor overblocks a substantial amount of speech."[4] The court ruled that public libraries cannot be forced to use Internet blocking systems because they might also block access to sites that contain information on subjects such as breast cancer, homosexuality, or sperm whales. As provided for in CIPA, the Department of Justice appealed the case directly to the Supreme Court, which upheld the constitutionality of CIPA on June 23, 2003 (see CRS Report 95-804). The

ALA decried the court's decision (see [http://www.ala.org/ ala/washoff/Woissues civilliberties cipaweb cipa.htm]).

2002 "Dot Kids" Act (P.L. 107-317)

The 107th Congress approached the issue from the aspect of creating or regulating the use of domain names. Website addresses actually are a series of numbers, but to make the Internet more user friendly, the Domain Name System was created to provide a simple address (e.g., [http://www.congress.gov]) that corresponds to the website's numerical address. Top Level Domains (TLDs) appear at the end of a Web address. They can be given a generic designation ("gTLD") such as .com, or a country code ("ccTLD") such as .us for the United States. TLDs are assigned by the Internet Corporation for Assigned Names and Numbers (ICANN), operating under a Memorandum of Understanding with the U.S. Department of Commerce. The .us ccTLD is owned by the Commerce Department, which contracts with a company, NeuStar, for its operation.

Congress passed the Dot Kids Implementation and Efficiency Act (HR. 3833, P.L. 107-317) in 2002. It creates a "dot kids" (.kids) second-level domain within the .us ccTLD as "a haven for material that promotes positive experiences for children and families using the Internet, provides a safe online environment for children, and helps to prevent children from being exposed to harmful material on the Internet" (H.Rept. 107-449, p. 5). Participation is voluntary, and the Commerce Department monitors the site to ensure that only material that is "suitable for minors and not harmful to minors" is posted there. "Minors" are children under 13. "Suitable for minors" is defined as material that is "not psychologically or intellectually inappropriate for minors, and serves the educational, informational, intellectual, or cognitive needs of minors, or the social, emotional or entertainment needs of minors." "Harmful to minors" is defined similarly to the way it is in COPA, although it omits obscene material and does not specify the types of material covered (communication, picture, image, etc.) The dot kids domain [http://www.kids.us] was opened for public registrations on September 4, 2003. NeuStar subcontracted with KidsNet, a Florida company, to provide content review and monitoring services. A House Energy and Commerce subcommittee held a hearing on May 6, 2004, at which a NeuStar witness stated that 1,700 .kids.us domain names have been sold, but there were only 13 "live sites"at that time. Critics have complained that the cost for obtaining a dot kids domain name, and paying for required content review, is too expensive, and the content requirements are too restrictive.[5]

2003 "Amber Alert" Act (P.L. 108-21) and Pending Amendments

The 108th Congress passed the PROTECT (Prosecutorial Remedies and Other Tools to End the Exploitation of Children Today) Act, also called the AMBER Alert Act (P.L. 108-21). Among its provisions, the act makes it a crime to knowingly use a misleading domain name to deceive a person into viewing obscenity on the Internet, or to deceive a minor into viewing material that is harmful to minors. Under the act, a domain name that includes a word or words that relates to the sexual content of a site, such as sex or porn, is not misleading. The term "harmful to minors" is defined similarly to CIPA, except that it applies to "any communication" rather than a "picture, image, graphic image file, or other visual depiction." The act also amends the Communications Decency Act so that it applies to child pornography transmitted via the Internet (discussed above), and prohibits "virtual" child pornography (see CRS Report 98-670). Legislation was introduced in the first session of the 109th Congress to increase the penalty. Under current law, an offender is to be fined, or imprisoned for no more than four years, or both. H.R. 2318/S. 956 would increase the maximum sentence to 10 years. H.R. 3132, which passed the House in September 2005, would impose a minimum sentence of 10 years and a maximum of 30 years. All three bills would make imprisonment mandatory.

Issues in the 109th Congress

Congress remains concerned about how to protect children using the Internet. Additional legislation has been introduced, and hearings held. In a statement before a November 10, 2005, Senate Judiciary subcommittee hearing (available at [http://judiciary.senate.gov]), Senator Hatch said that "The problem is not the Internet, the problem is pornography. But we must take seriously the unique and powerful ways the Internet can be used for evil rather than for good." The Senate Commerce Committee held a hearing on January 19, 2006, on these issues.

Taxing Pornographic Websites

The Internet Safety and Child Protection Act (H.R. 3479/S. 1507) would impose a 25% tax on the amounts charged by "regulated pornographic websites" as defined in the bill. The proceeds would be used to pay for enforcement of the act, for federal government programs such as Cyber Tip-line and the Internet Crimes Against Children Task Force, and other purposes related to protecting children who use the Internet. It would also set requirements on those sites to verify that anyone viewing the site is over 18. It appears that such a tax likely would be found unconstitutional, however. A 1987 Supreme Court decision (Arkansas Writers' Project, Inc. v. Ragland, 481 U.S. 221, 230) concluded that "official scrutiny of the content of publications as the basis for imposing a tax is entirely incompatible with the First Amendment's guarantee of freedom of the press."

Establishing an Adult (.Xxx) Domain Name

On June 1, 2005, the organization that manages assignment of Internet domain names, ICANN, announced that it had entered into negotiations with a registry company to operate a new ".xxx" domain for use by websites offering adult content. The extent to which a separate domain for such websites would reduce access to objectionable content by minors is unclear. Registering as a .xxx domain would be voluntary, with no requirement that adult website operators discontinue their existing sites. Use of a .xxx domain might make it easier to use filters to block .xxx websites, but similarly could make it easier to find adult-oriented material. ICANN has delayed consideration of final approval of the .xxx domain name at the request of the Department of Commerce and others. The Family Research Council, for example, opposes the idea because it might "do more harm than good" [http://www.frc.org/get.cfm?i=PR05F01]. See CRS Report RL33224 for an analysis of constitutional issues associated with the .xxx domain name concept. See CRS Report 97-868 for more information on domain names, generally.

Peer to Peer (P2P) Networks

Concern also exists about the availability of pornography on "peer-to-peer" (P2P) networks that use file-sharing software to allow individual users to communicate directly with each other via computer, rather than accessing websites. Such file-sharing programs are better known for their widespread use for downloading copyrighted works, raising concerns about copyright violations, but they can be used for sharing any type of files. Government Accountability Office (GAO) reports in 2003 (GAO-03-351) and 2005 (GAO-05-634), found that pornographic images are easily shared and accessed on P2P networks and juveniles are at risk of inadvertent exposure to them. The Federal Trade Commission issued a consumer alert [http://www.ftc.gov/bcp /conline/ pubs/alerts /sharealrt.htm] in 2003 and held a seminar in December 2004. In May 2004, the Justice Department announced the results of a major law enforcement effort against P2P networks that distribute child pornography [http: //www.usdoj.gov/opa/pr /2004/May /04_ crm_ 331.htm].

In: Child Abuse and Violence
Editors: T. Richardson, M. Williams, pp. 97-113
ISBN: 978-1-60456-128-9
© 2008 Nova Science Publishers, Inc.

Chapter VII

Intra-Familial Sexual Abuse (Incest) among Korean Adolescents

Kim Hyun Sil
Department of Nursing, Daegu Haany University, Daegu, South Korea
Kim Hun Soo
University of Ulsan School of Medicine, Seoul, South Korea

Introduction

Intra-familial childhood sexual abuse (incest) is now recognized as a major public health concern, both because of its widespread nature and because increasing evidence indicates that incest has a wide range of traumatic effects in childhood as well as serious long-term sequelae in adult life [Dong, Anda, Dube, Giles, & Felitti, 2003].

Despite the attention it has received in recent years, the sexual victimization of children or adolescents has not declined. However, the prevalence of intra-familial sexual abuse has proven difficult to determine. For example, the utilized methods of data collection and the reluctance or inability of children to disclose abuse have likely contributed to underestimation of the rates of intra-familial child sexual abuse [Kilpatrick, Edmunds, & Seymour, 1992]. The most widely used method for determining the extent to which members of a population acknowledge being sexually abused has been self-reporting surveys; however, estimates derived from such surveys vary dramatically depending on the population sampled (e.g., college students vs. clinical or special groups such as hospitalized psychiatric patients and runaway youth) [Barnett, Miller-Perrin, & Perrin, 1997]. In addition, underestimation may arise from the utilized definition of incest. In many studies, incest has been defined as sexual intercourse between participants who are related by some formal or informal bond of kinship that is culturally regarded as a bar to sexual relations [Kaplan & Sadock, 1998]. In practice, incestuous experiences may include a variety of acts, such as touching or fondling of sexual body parts, masturbation, oral sex, vaginal or anal intercourse, or penetration of those orifices by objects [Fergusson & Mullen, 1999].

Far fewer studies have examined intra-familial sexual abuse in Asian populations (e.g. Koreans) than in Western populations. Although several factors may contribute to the lack of attention paid to intra-familial sexual abuse among Asian societies, one of the most important factors may be the collective worldview of Asian societies versus the individual worldview of Western societies [Meston, Heiman, Trapnell, & Carlin, 1999]. In societies with a collective worldview, the identities of individuals are deeply embedded in the groups to which they belong (e.g., family, school, and country) and the needs of the group often take precedence over the needs of a given individual [Futa, Hsu, & Hansen, 2001]. Within a collective orientation, therefore, individual family members may be overlooked in order to protect the family from shame when problems such as incest arise, thus contributing to low rates of disclosure, strong denial, and underreporting of intra-familial sexual abuse [Okamula, Heras, Wong-Kerberg, 1995; Futa et al, 2001].

Indeed, in two representative Korean clinical cases presented below, incest was only identified following the victims' admission to psychiatric units for their mental problems and psychological turmoil.

Case 1

J, a high school girl, complained of depression, withdrawal, low academic performance, psychosomatic symptoms, sleeping difficulties, and troubled interpersonal relationships, beginning in the 11th grade (18 years old). She subsequently stopped attending school, became withdrawn and began to smile incessantly in a silly way, stopped eating, and complained of auditory hallucinations that blamed her. J was referred to our hospital for treatment of these symptoms, and was accompanied by her mother.

J was from a middle-class family in Seoul, and had grown up in her parents' home without any troubles by her mother. Although she was relatively timid and shy, she had harmonious relationships with her friends, sister and brother. Her father was chief manager of a construction company. When J was in the 10th grade, her father was transferred to another branch of the company in order to oversee construction of a new building located in an urban area apart from Seoul. Due to this transfer, her father moved away from the family home and lived alone. He found it difficult to perform many domestic chores, including cooking and cleaning, and J was asked to accompany her father to his new home. She transferred to a new high school located near where her father lived, and she helped him around the house. One evening at home, her father became drunk and sexually assaulted her while she was sleeping. J subsequently felt terribly guilty, ashamed and confused. After the first incident, her father repeatedly demanded that she have sex with him when he came home from work; this went on for several months.

J experienced conflict and guilty feelings toward her mother, and beginning the month prior to her referral, she started smiling in a silly way and talking to herself, and she experienced idea of reference, brief episodes of dissociation, and stopped attending school. On the last weekend of the month prior to her referral, she returned to her mother in Seoul without any explanation.

During the interview session, the therapist realized that J was a victim of incest. When the therapist brought this up with her parents, both vehemently denied that any incest had taken place. Her parents, especially her mother, also told the therapist that J was insane. J's siblings described their father as an indecisive, impulsive man, and their mother as an immature, irresponsible woman.

Case 2

L had worked as a clerk at a small law firm, but was fired for being foolish and inattentive to her duties. After she lost her job, L stayed in her home without any contact with family members. She began talking to herself, speaking incoherently, and became restless and smiled in a silly way. She wandered around every night for several weeks, developed a sleep disturbance and became unduly religious. Her family decided she needed professional psychiatric treatment and had her hospitalized. During her hospitalization, she told her therapist that several years earlier her elder brother had forced her to touch his genitals on multiple occasions and then had sexual intercourse with her. When confronted by the therapist, her parents denied L's accusation, telling the therapist, "Don't believe anything my daughter tells you about my son (who was not present). It's all a lie. As you know, she is crazy."

L continuously felt guilty and became to have a suicidal ideation. She was placed in a seclusion room close to the nurse's station for careful observation. Her chief complaints were low self-esteem, disorganized thoughts, poor concentration, headaches, dizziness, anorexia, sleep disturbances, nightmares, depressed mood, and difficulty in interpersonal relationships.

In response to these issues, we sought to examine the prevalence of incest among adolescents, and to identify the family problems, perceived family dynamics and psychological characteristics of adolescent victims of incest in South Korea and other countries.

Prevalence of Intra-familial Child Sexual Abuse (Incest) in Korea and Cross-cultural Comparison

In landmark reviews, Finkelhor [1994] and Fergusson and Mullen [1999] have observed that child sexual abuse (CSA) is common in all societies in which it has been measured. However, most of the studies published to date have been done in western nations. The situation in most non-English speaking countries remains relatively unexplored [Tang, 2002].

The studies in Western populations have identified three prominent trends. First, the prevalence is consistently high, with 80% of estimates from many studies of CSA of females ranging between 15% and 33% [Fergusson & Mullen, 1999]. Second, the risk of CSA is consistently two to three times higher among female children than among males [Dunne, Purdie, Cook, Boyle, & Najman, 2003; Tyler, 2002]. Third, although studies have not yet identified a distinct "sexual abuse syndrome," a consistent pattern of health and social problems has been observed among young people and adults who are or were the victims of

CSA; this pattern includes depression, suicidality, poor self-esteem, social withdrawal, aggression, and problematic drug use and sexual behavior. A growing consensus in the research literature is that the most serious health consequences arise when the sexual abuse is penetrative, protracted, and occurs at a young age [Fergusson & Mullen, 1999; Tyler, 2002].

In our recent study using a self-report questionnaire [Kim & Kim, 2005], the prevalence of incest among the 1,672 representative Korean adolescents examined was found to be 3.7% (see Table 1). In this study, incest was defined as having a clear and conscious memory of at least one incident of unwanted sexual penetration of bodily orifices by an older blood relative occurring either by threat or force. Incestuous experiences such as fondling were excluded from this definition because children may have difficulties in distinguishing a caring touch from sexual fondling.

Our results revealed that in this Korean population, females were more likely to be victims of incest than males, and delinquents were more likely to be victims than students. The perpetrator was usually male. These findings are similar to those obtained from surveys conducted in Western countries. The overall prevalence found in our study was higher than expected, suggesting that Korean victims may be more likely to self-disclose incest and sexual abuse now than in the past. Furthermore, since Koreans traditionally regard sexual affairs as secrets, the actual prevalence of incest is likely to be even higher than the 3.7% identified in our study [Kim & Kim, 2005]. The higher proportion of incest victims among delinquent adolescents from our study [Kim & Kim, 2005] compared to student adolescents may reflect the devastating long-term effects of intra-familial childhood sexual abuse, i.e. such abuse increased the tendency toward delinquency and deviant behavior.

When we classified the types of incest as father-daughter incest, sibling incest (brother-sister incest), and mother-son incest, we found that the sum of the rates of father (or stepfather)-daughter incest (1.0%) and male adult relative-daughter incest (1.3%) among Korean adolescents was higher than that of brother-sister incest (1.4%). Therefore, as in Western countries, male adults (fathers, stepfathers or male relatives) appeared to be more likely than other family members to initiate incest in Korea. Although in recent years an increasing number of victims of paternal incest have begun reporting the abuse, it is likely that many cases of father-daughter incest go unreported, primarily due to the daughters' fears of punishment, abandonment, or family disruption following a report. Thus, it is imperative that health professionals remain vigilant for signs of incest, particularly father-daughter incest, in the Korean population.

Over the past decades, several cross-cultural researches were done to find the similarities and differences in CSA rate among various populations. In a large sample of Chinese university students in Hong Kong, Tang [2002] found that prevalence estimates for a range of unwanted childhood sexual experiences were consistently much lower than those usually found in Western samples. Less than 1% of Chinese students reported sexual intercourse with an adult, compared to rates of between 6% and 10% in many Western countries [Tang, 2002].

In a Danish national survey in 1987 [Leth, Stenvig, & Pedersen, 1988], wherein a random sample of 2,000 adults aged 18-50 years with a response rate of 66% revealed that 14% of women and 8% of men reported having experienced sexual abuse before the age of 18. The reported abuse occurred during the period 1955-1987, when the respondents were children. However, police report disclosed CSA in 1998 was 1.0 per 1,000 children, and 0.6

per 1,000 excluding reported cases of indecent exposure. Half of intra-familial CSA were sentenced to conviction, compared to 40% of extra-familial CSA and 16% of indecent exposure [Helweg-Larsen, & Larsen, 2005].

In another survey conducted in western populations, the prevalence of child sexual abuse was found to range from 7% to 62% for females and from 3% to 16% for males [Wurtele & Miller-Perrin, 1992], whereas a separate telephone interview-based survey found that 15.3% of girls and 5.9% of boys reported having experienced attempted and/or completed sexual abuse [Finkelhor & Dziuba-Leatherman, 1994].

Table 1. Percentage of adolescents experiencing incest by group and gender (%)

Subgroup	Father-daughter Incest	Brother-sister Incest	Relative-child Incest	Non-Incest (%)	Total (%)
Student					
Male	0 (0)	0 (0)	2 (0.4)	556 (99.6)	558 (100)
Female	8 (1.6)	10 (2.0)	8 (1.6)	469 (94.8)	495 (100)
Delinquent					
Male	0 (0)	0 (0)	4 (0.7)	559 (99.3)	563 (100)
Female	10 (17.9)	13 (23.2)	7 (12.5)	26 (46.4)	56 (100)
Total	18 (1.0)	23 (1.4)	21 (1.3)	1,610 (96.3)	1,672 (100)

Adopted from Kim, H. S., & Kim, H. S. (2005). Incestuous experience among Korean adolescents; Prevalence, family problems, perceived family dynamics, and psychological characteristics. Public Health Nursing 22(6): 472-482.

Although the problem of child sexual abuse has been dealt with extensively, especially in North America and Western Europe, recent studies have also examined the problem in other countries. Finkelhor [1994] surveyed the international rate of child sexual abuse based on research conducted among non-clinical populations in English speaking and Northern European countries, as well as in Costa Rica, the Dominican Republic, Spain, and Greece. Finkelhor's survey and analysis revealed similar international rates of child sexual abuse in the United States and Canada, ranging from 7% to 36% for women and 3% to 29% for men [Haj-Yahia & Tamish, 2001]. In contrast, an epidemiological study from Norway reported that 5% of women had been victims of severe, repeated child sexual abuse [Kreyberg Normann, Tambs, & Magnus, 1992]. These findings indicate that the rates of sexual abuse vary not only among populations, but also according to the definition of sexual abuse used by the investigators [Kendall-Tacket & Marshall, 1998].

Internationally, epidemiological data on CSA are gathered from studies that may differ significantly in design and data collection methodologies. Most of these studies are based on retrospective approaches, but often differ in their definitions of childhood and sexual abuse. Furthermore, survey-type studies are often hampered by a low response rate, which has proven to be an important obstacle for trend studies and cross-national comparisons [Finkelhor, 1994; Leventhal, 2000]. These complications make it difficult for researchers to compare the results of international studies with the prevalence of intra-familial child sexual abuse obtained from studies in Western countries. In the future, it will be valuable for researchers to agree upon both data collection methods and definitions, thus allowing rational comparison of inter-population rates of child sexual abuse.

Psychological Consequences of Child Sexual Abuse

The psychological consequences of child sexual abuse are among the most widely examined and controversial aspects of research in this area. Although many researchers argue that child sexual abuse always has a detrimental effect on the victim, a considerable number of children who have experienced sexual abuse did not report any symptoms at the time of abuse or later in their life [Kendall-Tackett, Williams, & Finkelhor, 1993]. However, on the basis of a review of 45 empirical studies conducted in the 1980s and early 1990s, Kendall-Tackett et al. [1993] concluded that CSA is associated with a variety of psychological effects in different age groups. Among the youngest victims, usually toddlers and preschoolers, the most common symptoms were found to be anxiety, nightmares and inappropriate sexual behavior. Among school-age children, the most common symptoms were fear, mental illness, aggression, nightmares, problems at school, hyperactivity, and regressive behavior. Among adolescents, the most common symptoms were depression, withdrawal behavior, suicidal or self-injurious behavior, physical complaints, illegal acts, running away, and substance abuse [Haj-Yahia & Tamish, 2001].

Furthermore, over two decades of research have suggested that childhood intra-familial sexual abuse (incest) has many psychological sequelae, including low self-esteem, anxiety, depression, anger, aggression, posttraumatic stress, substance abuse, and sexual difficulties [Berliner & Elliott, 2002].

One maladjusted outcome that has been proposed to be associated with child sexual abuse (CSA) is poor academic achievement [Reyome, 1994]. On average, adolescents who have experienced CSA consistently display lower psychometric test scores on cognitive, academic achievement, and memory assessments compared to non-sexually abused age-matched control groups [Friedrich, Einbender, & Leucke, 1994]. In addition, adolescents who have experienced CSA have been shown to display increased school absenteeism [Leiter & Johnson, 1997], grade retention [Reyome, 1994], and greater involvement in special education programs [Reyome, 1994].

In research on child maltreatment, child sexual abuse has been considered a major risk factor for later negative outcomes such as psychological distress [Jumper, 1995] and/or the development of psychosomatic symptoms [Salmon & Calderbank, 1996], even more so if the abuse was severe [Banyard & Williams, 1996] or if the child was also exposed to cumulative trauma, such as physical abuse [Schaaf & McCanne, 1998] or other stressful life events [Swanston et al., 2003].

Some factors have been associated with a positive outcome and may function as protective factors against the negative effects of CSA; these include strong social support [Feiring, Taska, & Lewis, 1998], high coping abilities [Tremblay, Hebert, & Piche, 1999], and high self-esteem [Heller, Larrieu, D'imperio, & Boris, 1999]. However, studies conducted in France, the US, and other countries have consistently demonstrated that individuals with a history of sexual abuse exhibit a wide range of psychological and behavioral problems [Darves-Bornoz, 1997]. Depression, aggression, low self-esteem, substance abuse problems, sexualized behavior, excessive internalizing or externalizing behavior problems, school-based attainment problems, and relationship difficulties have all been found to be associated with CSA [Kendall-Tackett, Williams, & Finkelhor, 1993; Luster & Small, 1997]. Sexual victimization during childhood has been shown to be associated with cigarette smoking as well as other forms of substance abuse [DeFronzo & Pawlak, 1993]; a study of adolescent smoking and alcohol consumption revealed that children who had experienced physical or sexual abuse were almost three times more likely to smoke cigarettes than their non-abused counterparts [Simantov, Schoen, & Klein, 2000].

Sexual abuse during childhood has been shown to affect later psychological functioning in community-based studies [Fergusson, Horwood, & Lynskey, 1996] and amongst clinical subpopulations [Read, 1997]. In later life, CSA has been associated with depression and low self-esteem [Mullen, Martin, Anderson, Romans, & Herbison, 1996], eating disorders [Wonderlich, Wilsnack, Wilsnack, & Harris, 1996], suicide attempts [Plunkett, O'Toole, Swanston, Oates, Shrimpton, & Parkinson, 2001] and drug abuse [Wilsnack, Vogeltanz, Klassen, & Harris, 1997]. With regard to interpersonal functioning difficulty, CSA survivors report more difficulties in trusting and becoming intimate with others and tend to have problems sustaining healthy attachment relationships [Rumstein-McKean & Hunsley, 2001].

Recently, increased attention has been paid to the association between CSA and later parenting outcomes. Several studies have found important differences in parenting attitudes and beliefs between women who were sexually abused as children and women who were not. For example, women with a history of CSA reported a stronger desire to avoid motherhood [Herman, 1981], had lower confidence in their parenting abilities and reported less emotional control during interactions with their children [Cole, Woolger, Power, & Smith, 1992]. They also tended to have more negative views of themselves as parents [Banyard, 1997] and were more self-focused in parenting situations [Burkett, 1991]. Taken together, these findings suggest that CSA adversely impacts feelings of competence in parenting. As a result, women with a history of CSA may engage in parenting behaviors that differ from those of mothers without a history of CSA. In fact, a number of studies have suggested that CSA may have an inter-generational impact, in that mothers who experienced CSA were found to have an increased potential for physically abusing their own children [DiLillo, Tremblay, & Peterson, 2000], and were more likely to have children who became the victims of abuse by other perpetrators [Zuravin, McMillan, DePanfilis, & Risley-Curtiss, 1996].

Although not all survivors of CSA show adverse effects [Kendall-Tackett, Williams, & Finkelhor, 1993], these findings collectively indicate that child sexual abuse is an independent predictor of adult psychopathology, with more severe abuse associated with a greater chance of psychological problems in adulthood [Fergusson et al., 1996]. However, many of the reported studies have failed to control for various confounding or intervening factors that may be independently associated with poor adjustment and may also differ between abused and non-abused samples, such as the quality of family and peer relationships

[Lynskey & Fergusson, 1997], pre-abuse factors [Paradise, Rose, Sleeper, & Nathanson, 1994], family disruption and other stressors [Mannarino, Cohen, & Berman, 1994].

Although our recent study on the psychological characteristics of Korean victimized adolescents [Kim & Kim, 2005] had some research limitations, such as the use of a cross-sectional research design with a self-reported questionnaire, our results indicated that, compared to non-victimized adolescents, incest victims had lower academic performance and expressed significantly higher levels of various adverse psychological characteristics, including psychoticism, hostility, somatization, anxiety, phobic anxiety, paranoid ideation, depression, obsessive-compulsive behavior, and interpersonal sensitivity. These results were highly consistent with the findings of comprehensive studies conducted in other countries, collectively indicating that intra-familial sexual abuse has devastating psychological effects on victims [Kendall-Tackett, Williams, & Finkelhor, 1993; Haj-Yahia & Tamish, 2001]. The results of our study were also consistent with previous research findings regarding the association between childhood sexual abuse and long-term psychological distress. For instance, prior studies revealed that incest victims tend to suffer from poor self-esteem and feelings of guilt [Kim, Kim, Shin, & Min, 1990], chronic depression, eating and sleep disorders (including nightmares), diffuse anxiety, a variety of physical complaints not associated with observable organic pathologies [Bernstein, 1990], and sudden emotional flooding or numbness. Furthermore, our previous study [Kim, Kim, Shin, & Min, 1990] had shown that women incest victims often have trouble with normal sexual functioning later in life.

In sum, there does not appear to be a definitive pattern of symptoms associated with intra-familial childhood sexual abuse; the symptoms differ across age groups, and the findings across numerous studies suggest that the response to sexual abuse may be gradual and/or delayed.

Family Dynamics Associated with Child Sexual Abuse

Most studies on child sexual abuse have focused on the CSA experience itself. In the 1980s, however, Finkelhor and his colleagues pointed out that the long-term effects of CSA might not be solely a function of the sexual abuse, but could also include other pathological elements, such as psychological abuse, neglect, or family disorganization [Finkelhor, Araji, Baron, Peter, & Wyatt, 1986].

Over the past decade, an increasing number of studies have shown that children exposed to CSA were also physically and emotionally abused [Fergusson & Mullen, 1999]. In addition, psychological disorders and other complicating problems in adulthood have been linked to CSA [Davis & Petretic-Jackson, 2000; Molnar et al., 2001]. In a study of the impact of CSA on its victims, Burkhart and Fromuth [1996] found that CSA was associated with other forms of interpersonal violence in adulthood. Children who had been neglected, had a parent who abused alcohol, or had a battered mother were found to be at a significantly increased risk for CSA [Dube, Anda, Felitti, Croft, et al., 2001]. Thus, it is not sufficient to use simplistic, single-factor approaches to predicting abuse (including CSA) and neglect, because these strategies do not address the complexity of the events and their multiple determinants and modifiers [Sedlak, 1997].

In addition to attributing the long-term difficulties manifested in child sexual abuse (CSA) survivors to specific incidents of abuse, contextual theory [Gold, 2000] implicates a dysfunctional family environment in the development and maintenance of psychopathology. If this perspective is valid, one would expect to find high levels of dysfunction in the family of origin environments of CSA survivors, regardless of whether their abuse occurred within or outside the family [Gold, Hyman, & Andres-Hyman, 2004]. Consistent with this, numerous investigations have found that the family of origin environments of CSA survivors are characterized by greater dysfunction than those of non-abused individuals [Alexander & Schaeffer, 1994]. In discussing the reasons for these findings, Gold [2000] maintains that, in addition to sexual victimization, survivors of prolonged CSA often experience high levels of parental neglect and rejection, which contribute to a sense of alienation from others. Further, dysfunctional families interfere with adequate learning of the daily-living skills (e.g., social, coping, and instrumental skills) necessary for effective functioning in adulthood. This family dysfunction, Gold argues, predates the sexual abuse and is likely to foster childhood vulnerabilities, such as unassertiveness and unmet attachment needs, which appreciably increase a child's risk for being targeted for sexual abuse [Gold, 2000].

In the context of incest, family problems such as parental imprisonment for criminal acts, death, hospitalization, abandonment or divorce, have been found to be more common in incestuous families than in non-incestuous families [Smith & Israel, 1987]. Over two decades of research suggests that childhood intra-familial sexual abuse has many psychological sequelae, including low self-esteem, anxiety, depression, anger and aggression, posttraumatic stress, substance abuse, and sexual difficulties [Berliner & Elliott, 2002]. Therefore, in dealing with children, it is important for the health professional to obtain an accurate picture of both the child and his/her family, as the family is the primary unit of socialization for children. Parents are generally responsible for providing children and adolescents with a wide a variety of behavior patterns, attitudes, values, and norms. An abnormal family structure may be associated with abnormal and deviant behavior patterns (such as incest) and the family problems and family dynamics experienced by incest victims may contribute to the incestuous experience itself. For example, a family dynamic in which the father is authoritative and the daughter is passive may contribute to the occurrence of incest, as well as to an underreporting of father-daughter incest [Farrell, 1988]. Sexual contact between father and daughter places the daughter at risk for significant disruptions in the development of her personality and academic performance. Her home is no longer a place of safety and refuge, but instead becomes a place of high stress and sexual exploitation. In Western society, cases of father-daughter incest often result in the father's hospitalization or imprisonment, divorce, loss of financial support, family moves, and/or changes of schools [Browning & Boatman, 1977]. In the traditional patriarchal society of Korea, however, a father who perpetrates father-daughter incest faces fewer consequences, compared with those in Western countries, whereas a victimized daughter in Korea may suffer greater hardships than her Western counterparts. Indeed, the Korean family (including the perpetrator) may overlook the sufferings of the victim in an effort to preserve family dignity and honor. Tragically, the public revelation of incest or sexual violence between family members is often so humiliating that the family is forced to move to another place where their 'secret' can be maintained.

Consequently, a victim of incest in Korea is made to suffer twice after the act, once by keeping the secret, and the second by undergoing the psychological turmoil resulting from the incest. Historically, the study of intra-familial sexual abuse has been largely neglected among Asian populations compared with Western countries, perhaps due to the collective worldview of Asian societies as compared to the individual worldview of Western societies [Meston, Heiman, Trapnell, & Carlin, 1999]. Our experience in the clinical setting is that a substantial proportion of Korean incest cases are not disclosed until the victim has been admitted to a psychiatric unit due to mental problems and/or adjustment difficulties in school and social life.

Families in which incest occurs show a higher prevalence of problems such as the death, imprisonment, hospitalization of a family member, abandonment by one or both parents, and parental divorce [Smith & Israel, 1987]. Moreover, mounting evidence suggests that children reared in chemically dependent families are more likely to be exposed to abuse and neglect than children in the general population. Consistent with the first clinical case (father-daughter incest) described in our introduction, studies have shown that over 50% of intra-familial CSA incidents are related to alcohol [Finkelhor, Gelles, Hotaling, & Strauss, 1983]. Substantial researches have revealed a variety of problems in the dynamics of families that harbor parental substance abuse, including dysfunctional internal and external boundaries [Goglia, Jurkovic, Burt, & Burge-Callaway, 1992]; poor communication skills, low expressiveness, and high family conflict [Reich, Earls, & Powell, 1988]; chaotic or rigid interaction patterns [Preli, Protinsky, & Cross, 1990]; role distortion and role reversal [Moos & Moos, 1984; Mucowski & Hayden, 1992]; and generally low levels of family competence and adverse family environments [Sheridan & Green, 1993].

In our survey study [Kim & Kim, 2005], the responses of victimized Korean adolescents indicated that several family risk factors were associated with incest, including psychotic disorders, depression, criminal acts, and alcoholism among family members. These findings were consistent with the results of previous studies [Finkelhor et al., 1983; Smith & Israel, 1987; Kim et al., 1990]. In addition, we found that the families of adolescent victims of incest tended to have more dysfunctional characteristics than those of non-victimized adolescents, including higher levels of inconsistent parental child rearing patterns, rigid and autocratic parenting, dissatisfaction of family members toward their homes, unstable parental moods, parental rejection of children, conjugal disharmony, and alienation related to the mother working outside the home [Kim & Kim, 2005]. This finding supports assertions about the complex nature of the relationship between family dynamics and abuse. Specifically, the negative impact of family risk factors such as parental substance abuse and parental mental disorders may best be understood as having adverse consequences on family dynamics, which in turn increases the likelihood of exposure to child sexual abuse. However, the interactive nature of the cause-effect relationships between family dynamics and child sexual abuse will require further study.

Although our earlier study [Kim & Kim, 2002] indicated no association between mothers working outside the home and various types of problem behaviors among Korean adolescents, our more recent study [Kim & Kim, 2005] revealed that the incest victims had a significantly higher percentage of working mothers than did non-victimized adolescents. It is possible that factors restricting the availability of the mother to the family, such as the mother working outside the home, or the mother suffering from chronic depression, alcoholism, or a debilitating physical illness, may result in a role reversal between mother and daughter, indifference of the mother towards family members, and/or conjugal alienation, all of which may promote father-daughter incest.

In summary, our study [Kim & Kim, 2005] showed that 3.7% of Korean adolescents reported incestuous experiences. Dysfunctional family dynamics, alcohol abuse, mental problems, and criminal acts by parents or other family members were identified as familial risk factors for incest in South Korea, and we found that adolescent victims of incest tended to suffer from higher levels of psychological problems than non-victimized adolescents.

Conclusion

Despite the growing recognition that incestuous experiences have affected the lives of many people, few empirical studies have examined the health impact of sexual trauma. The taboo associated with incest may means that both victims and health professionals are frequently reluctant to explore incestuous histories. Incest victims may fear that catastrophic consequences will follow disclosure of the abuse, or they may feel intensely loyal to the perpetrator.

It is not so difficult to believe that incest occurs in highly dysfunctional, fragmented families, especially those with a history of drug and alcohol abuse. However, it is more difficult to contemplate that incestuous abuse also occurs in relatively intact and apparently functional families of all socioeconomic classes. Even when confronted by overt evidence, health professionals may be hesitant to believe that such an awful thing could take place in "such a perfect family," and may tend to dismiss the possibility. In particular, as the adoption and remarried family are steadily increasing not only in western countries but also in Korea, intra-familial child sexual abuse are likely to gradually rise owing to the weakening of family cohesion. Thus, clinicians and health professionals should always consider the possibility of sexual abuse within a family whenever children are seen in an emergency room or psychiatric unit.

When an allegation of intra-familial sexual abuse is made, health professionals should comprehensively evaluate the impact of the abuse on the child and family. This multifaceted assessment should include multiple data gathering methods (e.g. observation, interviews, and self-reporting questionnaires), and multiple respondents (e.g. the non-offending parent, child victim, siblings, and extra-familial sources such as teachers, former therapists, and child protection workers) [Friedrich, 1995]. Future studies aimed at obtaining a clearer picture of symptom patterns among victim of incest and their families will facilitate the development of individual intervention planning, and will provide a means for evaluating the effectiveness of various interventions.

The impact of sexual abuse is not solely a child problem; it is a family problem. In intra-familial sexual abuse cases, the family must participate to increasing the child's safety and parental support, and to reducing the risk of re-abuse. Treatment components for families affected by incest include treatment of the abused child, sibling treatment, non-offending parent treatment, offender treatment, and family treatment [Silovsky & Hembree-Kigin, 1994]. Health professionals working in psychiatric units, pediatric nursing, emergency care units, and public health nursing are responsible for providing all aspects of treatment, from assessment to intervention. To perform this role, they must be given assessment skills and knowledge about preventive strategies and interventions for incest victims. Thus, health education of medical and nursing professionals should be expanded into a multidisciplinary, collaborative approach.

Clearly, more research is needed if we are to understand the phenomenon of intra-familial sexual abuse, treat its medical and psychological sequelae, and prevent its occurrence. As the number of reported cases of incest increases, the need for treatment and preventive intervention increases as well. However, effective and culturally sensitive strategies have not yet been developed to help diminish the medical and psychological impacts of incestuous experiences in Korea.

Our findings [Kim & Kim, 2005] identified some of the family problems and dysfunctional family dynamics may associated with intra-familial child sexual abuse in Korea, and hence may be of use in planning future treatment and prevention programs. Our identification of risk factors for incest, such as parental alcohol abuse, could potentially be used as the basis for a combined effort between intra-familial child sexual abuse prevention and alcohol rehabilitation programs. Furthermore, ongoing public health surveillance programs will be vital for monitoring the need for and effectiveness of various interventions aimed at preventing intra-familial child sexual abuse.

References

Alexander, P. C., & Schaeffer, C. M. (1994). A typology of incestuous families based on cluster analysis. *Journal of Family Psychology,* 8, 458-470.

Barnett, O. W., Miller-Perrin, C. L., & Perrin, R. D.(1997). Family violence across the life-span. Thousand Oaks, CA: Sage.

Banyard, V. (1997). The impact of childhood sexual abuse and family functioning on four dimensions of women's later parenting. *Child Abuse & Neglect,* 21, 1095-1107.

Banyard, V. L., & Williams, L. M. (1996). Characteristics of child sexual abuse as correlates of women adjustment: A prospective study. *Journal of Marriage & the Family,* 58, 853-865.

Berliner, L., & Elliott, D. M. (2002). Sexual abuse of children. In J. E. B. Myers, L. Berliner, J. Briere, C. T. Hendrix, T. Reid, & C. Jenny (Eds.), *The APSAC handbook on child maltreatment* (2nd ed., pp. 55-78). Newbury Park, CA: Sage Publications.

Bernstein, A. E. (1990). Incest: The unknowable trauma. *JAMWA ,* 45(1), 23-26.

Browning, D. H., & Boatman, B. (1977). Incest: Children at risk. *American Journal of sychiatry,* 134, 69-72.

Burkett, L. (1991). Parenting behaviours of women who were sexually abused as children in their families of origin. *Family Process,* 30, 421-434.

Burkhart, B. R., & Fromuth, M. E. (1996). The victim: Issues in identification and treatment. In T. L. Jackson(Ed.), *Acquaintance rape: Assessment, treatment and prevention* (pp. 145-176). Sarasota, FL: Professional Resources Press.

Cole, P. M., Woolger, C., Power, T., & Smith, K. (1992). Parenting difficulties among adult survivors of father-daughter incest. *Child Abuse & Neglect,* 16, 239-249.

Darves-Bornoz, J. M. (1997). Rape-related psychotraumatic syndromes. *European Journal of Obstetrics & Gynecology and Reproductive Biology,* 71, 59-65.

Davis, J. L., & Petretic-Jackson, P.A.(2000). The impact of child sexual abuse on adult interpersonal functioning: A review and synthesis of the empirical literature. *Aggression and Violent Behavior,* 5, 291-328.

DeFronzo, J., & Pawlak, R. (1993). Effects of social bonds and childhood experiences on alcohol abuse and smoking. *Journal of Social Psychology,* 133(5), 635-642.

DiLillo, D., Tremblay, G. C., & Peterson, L. (2000). Linking childhood sexual abuse and abusive parenting: The mediating role of maternal anger. *Child Abuse & Neglect,* 24, 767-779.

Dong, M., Anda, R. F., Dube, S. R., Giles, W. H., & Felitti, V. J. (2003). The relationship of exposure to childhood sexual abuse to other forms of abuse, neglect, and household dysfunction during childhood. *Child Abuse & Neglect,* 27(6), 625-639.

Dube, S. R., Anda, R. F., Felitti, V. J., Croft, J. B., Edwards, V. J., & Giles, W. H. (2001). Growing up with parental alcohol abuse: Exposure to childhood abuse, neglect and household dysfunction. *Child Abuse & Neglect,* 25, 1627-1640.

Dunne, M. P., Purdie, D. M., Cook, M. D., Boyle, F. M., & Najman, J. M. (2003). Is child sexual abuse declining? Evidence from a population-based survey of men and women in Australia. *Child Abuse & Neglect,* 27, 141-152.

Farrell, L. T. (1988). Factors that affect a victim's self-disclosure in father-daughter incest. *Child Welfare,* 67(5), 462-468.

Feiring, C., Taska, L., & Lewis, M. (1998). Social support and children's and adolescents' ---
----

Fergusson, D. M., & Mullen, P. E. (1999). *Childhood sexual abuse: an evidence based perspective.* Thousand Oaks, CA: Sage.

Fergusson, D. M., Horwood, L. J., & Lynskey, M. T. (1996). Childhood sexual abuse and psychiatric disorders in young adulthood: Psychiatric outcomes of childhood sexual abuse. *Journal of the American Academy of Child and Adolescent Psychiatry,* 34, 1365-1374.

Finkelhor, D., Araji, S., Baron, L., Peter, S. D., & Wyatt G. E. (1986). *A source book on child sexual abuse.* Thousand Oaks, CA: Sage.

Finkelhor, D. (1994). The international epidemiology of child sexual abuse. *Child Abuse & Neglect,* 18, 409-417.

Finkelhor, D., & Dziuba-Leatherman, J. (1994). Children as victims of violence: A national survey. *Pediatrics,* 94, 413-420.

Finkelhor, D., Gelles, R. J., Hotaling, G. T., & Strauss, M. A.(Eds.) (1983). *The dark side of families: Current family violence research.* Beverly hills, CA: Sage Publications.

Friedrich, W. N.(1995). *Psychotherapy with sexually abused boys: An integrated approach.* Thousand Oaks, CA: Sage.

Friedrich, W. N., Einbender, A. J., & Leuke, W.J.(1994). *Cognitive and behavioral characteristics of physically abused children Journal of Consulting and Clinical Psychology,* 51, 313-314.

Futa, K. T., Hsu, E., & Hansen, D. (2001). Child sexual abuse in Asian American families: An examination of cultural factors that influence prevalence, identification and treatment. *Clinical Psychology: Science and Practice,* 8, 189-209.

Goglia, L. R., Jurkovic, G. J., Burt, A. M., & Burge-Callaway, K. J. (1992). Generational boundary distortions by adult children of alcoholics: Child –as-parent and child-as-mate. *American Journal of Family Therapy,* 20(4), 291-299.

Gold, S. N. (2000). *Not trauma alone: Therapy for child abuse survivors in family and social context.* Lillington, NC: Taylor & Francis.

Gold, S. N., Hyman, S. M., & Andres-Hyman (2004). Family of origin environments in two clinical samples of survivors of intra-familial, extra-familial, and both types of sexual abuse. *Child Abuse & Neglect,* 28, 1199-1212.

Haj-Yahia, M. M., & Tamish, S. (2001). The rate of child sexual abuse and its psychological consequences as revealed by a study among Palestinian university students. *Child Abuse & Neglect,* 25, 1303-1327.

Heller, S. S., Larrieu, J. A., D'Imperio, R., & Boris, N. W. (1999). Research on resilience to child maltreatment : Empirical considerations. *Child Abuse & Neglect,* 23(4), 321-338.

Helweg-Larsen, K., & Larsen, H. B. (2005). A critical review of available data on sexual abuse of children in Denmark. *Child Abuse & Neglect,* 29, 715-724.

Herman, J. L. (1981). *Father-daughter incest.* Cambridge, MA: Harvard University Press.

Jumper, S. A. (1995). A meta-analysis of the relationship of child sexual abuse to adult psychological adjustment. *Child Abuse & Neglect,* 19(6), 715-728.

Kaplan, H. I., & Sadock, B. J. (1998). *Kaplan and Sadock's Synopsis of Psychiatry.* 8th ed., Baltimore: Williams & Wilkins, 850-851.

Kendall-Tackett, K. A., & Marshall, R.(1998). Sexual victimization of children: incest and child sexual abuse. In R. K. Bergen (Ed.), *Issues in intimate violence* (pp. 47-63). Thousand Oaks, CA: Sage.

Kendall-Tackett, K. A., Williams, L. M., & Finkelhor, D.(1993). The effects of sexual abuse on children: a review and synthesis of recent empirical studies. *Psychological Bulletin,* 113, 164-180.

Kilpatrick, D. G., Edmunds, C. N., & Seymour, A. K. (1992). *Rape in America: A report to the nation.* National Victim Center.

Kim, H. S., & Kim, H. S. (2002). Structural model of delinquent behavior influencing by media violence. in South Korea. *International Nursing Perspectives,* 2(2), 63-78.

Kim, H. S., & Kim, H. S. (2005). Incestuous experience among Korean adolescents: Prevalence, family problems, perceived family dynamics, and psychological characteristics. *Public Health Nursing,* 22(6), 472-482.

Kim, H. S., Kim, H. S., Shin, H. S., & Min, B. K. (1990). A review and cases report about incest. *The Bulletin of Department of Neuropsychiatry,* College of Medicine, Korea University, 7(4), 2- 26.

Kreyberg Normann, E., Tambs, K., & Magnus, P. (1992). *Seksuelle overgrep mot barn – et folkehelse problem?* (in Norwegian: Child sexual abuse – a major health problem). Nordisk Medisin, 107, 326-330.

Leiter, J., & Johnson, M. (1997). Child maltreatment and school performance declines: An event-history analysis. *American Educational Research Journal,* 34, 563-589.

Leth, I., Stenvig, B., & Pedersen, A. (1988). Sexual assaults against children and adolescents. *Nordisk Psykologi,* 40, 383-393 (In Danish).

Leventhal, J. M. (2000). Sexual abuse of children: Continuing challenges for the new millennium. *Acta Paediatrica,* 89, 268-271.

Luster, T., & Small, S. A. (1997). Sexual abuse history and problems in adolescence: Exploring the effects of moderating variables. *Journal of Marriage and the Family,* 59, 131-142.

Lynskey, M. T., & Fergusson, D. M. (1997). Factors protecting against the development of adjustment difficulties in young adults exposed to childhood sexual abuse. *Child Abuse & Neglect,* 21(12), 1177-1190.

Mannarino, A. P., Cohen, J. A., & Berman, S. R. (1994). The relationship between preabuse factors and psychological symptomatology in sexually abused girls. *Child Abuse & Neglect,* 18(1), 63-71.

Meston, C. M., Heiman, J. R., Trapnell, P. D., & Carlin, A. S. (1999). Ethnicity, desirable responding, and sell-reports of abuse: A comparison of European-and Asian-ancestry undergraduates. *Journal of Consulting and Clinical Psychology,* 67, 139-140.

Molnar, B. E., Buka, S. L., & Kessler, R. C. (2001). Child sexual abuse and subsequent psychopathology: Results from the national comorbidity survey. *American Journal of Public Health,* 91, 753-760.

Moos, R. H., & Moos, B. S. (1984). The process of recovery from alcoholism: III. Comparing functioning in families of alcoholics and matched control families. *Journal of Studies on Alcohol,* 45(2): 111-118.

Mucowski, R. J., & Hayden, R. (1992). Adult children of alcoholics: Verification of role typology. *Alcoholism Treatment Quarterly,* 9(3-4), 127-140.

Mullen, P.E., Martin, J. L., Anderson, J. C., Romans, S. E., & Herbison, G. P. (1996). The long-term impact of the physical, emotional, and sexual abuse of children: A community study. *Child Abuse & Neglect,* 20(1), 7-21.

Okamura, A., Heras, P., & Wong-Kerberg, L. (1995). Asian, Pacific Island, and Filipino Americans and sexual child abuse. In L. Fontes (ed.), *Sexual abuse in nine North American cultures: Treatment and prevention* (pp.67-96). Thousand Oaks, CA: Sage.

Paradise, J. E., Rose, L., Sleeper, L. A., & Nathanson, M. (1994). Behaviour, family function, school performance and prediction of persistent disturbance in sexually abused children. *Pediatrics,* 93, 452-459.

Plunkett, A., O'Toole, B. I., Swanston, H., Oates, R. K., Shrimptona, S., & Parkinson, P. (2001). Suicide risk following child sexual abuse. *Journal of the Ambulatory Pediatric Association,* 5, 262-266.

Preli, R., Protinsky, H., & Cross, L. (1990). Alcoholism and family structure. *Family Therapy,* 17(1), 1-8.

Read, J. (1997). Child abuse and psychosis: A literature review and implications for professional practice. *Professional Psychology: Research Practice,* 28(5), 448-456.

Reich, W., Earls, F., & Powell, J. (1988). A comparison of the home and social environments of children of alcoholic and nonalcoholic fathers. *British Journal of Addiction,* 83, 831-839.

Reyome, M. D. (1994). Teacher ratings of the academic achievement related classroom behaviors of maltreated and non-maltreated children. *Psychology in the Schools,* 31, 253-260.

Rumstein-McKean, O., & Hunsley, J. (2001). Interpersonal and family functioning of female survivors of childhood sexual abuse. *Clinical Psychology Review,* 21, 471-490.

Salmon, P., & Calderbank, S. (1996). The relationship of childhood physical and sexual abuse to adult illness behavior. *Journal of Psychosomatic Research,* 40(3), 329-336.

Schaaf, K. K., & McCanne, T. R. (1998). Relationship of childhood sexual, physical, and combined sexual and physical abuse to adult victimization and posttraumatic stress disorder. *Child Abuse & Neglect,* 22(11), 1119-1133.

Sedlak, A. J. (1997). Risk factors for the occurrence of child abuse and neglect. *Journal of Aggression, Maltreatment & Trauma,* 1, 149-187.

Sheridan, M. J., & Green, R. G. (1993). Family dynamics and individual characteristics of adult children of alcoholics: An empirical analysis. *Journal of Social Service Research,* 17(1/2), 73-97.

Silovsky, J. F., & Hembree-Kigin, T. L. (1994). Family and group treatment for sexually abused children: A review. *Journal of Child Sexual Abuse,* 3, 1-20.

Simantov, E., Schoen, C., & Klein, J.D. (2000). Health-compromising behaviors: Why do adolescents smoke or drink? *Archives of Pediatrics & Adolescent Medicine,* 154(10), 1025-1033.

Smith, H., & Israel, E. (1987). Sibling incest: A study of the dynamics of 25 cases. *Child Abuse and Neglect,* 11, 101-108.

Swanston, H. Y., Plunkett, A. M., O'Toole, B. I., Shrimpton, S., Parkinson, P. N., & Oates, R. K. (2003). Nine years after child sexual abuse. *Child Abuse & Neglect,* 27(8), 967-984.

Tang, C. S.K.(2002). Childhood experience of sexual abuse among Hong Kong Chinese college students. *Child Abuse & Neglect,* 26, 23-37.

Tremblay, C., Hebert, M., & Piche, C. (1999). Coping strategies and social support as mediators of consequences in child sexual abuse victims. *Child Abuse & Neglect,* 23(9), 929-945.

Tyler, K. A. (2002). Social and emotional outcomes of childhood sexual abuse: A review of recent research. *Aggression and Violent Behavior,* 7, 567-589.

Wilsnack, S. C., Vogeltanz, N. D., Klassen, A. D., & Harris, T. R. (1997). Childhood sexual abuse and women's substance abuse: National survey findings. *Journal of Studies on Alcohol,* 58(3), 264-271.

Wonderlich, S. A., Wilsnack, R. W., Wilsnack, S. C., & Harris, T. R. (1996). Childhood sexual abuse and bulimic behavior in a nationally representative sample. *American Journal of Public Health,* 86(8 Pt. 1), 1082-1086.

Wurtele, S. K., & Miller-Perrin, C. L. (1992). *Preventing child sexual abuse: sharing the responsibility.* Lincoln, NE: University of Nebraska Press.

Zuravin, S., McMillan, C., DePanfilis, D., & Risley-Curtiss, C. (1996). The intergenerational cycle of child maltreatment: Continuity versus discontinuity. *Journal of Interpersonal Violence, 7,* 471-489.

In: Child Abuse and Violence
Editors: T. Richardson, M. Williams, pp. 115-119

ISBN: 978-1-60456-128-9
© 2008 Nova Science Publishers, Inc.

Chapter VIII

Model of Abuse Prophylaxis for Academy Community

Elizabeth Krawczyk
Collegium Meducum, Jagiellonian University,
Cracow

Abstract

The problem of the use of psychoactive substances has not always been considered as the main issue in Poland. It is regarded that the 90's apart from the positive changes following the transformation of the system, contributed to a considerable increase of undesirable problems. Thus, the use of drugs and abuse of alcohol became popular as a style among young people. Students established a specific community of young-adults. The problem following the use of psychoactive substances seemed not to concern them.

Even so, the real scale and range of the problem isstill obscure. The initial results of research shows that about 40 % of researched had had drug initiation, 84 % faced the problem in their environment. Special attention should be paid to unknown substances provided by legal drugs which often were used by young people. In Poland the problem of abuse of diverse drugs has been increasing. This group is treated marginally and is not included in preventive projects.

Only by monitoring a series of changes which happen during the process of studying Are we able to define the influence of the university environment on the use of psychoactive substances. This enables us to define the frequency and changeableness of the determinant. The results of research show that students in different forms gain different experiences in the use of psychoactive substances. Current knowledge shows that particular substances and the features which lead to or prevent against destructive behavior are the main factors. The data are very essential and helpful for creating projects covering prevention.

Our model of prevention against drug addiction among young adults is based on the belief that all people have the right of choice. The only way of making the right decisions (including health) is to acquire good knowledge and to understand yourself.

Salutogenesis and the theory of coherency allow us to look at the whole problem in a different way. We have to try to understand which psychological and social factors are a predisposition to healthy or unhealthy behaviors. Some substances are "welcome" among students of each specialization. The choice of substance may depend on specific deficits in coping and conditions of study.

The model includes both forms: educational (information about drugs) and practical (strengthening resources for healthy decisions). Essential subject and reinforcement each resource depends on a specific character of specialization and what we have to precede by is a public opinion-pool. Prophylaxis can be effective on the condition that it is adapted to the peculiarity of the recipient.

The phenomenon of the use of psychoactive substances in Poland has been the subject of widespread debate in a relatively short time.

The fact is that drugs entered a life of subculture in the mid-60's. In the middle of the 70's, when Polish students produced Polish heroin – (kompot), an outbreak of drug abuse occurred. An increasing slump in the demand for drugs was gradual over the next 20 years. The 90' brought Poland a lot of positive change in the political system but negative social phenomenons also. Known and unknown drugs were coming to Poland. Previously, this problem could be treated lightly because it concerned only so-called dregs of society. In the last few years, the problem of drug abuse has spread and has affected every group of society.

We are interested in the academic environment. It is a specific group of young adults- university and college students who aspire to fulfill important, reliable social roles. This group was passed over in discussions about drug problems until recently. Even the police were not able to enter an academic campus of many Polish universities.

The first all-Poland study, in 2000, drew attention to students as a group where thr phenomenon of drug use is not alien [3].

One year later, the president declared a country-wide campaign to keep "Universities Drug Free". The aim was cooperation among organizations and university residents to take diagnostic and preventive action against the spread of drug use among students.

As a part of the campaign (2004), Sierosławski did research. The aim of this study was the measurement of the intensity and circumstances of drug use.

According to this study 41% of respondents had contact with psychoactive substances. One fifth had taken drugs in the last year and almost 12% of them in the month before research. The most popular was marihuana. Cannabis products were perceived as not as risky. Interestingly 80% of the students admitted accepting effective anti-drug campaigns at the university [7]. This study showed the need of primary and secondary prevention.

As a part of a campaign on February 23, 2005 a presidential Control Committee was set up. The name of the campaign was changed to "All-Poland Network Universities Addiction Free". About 120 universities and colleges are participating in the project.

The fundamental task of the Network is the diagnosis of the phenomenon of psychoactive substance use in an acedemic community and the creation of appropriate prophylaxis programme. Jagiellonian University in Cracow has been entrusted with organizing research. We have taken responsibility for constructing the tool (survey) and the penetrating analysis of results.

We assume that most important for effective prophylaxis is to accurately determine the specificity of the group. The survey contains questions concerning opinions about the scope of the phenomenon in the students' environment, experience in psychoactive substance taking, knowledge about substances and qualities or skills predisposed to addiction or tp protection. The most important effective prevention programme factors are included in the survey and will be taken into consideration during analysis. The factors contained in the survey are subordinated to assumptions which were made as a basis of an efficient programme. First of all an effective programme must be adjusted to the audience of the prophylaxis actions.

A theoretical outline of our programme is a biopsychosocial, interactive point of view of the addiction problem. In accordance with biological, environmental and psychological determinants individual persons are at a different extended risk for drug use, abuse, and dependence. Interaction among those factors determine the possibility of deviant behaviour. So, we can see the risk of addiction as a continuum (low risk – revised risk). The place on the continuum depends also on an inner store of life management skills which we can increase.

According to salutogenesis [1] we focus our attention on pro-healthful activities (eliminate deficites and improve stores). First of all we have to get to know about deficits and stores in our group. The theory of coherency lets us consider prophylaxis in another way. According to this theory, a sense of comprehension, resourcefulness and sense determine the place on the continuum health – illness. We need to understand which psychological and social factors are a predisposition to healthy and unhealthy behaviors.

The survey contains questions about this. In our opinion, it is important for us to make it in front of audiences (to adjust to needs) whereas for students it is a first step to autoreflection and autodiagnosis).

When we were formulating the survey, we thought about the theory of health/illness and about the situation and experience of young adult – students.

The time of study is a peculiar life period. Students are adults but are still dependent on parents. Very often they leave the parent's home and move to another place. Facing a new environment, exam stress, parent's expectations, - they make an attempt at self-reliance; moreover, they enjoy freedom.

A lot of students have a drug use experience. Cracow's research [6] suggested that initiation occurred before the study. 38,3% first- year students took drugs any time before. 84 % faced the problem in their environment. A similar result appeared in research of college students in a Polish town where 34,3 % first-year students had an initiation into drugs [5]. Special attention should be paid to unknown substances provided by legal drugs which often were used by young people. In Poland the problem of abuse of diverse drugs has been increasing. This group of drugs is treated marginally and is not included in prevention projects. That is why a preventive programme directed toward students should include elements of primary and secondary prophylaxis [8].

Separate universities or colleges differ in the number of users after initiation, in the sort of popular drugs, and in psychoactive substance knowledge and attitudes. Students are the group of adults who have some experience, knowledge and opinion about drugs and addiction. Everyone who has taken drugs or has contact with people after initiation believe that psychoactive substances provide some nice experiences and they very often can not see any negative consequences. Pass-on information should be honest – students should know potential profits and losses. A student can make a decision autonomously but needs solid knowledge for making an appropriate decision.

One of the elements in a student's life are social gatherings (pubs, disco, parties) and psychoactive substances are common at those meetings [5, 6]. Students ought to find the distinction among use, abuse and addiction and take into consideration that it is a continuum.

That is why education's part of prophylaxis and should take into consideration experience and knowledge level.

A proposed programme should include not only education but also training in life skills significant for psychological health.

Cognitive, emotional and behavioral strategies should be combined for effective prophylaxis. The offer should be fitted to individuals. The university should be prepared to offer both primary prevention, intervention and professional, therapeutic help. The model includes both forms: educational (information about drugs) and practical (strengthening resources for healthy decisions) [2, 8].

Only by monitoring a series of changes which happen during the process of research, are we able to define the influence of the university environment on the use of psychoactive substances. This enables us to define the frequency and changeableness of the determinant. Prevention and health promotion should be helpful but sometimes iatrogenic effects made them even harmful [9] Monitoring is essential for honest evaluation that can be handy to new projects. Our model of prevention against drug addiction among young adults is based on the belief that all people have the right of choice [2]. The only way of making the right decisions (including health) is to acquire good knowledge and to understand yourself.

References

[1] Antonowsky, A. (1995). *Unraveling the Mystery of Health*. Warszawa: Wydawnictwo IPN.

[2] Krawczyk, E., Kroch, S., and Satora, L. (2005). An addiction counteraction model on academic community In Cracow. *Przegl. Lek.* 62, 6, 339 - 341.

[3] Mellibruda, J., Nikodemska, S. and Fronczyk, K. (2003). Using and abuse of alcohol and other psychoactive substances among Polisch students. *Med. Wieku Rozwoj*, VII, 1, 135-55.

[4] Pach, J., Tobiasz-Adamczyk, B., Chodorowski, Z., Krawczyk, E., Satora, L., Brzyski, P., Sein Anand, J., Ogonowska, D., and Morawska, J. (2006). Using of psychoactive substances among students of Nowy Sacz. *Przegl. Lek.*, 6, 385 - 392.

[5] Pach, J., Tobiasz-Adamczyk, B., Jabłoński, P., Brzyski, P., Krawczyk, E., Satora, L., Targosz, D., and Morawska, J. (2005). The drug free Universities – trends in illicit drug use among the Kraków's students. *Przegl. Lek.* 62. 6, 342 – 350.

[6] Ross, C., Richard, L., and Potvin, L., (1998). One year outcome evaluation of an alcohol and drug abuse prevention programme in Quepec high school. *Rev. Can. De Sante Publ.*, 89, 166 – 170.

[7] Sierosławski, J. (2004). Questionnaire survey of using of psychoactive substances by students – report. STUDENCI 2004, http://www.narkomania.gov.pl.

[8] Werch, C.E., Pappars, D.M., Carlskon, J.M., DiClemente, C.C., Chany, P.S.,and Sinder, J.A. (2000). Results of social norm intervention to prevent binge drinking among first-year residential college students. *J.Amer.Coll.Hlth* 49, 85 – 92.

[9] Whitaker, L. (2001) Substance abuse prevention: What works and what doesn't. Adwances. The Robert Wood Johnson Fundation, *Quarterly Newsletter*, 2, 1-2.

In: Child Abuse and Violence
Editors: T. Richardson, M. Williams, pp. 121-162
ISBN: 978-1-60456-128-9
© 2008 Nova Science Publishers, Inc.

Chapter IX

Outcomes of Parental Corporal Punishment: Psychological Maladjustment and Physical Abuse

Piyanjali de Zoysa[4]
University of Colombo, Kynsey Road, Colombo 8, Sri Lanka;
Peter A. Newcombe
University of Queensland, Brisbane, Australia 4072
Lalini Rajapakse
University of Colombo, Kynsey Road, Colombo 8, Sri Lanka

Abstract

The use of corporal punishment as a disciplinary method is a much debated topic in the area of parent-child relations. Recent research has shown that such punishment is associated with adverse psychological and physical outcomes for children. This chapter will address this issue in the cultural context of Sri Lanka where specific information about the experiences of disciplining children and its outcomes is lacking. The research reported here is part of a larger study of the outcomes of child-directed violence on 12-year-old children. The study incorporated a number of measures including the Parent-Child Conflict Tactic Scale [CTSPC: Straus, Hamby, Finklehor, Moore, & Runyan, 1998] and Personality Assessment Questionnaire [PAQ: Rohner, 1999] which were translated, adapted and validated for the Sri Lankan context. A Psychosocial Questionnaire (PSQ) was also designed specifically for this study to assess selected correlates (including non-parent-to-child violence, children's attitude to corporal punishment, parent-child relationship, and children's support network) hypothesized to be associated with parental use of corporal punishment and its psychological outcomes.

The validated instruments were used in a cross-sectional study of 12-year-old Sinhala speaking government school children in the Colombo district. Participants were

---
[4] Tel -: +94 11 2695300; Fax -: +94 11 2669003; ptdz@sltnet.lk

chosen according to a stratified random sampling technique. The final sample size was 1226 (M age = 11.83 years, SD = 0.51 years; 61% females). The children reported a high prevalence of corporal punishment and physical abuse. A predictive model examining the association between corporal punishment and psychological maladjustment was tested. It was found that not only did corporal punishment directly predict a child's maladjustment but that non-parent-to-child violence (i.e., domestic, school, peer, and community violence) significantly impacted this association. A predictive model examining the association between corporal punishment and physical abuse was also tested. The results showed that corporal punishment is moderately but significantly associated with physical abuse.

Taken together, these findings inform our understanding of children's perceptions of parenting behaviors and their impact on children. In particular, they highlight that, though many Sri Lankans believe in the efficacy of corporal punishment, it does appear to be associated with negative outcomes for children. It is hoped that the empirical findings from this research program can assist and support social policy-makers as they plan guiding principles for positive parenting and develop programs aimed at raising awareness among Sri Lankan parents on healthy disciplinary methods.

Sri Lanka (formerly known as Ceylon) is an island lying off the South-Eastern tip of India. About ten ethnic groups can be distinguished in present day Sri Lanka. The two main ethnic groups are the Sinhaleese (of Indo-Aryan origin), who tend to be Buddhist and approximately 74% of the population, and the Tamils who are largely Hindu, forming approximately 18% of the population. Sinhala is the official language in the country, but Tamil is also a national language. English is spoken by about 10% of the population and commonly used for official purposes. Sri Lanka has a mixture of religions with Buddhist (68%), Hindu (15%), Christian (8%) and Muslim (8%).

Introduction

Disciplining children is a key aspect of parenting. There is currently much interest on what constitutes healthy versus unhealthy disciplinary methods, especially with regards to corporal punishment [Parke, 2002]. An informed examination of corporal punishment requires an understanding of its nature and thus, a definition of its constructs. However, there is no globally accepted definition of corporal punishment. In such an absence, the present study adopted the following definition which is based on Straus (1994) and supported by interviews and focus groups in Sri Lanka [De Zoysa, 2005]: Corporal punishment "is the use of physical force with the intention of causing a child to experience pain but not injury for the purposes of correction or control of the child's behavior" [Straus, 1994, p. 4]. Corporal punishment therefore includes strategies such as spanking, slapping, pinching, or hitting with objects such as sticks or belts [Straus & Stewart, 1999].

The historical record on corporal punishment: Globally and in Sri Lanka

Since ancient times, parental use of corporal punishment on children has been recorded in literature, art and science [Ten Bensel, Rheinberger, Radbill, 1997]. Similarly, for centuries, there have also existed persons who have protested against the use of such physical punishment. For instance, educationists such as Quintilian, and philosophers such as Locke and Rousseau have argued against or called for moderation in parental use of corporal punishment [Peisher, 1989].

For more than 70 years, psychologists have been investigating the effectiveness of corporal punishment. Both Thorndike and Skinner claimed that such punishment was ineffective in producing significant and lasting behavioral changes in children [Hall & Lindzey, 1991]. Instead, these behaviorists espoused that children's behavior be molded by rewards for their positive actions. Freudian thought raised the issue of long-term psychic damage that corporal punishment might cause children and an examination of the motives of the parent dispensing it [Hall & Lindzey, 1991]. Incorporating these insights, by the 1940's, psychologists and psychiatrists involved in childcare were offering parents advice on how to raise their children. In contrast to these earlier decades of the 20th century, the literature during the middle decades propounded that spanking could be a beneficial tool in parenting. However, it asserted so cautiously, advocating its use only in situations where parents assessed its potential benefits and harm [Spock, 1946, cited in Howard, 1996]. Hence, corporal punishment began to be viewed as part of a range of disciplinary methods that was available in appropriate parenting. Some even considered corporal punishment and discipline as synonymous whilst other childcare professionals considered these as separate, but related concepts [Howard, 1996]. Nevertheless, and despite tacit support, many professionals felt that corporal punishment was not an optimal disciplinary method as it was open to misuse. This acknowledgement was primarily due to the child development movement establishing normative patterns of behavior for children of different ages, and its suggestion that many of the behavioral problems of children who had warranted corporal punishment in the past were actually indications of normal development.

In Sri Lanka, Moldrich [1986] has presented evidence of ancient Sri Lankan kings who declared laws prohibiting any bodily harm, by way of punishment, to children or adults. For instance, Moldrich [1986] has exemplified King Vijayabahu II (1186 - 1187) and King Vijayabahu III (1232 - 1236) who were especially credited for their compassion towards children. Children hit by their parents have been reported to come to King Vijayabahu III and tell him of their woes, with the king then exhorting their parents not to beat the children any longer [Moldrich, 1986]. In ancient Sri Lanka, Buddhist monks were often advisors to kings and to the local community. They were also teachers as children were taught at "Pirivenas" (temple-based schools). Hence, in keeping with the Buddhist values of compassion and non-violence [Narada Thera, 1972], corporal punishment may not have been encouraged or propagated among parents in those times [De Silva, De Zoysa, Kannangara, 2000].

With the Portuguese, Dutch and British colonization of Sri Lanka (1505 - 1948), certain aspects of ancient Sri Lankan culture, including its parenting practices, appear to have been replaced by those practiced by the colonial powers. Though these new practices may have been initially thrust on the Sri Lankans by force of law [Moldrich, 1986], with time it may have pervaded the deeper fabric of Sri Lankan society. Therefore, the use of corporal punishment in parenting, though considered contrary to cultural and religious values in ancient Sri Lanka, may have consequently been accepted as a normative practice in parenting. For instance, Moldrich [1986] has reported that during the British period (1796 - 1948), if a Sri Lankan child was caught flying a kite, he or she was ordered by law to be given 20 lashes for doing so. Such laws, established during colonial times, may have, with time, become normative modes of disciplining children. The Ganadevi Hella [cited in De Silva, 2001], a series of traditional Sri Lankan verses, also exemplifies the widespread use of corporal punishment by parents and teachers during those colonial times.

Corporal punishment: The controversy

Corporal punishment is the most controversial topic in the domain of parental discipline [Holden, 2002]. There is evidence that the experience of such physical force is associated with detrimental psychological and physical outcomes for children [Gershoff, 2002], even when used by loving and supportive parents [Straus, 1994; Straus, Sugarman, & Giles-Sims, 1997]. Nevertheless, many lay persons as well as professionals involved in childcare advocate its use [De Silva, 2001; White, 1993].

The use of corporal punishment

The main debate is whether corporal punishment is wholly negative [American Academy of Pediatrics, 1998; McCord, 1997a], or whether it is effective if used within certain conditions [Larzelere, 1994, 2001]. Those who advocate for corporal punishment promote their position by pointing out methodological limitations in studies that show harmful outcomes of such discipline [Larzelere, Silver, & Polite, 1997]. They also illustrate that, although corporal punishment may not be suitable in all situations, it generally has advantages if used within prescribed conditions [e.g., Gunnoe & Mariner, 1997; Larzelere, 1994; Simons, Lin, & Gorden, 1998]. These conditions include (i) spanking limited to a maximum of two slaps to the buttocks with an open hand, (ii) the child being between the ages of two- and six-years of age, (iii) spanking used to supplement positive parenting, not to replace it, and (iv) spanking used primarily to back-up less aversive disciplinary responses, such as verbal correction or time-out [Larzelere, 1994].

The cross-cultural dimension of corporal punishment

In exploring corporal punishment, it is important to acknowledge the existing parenting practices in a particular culture. However, not infrequently, cultural rationalization of harmful behavior towards children, in the guise of discipline, is accepted blindly as proof that this treatment is neither abusive nor harmful [Kempe, 1991]. Due to the cultural variations in its acceptance, a culturally relative model of socialization has considered the possibility that child outcomes of corporal punishment may vary across cultural groups [Deater-Deckard, Dodge, Bates, & Pettit, 1996]. Larzelere et al. [1997] has further pointed out the importance of understanding the attitudes to corporal punishment within a given culture before evaluating the incorrectness or criminality of using such discipline within that culture. Though some empirical evidence for this model has been reported [Larzelere et al., 1997], the results are as yet not conclusive.

Based on his studies on corporal punishment and cultural context, Straus [1994] has presented a universal harm view of corporal punishment. His findings support the culturally relative model to some extent, as there appear to be some differences in the negative outcomes of corporal punishment among ethnic groups. However, his studies appear to better support the universal harm view as negative outcomes of corporal punishment were present in all ethnic groups.

These facets of the controversy surrounding corporal punishment have led to a number of debates on what corporal punishment does, and does not do, for children [e.g., Freidman & Schonberg, 1996]. In order to understand these dynamics of corporal punishment, extensive research has been conducted in many societies [e.g., Lau, Liu, Cheung, Yu, & Wong, 1999; Straus & Stewart, 1999; Yamamoto, et al., 1999; Youssef, Attia, & Kamel, 1998]. Such empirical studies have usually been undertaken to better understand this controversial topic, and thus to influence child protection policies and design appropriate parent education programs. Though interest and research on corporal punishment has been evident in many countries, there is a dearth of such studies in Sri Lanka [De Silva, 2001]. Culture-specific empirical information is essential, as there is a global awakening to the potential negative outcomes of corporal punishment, evidenced by several countries taking measures to ban its use [Save the Children, 2002]. Today, corporal punishment still has much relevance in Sri Lanka as it is not unusual for parents (and teachers) to believe that they have the right to use such discipline on children. Thus, Sri Lanka, without culture specific information, is not in a position to take an evidence-based stand on this matter.

Psychological maladjustment as an outcome of corporal punishment

Although the merits and demerits of parental corporal punishment have been argued for decades, a thorough understanding of whether, and how, corporal punishment impacts on children has not yet been reached [Gershoff, 2002]. Childcare professionals are divided in their opinion as to whether the benefits of corporal punishment might outweigh any potential hazards.

The primary reason that most parents use corporal punishment is to stop children from misbehaving, immediately [Gershoff, 2002]. Laboratory research on learning has confirmed that corporal punishment is indeed effective in securing such short-term compliance [Newsom, Flarell, & Rincover, 1983]. However, it may not lead to long-term compliance [Lepper, 1983] or moral internalization of the disciplinary message intended by the parents [Grusec, 1993]. Studies have shown that corporal punishment may not facilitate such moral internalization because it does not teach children the need to behave correctly, does not involve the communication of the effects of children's misbehavior on others, and because it may teach children the desirability of not getting caught [Grusec, 1993].

The potential for corporal punishment to disrupt the parent-child relationship is a main disadvantage of its use. The painful nature of corporal punishment can evoke feelings of anger, fear and anxiety in children, thus making them avoid the parent [Grusec & Goodnow, 1994].

Corporal punishment has been significantly associated with adolescent's depression symptomatology and distress, even after controlling for gender, family socio-economic status and history of physical abuse [McLoyd, Jayaratne, Ceballo, Borquez, 1994]. A study by Straus [2000] has led to similar findings where higher the level of corporal punishment experienced as a teenager, greater the level of depressive symptomatology and thoughts of committing suicide as an adult. This finding stood, regardless of whether there was marital violence, for both genders, for high and low socio-economic persons, for those who did and did not have an alcohol problem, and for those who had witnessed violence between their parents and those who had not. In fact, Greven [1991] has postulated that "depression often is a delayed response to the suppression of childhood anger ... from being physically hit and hurt ... by adults ... whom the child loves and on whom he or she depends for nurturance and life itself" [p.129]. Coercive disciplinary techniques have also been associated with decreases in children's level of confidence and assertiveness and with increases in feelings of humiliation and helplessness [Lasky, 1993].

The association between corporal punishment and children's aggression is one of the most studied and debated findings in the literature on parenting [Coie & Dodge, 1998]. Corporal punishment is thought to predict an increase in children's aggression because it models aggression [Avonfreed, 1969, cited in Coie & Dodge, 1998], promotes hostile attributions which predict violent behavior [Dishion & Patterson, 1999], and because it initiates cycles of coercive behavior between the child and the parent [Dodge, Pettit, & McClaskey, 1986]. Early experiences with corporal punishment may lead to modeling and legitimizing the use of violence throughout an individual's life [Simons et al., 1998]. In fact, the experience of corporal punishment in childhood has been shown to be the strongest predictor of adolescent's aggression eight years later [Cohen, Brook, Cohen, Velez, & Garcia, 1990].

Corporal punishment has also been implicated in the etiology of criminal and anti-social behavior in both children and adults [Wilson & Herrnstein, 1985]. It is postulated that this is because of corporal punishment's capacity to erode the parent-child relationship which in turn may decrease the child's motivation to internalize the parent's and the society's moral values [Hirschi, 1969, cited in Gershoff, 2002]. Research such as Glueck and Glueck's [1964, cited in Gershoff, 2002] and McCord's [1997b] longitudinal studies on corporal punishment and criminality have supported the above hypothesis where the extent to which parents were aggressively punitive predicted their children's arrest rate at 17-years and their criminal behavior as adults. With regards to antisocial behavior, a study by Straus et al.'s [1997] has shown that the more corporal punishment children experienced, the greater was their antisocial behavior subsequent to such discipline. This effect was consistent across all ethnic groups in the study.

Many of the previous studies linking corporal punishment and antisocial behavior had not taken into account the possibility that aggression and other behavior problems in children may lead parents to use corporal punishment, rather than vice versa. That is, the child may have been aggressive and antisocial even before the start of corporal punishment and thus parental corporal punishment may have been due to the child's temperament rather than the child's antisocial behavior being due to corporal discipline. Straus et al.'s [1997] study that explored this latter possibility supported a causal link between corporal punishment and antisocial behavior in children.

It has been hypothesized that if corporal punishment is associated with a general tendency towards aggression in adulthood, this may manifest itself in relationships with others, such as with children, spouse/partner or both. Research findings have supported this hypothesis. For instance, there appears to be a strong disposition for parents who had experienced corporal punishment in their childhood to continue that practice with their own children [Fry, 1993; Holden Thompson, Zambarano, & Marshall, 1997]. Similarly, childhood experience of corporal punishment has been shown to be associated with an increase in an individual's likelihood of acting violently with an adult romantic partner [Straus & Yodanis, 1996; Swinford, De Maris, Cernkovich, & Giardano, 2000].

It has been suggested that if parents avoided corporal punishment, they would be more likely to engage in verbal methods of behavior control such as explaining and reasoning [Straus, 2001]. As talking to children (including pre-speech infants) has been associated with an increase in the neural connections in the brain and children's cognitive performance [Vander Zanden, 1997], this increased verbal interaction would in turn enhance children's cognitive ability [Straus, 2001]. This theory has been substantiated by a study that showed a greater probability of above average cognitive growth in children being associated with less experience of corporal punishment [Straus, 2001]. Though the proponents of qualified use of corporal punishment [e.g., Baumrind, 1996, Larzelere, 1996] have suggested corporal punishment is best used with two- to six-years-olds, Straus [2001] has opined that this recommendation is not evidence-based and has argued that corporal punishment at these ages will have the most adverse effects on children's cognitive development.

Corporal punishment also appears to have a dampening effect on occupational and economic achievement [Straus & Gimpel, 1992]. Straus and Gimpel [1992] have postulated that experiencing corporal punishment in childhood increases the probability of children becoming alienated, depressed and violent, which in turn may result in their low educational attainment (in terms of graduation) [Straus 1994]. A study by Straus and Mathur [1995] which has substantiated Straus and Gimpel's [1992] explanation has found that academic achievement requires a self-directed commitment to learn, but that the experience of corporal punishment may teach obedience more than such self-direction. Straus and Gimpel [1992] and Straus and Mathur [1995] have however emphasized the need to further substantiate their preliminary data on corporal punishment and academic and economic achievement.

It is important to acknowledge that most studies examining the association between corporal punishment and its psychological outcomes were of cross-sectional design and thus prevent any conclusions on causality. Such causality could only be determined in a longitudinal study [e.g., Cohen et al., 1990] or an experimental study where the outcomes of interest could be controlled at Time 1, before the onset of corporal punishment, and where the development of the outcome, if any, could be measured across a time period. Therefore, most of the above research studies do not offer directional conclusions but instead only allow an understanding of whether corporal punishment and certain identified outcomes are associated

Psychosocial correlates impacting the association between corporal punishment and psychological maladjustment

There is great variability in the type and extent of difficulties among children who have experienced corporal punishment [Farber & Egeland, 1987]. This variability is present because corporal punishment occurs within the broader context of an individual's life and hence individual correlates and diverse life circumstances influence the presentation of its signs and symptoms. Thus, "even when there is a strong statistical association between a risk factor and a disease (or problem), this does not mean that all individuals with that risk factor will necessarily develop the disease, nor that the absence of the risk factor will ensure absence of the disease (or problem)" [Mrazek & Haggerty, 1994, p. 127]. The inability to identify all the factors or correlates contributing to such risk limits the ability to predict for individuals [Mausner & Kramer, 1985]. Thus, not all people exposed to even strong risk factors will eventually develop the problem. This resilience may be due, at least in part, to protective factors that blunt the impact of risk factors. Thus, protective factors are buffers of risk because they interact with risk factors in predicting the occurrence of a problem [Heyman & Smith Slep, 2001]. Therefore, an understanding of the multitude of risk and protective factors associated with the psychological outcomes of corporal punishment is important as it can provide an empirical basis for designing scientifically informed preventive and intervention programs.

Research has identified several risk and protective factors associated with corporal punishment and its psychological outcomes Perpetrator-related risk and protective factors include: (i) demographic variables including gender [Biernat & Wortman, 1991, Hart & Robinson, 1994; Straus & Stewart, 1999], age [Culp, Culp, Dengler, & Maisano, 1999; Wissow, 2001; Xu, Tvng, & Dunaway, 2000], socio-economic status of the family [Pinderhughes, Dodge, Bates, Pettit, & Zelli, 2000; Straus & Stewart, 1999; Xu et al., 2000], race [Loeber et al., 2000; Pinderhughes et al., 2000; Straus & Stewart, 1999; Whaley, 2000; Wissow, 2001], religion [Gershoff, Miller, & Holden, 1999; Stolley & Szinovacz, 1997; Xu et al., 2000], and number of children in the family [Asdigian and Straus 2001], (ii) personal history variables [Straus & Smith, 1992; Rodriguez & Sutherland, 1999], and (iii) perpetrator personality and mental health including temperament and genetic contribution [Bank, Forgatch, Patterson, & Fetrow, 1993; DiLalla & Gottesman, 2000], psychological functioning [Holden, Coleman, & Schmid, 1995; Paquette, Bolte, Tucotte, Dubeau, & Bouchard, 2000], parenting style and beliefs [Darling & Steinberg, 1993; Straus & Mouradian, 1998; Wissow, 2001] and emotional state [Pinderhughes et al., 2000; Wissow, 2001].

Child-related risk and protective factors comprise (i) demographic variables including gender [Day, Peterson, McCrackors, 1998; Houston, 1983; Mahoney, Donnelly, Lewis, Maynard, 2000; Smith & Brooks-Gunn, 1997; Straus & Stewart, 1999], and age [Loeber et al., 2000; Mahoney et al., 2000], (ii) personality and mental health including temperament and genetic contributions [Ge et al., 1996; O'Connor, Deater-Deckard, Fulker, Rutter, & Plomin, 1998], and developmental disabilities [Ammerman, Hersen, Van Hasselt, Lubetsky, & Sieck, 1994], and (iii) perception and acceptance of parent's disciplinary message [Grusec & Goodnow, 1994; Gunnoe & Mariner, 1997; Deater-Deckard & Dodge, 1997]. Family related risk and protective factors [Pinderhughes et al., 2000; Simons, Lorenz, Wu, & Congeer, 1993; Xu et al., 2000] and social-community-cultural-related risk and protective factors [Greenfield & Suzuki, 1998; Grusec et al., 1997] have also been studied. In summary, the findings from these studies have not been unequivocal and, in fact, have often yielded contradictory information [Gershoff, 2002].

Physical abuse as an outcome of corporal punishment

Some childcare professionals postulate that corporal punishment and physical abuse lie along a continuum of physical force, where abuse may occur when corporal punishment escalates beyond parental control [e.g., Haeuser, 1991; Straus, 2000; Straus & Yodanis, 1994]. They believe that corporal punishment is a risk factor for physical abuse. This position is supported by studies of individuals who have been convicted of child physical abuse. In most of these cases, the individuals convicted were "normal" persons, apparently exercising their prerogative of disciplining a child whose behavior they found was in need of correction [Gil, 1970, cited in Gershoff, 2002], but where they lost control of their anger or underestimated their strength [Zigler & Hall, 1989]. For instance, findings of a New Zealand study indicated that, in a majority of physical abuse cases, the parents started out with the intention of disciplining their child but went too far [Ritchie & Ritchie, 1981]. Similarly, studies in the USA [Kadushin & Martin, 1999] and Finland [Peltoniemi, 1983] have shown that a majority of physical abuse cases began as corporal punishment. Therefore, these childcare professionals are of the view that both corporal punishment and physical abuse should be legally condemned, as the latter is a risk factor for the former. On the other hand, other researchers and childcare professionals view corporal punishment and physical abuse as two distinct phenomena [e.g., Strassberg, Dodge, Pettit, & Bates, 1994], or believe that only in certain instances could corporal punishment lead to abusive levels [e.g., Baumrind, 1996, 1997; Larzelere, 1994]. In fact, these pro-corporal punishment scholars postulate that if corporal punishment is paired with reasoning, it could actually reduce the risk of physical abuse [e.g., Larzelere et al., 1997; Lyons & Larzelere, 1996]. They reason that, through such pairing, parents could control children's misbehavior at the onset itself rather than allowing it to escalate. They argue that if children's misbehaviors are allowed to escalate, frustrated parents may then resort to disciplinary strategies that can be considered physically abusive. Further, they believe that replacing corporal punishment with non-physical discipline only will not necessarily give better results and suggest that parents should use a wide range of disciplinary methods, including physical means, depending on the child's temperament and the misbehavior.

The present study: The theoretical model

As has been shown above, an array of findings on the psychological and physical outcomes and psychosocial correlates of parental use of corporal punishment on their children have been demonstrated. The identification of these outcomes and correlates has been the result of several research programs conducted over the years and in several countries. In the present study, a number of selected outcomes and correlates, hypothesized to be associated with parental corporal punishment, were investigated. The number of outcomes and correlates chosen was influenced by the need to be as comprehensive as possible whilst being conscious of the demands placed on children in responding to lengthy questionnaires.

The key outcomes and correlates explored in the present study are presented in Figure 1 (i.e. the theoretical model). Based on previous research [Gershoff, 2002], the model hypothesized that the experience of parental corporal punishment would be directly and significantly associated with psychological maladjustment in children. Corporal Punishment was assessed through two indicators: Prevalence of Corporal Punishment and Frequency of Corporal Punishment. Psychological Maladjustment was assessed through seven personality indicators: Aggression and Hostility, Dependency, Negative Self-Esteem, Negative Self-Adequacy, Emotional Unresponsiveness, Emotional Instability, and Negative World View. Following a literature review, it was also hypothesized that this direct and significant association between Corporal Punishment and Psychological Maladjustment would be mediated by select third variables including Children's Attitude to Corporal Punishment, the Parent-Child Relationship, Non-Parent-to-Child Violence, and Children's Support Network.

Specifically, the model hypothesized that children's favorable attitude to corporal punishment would mediate its negative psychological impact for them. Children who believed that their parents were acting in their best interests [Dix, 1992], who viewed discipline as appropriate to their misdeed [Grusec & Goodnow, 1994], and who considered their parent's use of force as legitimate [Baumrind, 1997; Gunnoe & Mariner, 1997], were hypothesized to accept their parent's message, which would in turn buffer the negative impact of corporal punishment on them. The model also hypothesized that frequent exposure to corporal punishment may also foster the acceptance of such discipline as an acceptable means of dealing with problems [Rutter, Giller, & Hagell, 1998]. Therefore, if corporal punishment was normative in the family culture, children may view their parent's use of it as legitimate [Deater-Deckard & Dodge, 1997; Gunnoe & Mariner, 1997].

It was also hypothesized that the nature of the parent-child relationship would mediate the corporal punishment-psychological maladjustment association [Kuczynski & Hilderbrant, 1997]. Children who reported a more positive relationship with their parents may report less psychological maladjustment. It was hypothesized that parental nurturance encourages feelings of trust in, and reciprocation towards, the parent [Grusec & Goodnow, 1994] which in turn may buffer the potential harmful outcomes of corporal punishment [Deater-Deckard & Dodge, 1997]. However, if corporal punishment were to occur within a negative parenting style, it may be associated with more negative child outcomes [Campbell & Frabutt, 1999]. Exceptions to this buffering role of parenting style do exist. Straus & Mourdian [1998] for instance, found no interaction between parental nurturance and use of corporal punishment in predicting children's antisocial behavior. McCord [1997b] has similarly reported that children's tendency for criminality could be predicted by their parent's use of corporal punishment, regardless of whether the parents had been rated as being warm during their childhood.

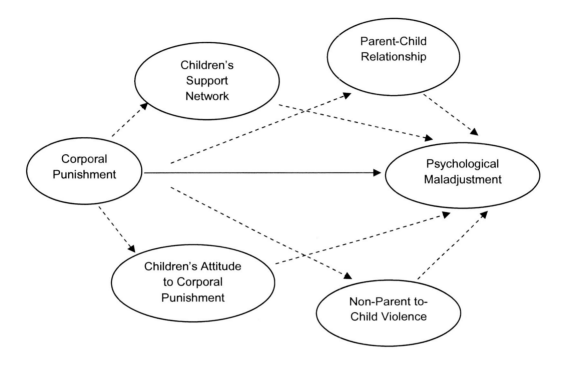

Figure 1. The theoretical model tested in the present study

Note: ———▶ represent hypothesized direct pathways
 - - - - - ▶ represent hypothesized indirect (mediated) pathways

An inconsistent parenting style was also postulated to compound the negative outcomes of corporal punishment. For instance, inconsistent parenting has predicted children's aggressive delinquent behavior, sometimes over and above parental use of corporal punishment [Simons, Whitbeck, Melby, & Wu, 1994]. Therefore, corporal punishment used in a consistent manner [Simons et al., 1994] has been considered to mitigate its negative outcomes because it would be accepted and expected. Similarly, children's perceived fairness of corporal punishment [Rohner, Bourque, & Elordi, 1996] and parent-child dialogue when using such punishment [Larzelere & Merenda, 1994] has also been considered to ameliorate its negative outcomes.

The children's experience of non-parent-to-child violence was hypothesized to have an additive effect on the psychological maladjustment, if any, resulting from their experience of parental corporal punishment. The experience of corporal punishment and its outcomes has been linked to the child witnessing/experiencing other forms of violence [Kim, Kim, Park, Zhang, & Lu, 2000] such as domestic [Pinderhughes et al., 2000] and community [Dietz,

2000] violence. For instance, parents in abusive marriages, as compared to those in happy ones, have shown to be more likely to use corporal punishment when managing their children [Pinderhughes et al., 2000; Simons et al., 1993; Xu et al., 2000]. In these families, aggressive conflict resolution may be normative. Further, studies have shown that parents living in communities where aggression is frequently encountered tend to use corporal punishment more [Dietz, 2000]. Hence, those who are socialized in an environment that promotes aggression would be more likely to use corporal punishment in their parenting role [Dietz, 2000]. Being a recipient/witness of such violence has been associated with several psychological problems in the child [Gershoff, 2002; Straus, 1994]. Such psychological difficulties may lead to a deficit in coping skills predisposing such children to be further victimized in non-family situations such as in school [Hughes, 1998; Silverman, Reinherz, & Gioconia, 1994], by teachers and/or peers [Kim et al., 2000].

Finally, and based on the research of Mason, Cauce, Gonzales, & Hiraga [1996], the extent of children's support network was hypothesized to mediate (or buffer) the psychological maladjustment associated with corporal punishment. For instance, the existence of a supportive relationship with a non-parental adult figure [Milner, Robertson, & Rogers, 1990], has been shown to buffer the intergenerational transmission of corporal punishment [Durrant & Rose-Krasnor, 1995]. The existence of such a support network was hypothesized to buffer the impact of the stress associated with experiencing corporal punishment.

At this time of global controversy on the appropriateness of parental use of corporal punishment on children, a country needs reliable culture-specific information in order to take a stand on the matter. Hence, research on its dynamics should be conducted within that relevant country. Hence, the present study, a comprehensive and representative study of parental use of corporal punishment on Sri Lankan children, had as its objective to explore the nature of the association between corporal punishment and its psychological and physical outcomes on children. It also investigated if the association between corporal punishment and psychological maladjustment was significantly mediated by the selected variables of children's experience of non-parent-to-child violence, children's support network, the parent-child relationship and the children's attitude to corporal punishment.

This study is Sri Lanka's first documented contribution to the national and international literature on parental use of corporal punishment on children. It is also one of the few non-Western studies on corporal punishment and hence, it will be a contribution to the dearth of such studies from traditional cultures such as Sri Lanka. Importantly, it was also envisaged that the study results would shed further light and understanding on the dynamics and outcomes of the use of physical force in times of human conflict.

Method

Participants

Children (N = 1319) studying in grade seven, in the Sinhala medium, in 45 government schools in the Colombo district participated in this study. Of these, twenty-seven children returned incomplete instruments and these were excluded from the analyses. From the 1292 who returned completed instruments, data from 66 participants were removed due to the statistical assumptions of multivariate normality and outliers for estimating the models being violated [Tabachnick & Fidell, 1996]. Hence, the final sample size on which this research program was based was 1226 (60.8% girls) with a mean age of 11.83 yrs (median = 12 yrs.; SD = 0.51) where 84.8% of the sample were Buddhist (6.4% Muslim; 4.1% Roman Catholic; 3.4% Christian; 1.2% Hindu) and 90.2% were of Sinhaleese ethnic origin (1.8% Muslim; 2.4% Sri Lankan Tamil; 0.6% Malay; 0.6% Burgher; 0.4% Indian Tamil; 0.1% Other).

School attendance is good in Sri Lanka (Department of Census & Statistics, 1997]. Therefore, as school is an institution that most children attend, it was considered an appropriate population for the present study. Further, 12-year-old children, in terms of their intellectual development, understand written language. Sri Lankan children are familiar with self-administered formats, such as those in the instruments used in the present study, as most of their school exams are designed in such a manner. Logistic and time constraints led to the present study being conducted solely on Sinhala speaking children attending government schools in the Colombo district.

The children were chosen by a stratified random sampling technique that comprised of all Sinhala language government schools in the Colombo district. Permission for the study was gained from the appropriate Ministry and ethical approval was gained from the Faculty of Medicine, University of Colombo. Informed consent from the participants was assumed by their verbal consent to take part in the study.

Materials

Instrument package

The instruments detailed were chosen and validated/developed to suit the objectives of a larger study on child-directed violence on 12-year-old Sri Lankan school children, its prevalence, psychosocial correlates and psychological outcomes.

The Parent-Child Conflict Tactic Scale [CTSPC: Straus et al., 1998]:

The original CTSPC has three scales and 22 items. Scale items are disciplinary strategies. A respondent indicates if a particular disciplinary strategy never occurred or occurred once, twice, three-five times, six-ten times, 11-20 times, or more than 20 times in the referent period assessed. The response option of "did not happen in the referent period assessed, but did happen before" is also available. The referent period may vary (e.g., past month, past year, lifetime), depending on the research objectives. The CTSPC scales [Straus et al., 1998] include: (i) Nonviolent Discipline (n items = 4: these are disciplinary strategies that are widely used alternatives to corporal punishment. e.g., "explained why something was wrong"); (ii) Physical Assault (n items = 13: at the lower severity level of the Minor Physical Assault sub-scale, the items relate to corporal punishment that has been traditionally used by parents in response to child misbehavior. e.g., "shook you". Items of higher severity in the Severe Physical Assault and Very Severe Physical Assault sub-scales include indicators of physical abuse. e.g., "grabbed you around the neck and choked you"); and (iii) Psychological

Aggression (n = 5 items: these are verbal and symbolic acts by the parent intended to cause psychological pain or fear in the child. e.g., "swore or cursed at you").

Supplemental scales on Discipline in the Previous Week, Child Neglect, and Child Sexual Abuse are also included in the CTSPC. It has an average testing time of about six to eight minutes if only the three main scales are used and 10 to 15 minutes if the supplemental scales are also included.

The minor physical assault (i.e. corporal punishment) sub-scale of the CTSPC was used to determine the annual prevalence and frequency of corporal punishment. The severe and very severe physical assault sub-scales of the CTSPC were used to determine the annual prevalence and frequency of physical abuse. The adaptation, validation, psychometric properties, and scoring of the Sinhala version of minor physical assault scale of the CTSPC is discussed elsewhere [De Zoysa, Rajapakse, & Newcombe, 2005].

Test-retest (a 14-day interval) and internal consistency reliabilities for the full CTSPC and its scales/sub-scales are presented in Table 1. Though the CTSPC was developed for use in a classroom, when it was used so in Sri Lanka (i.e. large group, n = 40), the results were not encouraging. Hence, it was administered to small groups (n = 20) where children having an opportunity to be in close contact with the instrument administrator and with greater opportunity to clarify questions, the obtained information would be more reliable. As can be seen from Table 1, the reliability results for the full instrument, its scales and sub-scales were superior in the small than in the large group. A "rule of thumb" acceptability of test-retest reliability is an Inter-Class Correlation Coefficient (ICC) of at least 0.7 and an internal consistency alpha value of at least 0.6 [De Vaus, 1991]. All reported ICC and alpha values for the small group were above these acceptable values, indicating that the CTSPC's Sinhala version, used in small groups, have good test-retest reliability and internal consistency [De Zoysa et al., 2005].

Table 1. Reliability estimates of the CTSPC's original and Sinhala version: full instrument/scales/sub-scales for the large and small group administration

CTSPC scales	Internal Consistency (Alpha) Sinhala version Large group	Internal Consistency (Alpha) Sinhala version Small group	Internal Consistency (Alpha) USA version ***	Test-Retest (Inter-Class Correlation) Sinhala version Large group	Test-Retest (Inter-Class Correlation) Sinhala version Small group
Full instrument	0.81	0.95	-	0.62*	0.88*
Nonviolent discipline	0.72	0.62	0.70	0.64*	0.81*
Psychological aggression	0.63	0.81	0.60	0.69*	0.72*
Minor physical assault (Corporal punishment)	0.80	0.89	-	0.47*	0.82*
Severe physical assault **	0.39	0.77	-0.02	0.35*	0.83*
Very severe physical assault **	0.80	0.82	-	0.13	0.79*

* $p<0.001$

** These two sub-scales form the physical abuse scale

*** Source: Straus *et al.* 1998.

Personality Assessment Questionnaire [PAQ: Rohner, 1999]:

The PAQ is a self-report instrument designed to assess an individual's perception of him or her self (or of his or her child) and is used to assess the presence or absence of psychological maladjustment in a child. It has 42 items, arranged in a cyclical order, assessing seven personality dimensions/scales (each scale has six items). Some items are reverse-worded in order to minimize response bias. The items are in the form of statements and a respondent indicates whether an item is "almost always true of me", "sometimes true of me", "rarely true of me", or "almost never true of me". The PAQ scales include:

(i) Hostility and Aggression - Hostility is conceptualized as an emotional reaction or feeling of anger directed towards another person, situation or oneself. Hostility is expressed behaviorally in the form of aggression, usually towards another person, but sometimes towards oneself (e.g., "I think about fighting or being mean").

(ii) Dependency - Dependence is conceptualized as the emotional reliance of one person on another for comfort, guidance, or decision-making (e.g., "I like my parents to give me a lot of love").

(iii) Negative Self-Esteem - Negative self-esteem implies that a person is uncomfortable with oneself, perhaps feels inferior to others, and perceives oneself as essentially a worthless person (e.g., "I get unhappy with myself").

(iv) Negative Self-Adequacy - Negative self-adequacy implies that a person feels that he or she is an incompetent person, lacks confident self-assurance, and sees oneself as a failure (e.g., "I feel I can do the things I want as well as most people").

(v) Emotional Unresponsiveness - An emotionally unresponsive person may be friendly and sociable, but their friendships tend to be impersonal and emotionally inexpressive. Emotionally unresponsive people often have difficulty or are unable to give or receive normal affection (e.g., "I have trouble showing people how I feel").

(vi) Emotional Instability - Emotionally unstable people are subject to fairly wide, frequent and unpredictable mood shifts where small setbacks often upset them (e.g., "I feel bad or get angry when I try to do something and cannot do it").

(vii) Negative World View - World view is a person's overall evaluation of life as being essentially a positive or negative place. The evaluation is seen as being basically a good, unthreatening place (positive world view), or as being a bad, threatening, or uncertain place (negative world view) (e.g., "I feel that life is nice").

Three versions of the PAQ have been developed. One asks adults to reflect on their own behavioral dispositions (Adult PAQ); a second asks children to reflect on their behavioral dispositions (Child PAQ); and the third asks mothers (or other caretakers, such as teachers) to reflect on the child's behavioral depositions (Mother PAQ). The version used in this study, the Child PAQ, has been developed for use with children aged seven to 12 years. The test author has suggested that the instrument be self-administered, though if the child is a poor reader, it may be read out to him or her [Rohner, 1999]. The adaptation, validation and psychometric properties of the PAQ for use in the Sri Lankan context is reported elsewhere [De Zoysa, Rajapakse, & Newcombe, 2003].

Table 2. Reliability estimates of the PAQ's original and Sinhala version: full instrument and scales for the large and small group administration

PAQ scales	Internal Consistency (Alpha) Sinhala version Large group	Internal Consistency (Alpha) Sinhala version Small group	Internal Consistency (Alpha) USA version **	Test-Retest (Inter-Class Correlation) Sinhala version Large group	Test-Retest (Inter-Class Correlation) Sinhala version Small group
Full instrument	0.79	0.82	0.83	0.70*	0.84*
Hostility & aggression	0.62	0.62	0.66	0.48*	0.81*
Dependency	0.44	0.47	0.47	0.40*	0.59*
Negative self-esteem	0.41	0.42	0.66	0.67*	0.73*
Negative self-adequacy	0.55	0.63	0.63	0.61*	0.62*
Emotional unresponsiveness	0.52	0.57	0.46	0.57*	0.70*
Emotional instability	0.28	0.55	0.52	0.44*	0.74*
Negative world view	0.75	0.65	0.74	0.71*	0.76*

* $p<0.001$
** Source: Khaleque & Rohner 2002

As with the CTSPC, A test-retest (a 14-day interval) and internal consistency reliability for the full PAQ and its scales were determined via a large and small group administration and are presented in Table 2. The test-retest reliabilities for the full instrument and the scales were higher in the small group than in the large group administration. In the small group administration, all ICC values except for the Dependency (ICC = 0.59) and Negative self-Adequacy (ICC = 0.62) scales were at above the minimum acceptable criterion of 0.7 [De Vaus, 1991]. The internal consistency with the small group administration also exceeded the minimum acceptable criterion of 0.6 [De Vaus, 1991], and thus the full instrument could be confidently used in research, clinical and applied settings in Sri Lanka - provided it is used in small groups. The scale alphas of the small group administration were consistent with originally reported values [Rohner, 1999].

Psychosocial Questionnaire (PSQ):

The PSQ was designed especially for the larger study on child-directed violence and comprised of 66 items assessing select variables that have been shown in previous research to be associated with parental use of physical force and its outcomes. Correlates identified in individual interviews with parents and professionals who work with children (N=10), and focus group discussions with 25 twelve-year-olds were also included in the PSQ. The PSQ consisted of several scales/sub-scales: Socio-demographics (n items = 3); Family Structure (n items = 8); Family Support Network (n items = 2); Children's Support Network (i.e. Peer Support and Adult Support) (n items = 12); Non-Parent-to-Child Violence (n items = 15); Parent-Child Relationship (n items = 16); Sexual Abuse (n items = 4); Parent-to-Child Corporal Punishment (n items = 5); and Children's Attitude to Corporal Punishment (n items = 4).

Four areas of non-parent-to-child violence were included - domestic (2 items: e.g., "Have you ever seen or heard your parents hitting each other?"), community (3 items: e.g., "In the past year, have you seen or heard household items being smashed or windows being broken in your neighbor's houses?"), peer (9 items: e.g., "Has any student ever hit you with the hand or an object, kicked you, or shoved you?"), and teacher (9 items: e.g., "Has an teacher hit you on the head with the knuckles?). Children responded on a dichotomous scale ("yes/no") for these sub-scales. Scores for each were summed to give a sub-scale score.

For the children's support network scale, there were two sub-scales - peer (3 items: e.g., "If you missed school for say, two weeks, do you have a friend who will give you their books for you to copy notes from?") and adult (3 items: e.g., "Do you know an adult - who is not your parent - whom you feel has a special interest in yourself and your activities?"), with children again responding on a dichotomous scale ("yes/no"). Scores for each were summed to give a sub-scale score.

The parent-child relationship scale consisted of 4 sub-scales - parental nurturance (7 items: e.g., "Do your parents help you when you are unhappy"), consistency in using corporal punishment (2 items: e.g., "You know the situations when your parents will punish you"), children's perceived fairness of corporal punishment (2 items: e.g., "You think you deserve it when your parents punish you"), and parent-child dialogue when using corporal punishment (2 items: e.g., "When your parents punish you for doing something wrong, the explain to you the reason for doing so"). Response alternatives ranged from 1 (never) to 5 (always) for the nurturance sub-scale and 1 (never) to 4 (always) for the consistency, fairness and dialogue sub-scales. Scores for each were summed to give a sub-scale score.

Finally, the children's attitude to corporal punishment was measured with 4 items that related to a short story the children read (e.g., "Anil and Kumari's parents' should hit them when they misbehave"). The children responded on a 4-point scale ranging from 1 (completely unfavorable) to 4 (completely favorable). Scores were summed to give a scale score.

For ease of responding, the PSQ was formatted in a skip response pattern. Depending on children's answer to a given item, arrows then directed the children to the next relevant item. Some items were reverse-worded in order to minimize response bias. General (e.g., questions on socio-demographic) items were presented first and emotionally charged items (e.g., questions on sexual abuse) were presented later in the instrument. The PSQ was developed in Sinhala and used the same validation procedure as with the CTSPC [De Zoysa, 2005].

The test-retest and internal consistency reliabilities of the PSQ were determined by a small group administration only and are presented in Table 3. A full instrument test-retest or internal consistency reliability was not calculated as such statistics would not be theoretically applicable to an instrument (such as the PSQ) that is designed to gather descriptive information from diverse, possibly conceptually unrelated, constructs. Certain PSQ sub-scales (e.g., Peer Support, Adult Support, Domestic Violence,) were categorized into two dimensions when determining reliability. This categorization enabled conceptual meaningfulness within groups of items measuring a broader concept. For example, the Peer Support sub-scale was categorized as Peer Support Occurrence and Peer Support Frequency. Peer Support Occurrence items reported if there was peer support whilst Peer Support Frequency items reported the extent of such peer support. Overall reliabilities for these PSQ sub-scales were therefore not computed as they measured two mutually exclusive aspects of the broader concept.

Table 3. Reliability estimates of the PSQ scales/sub-scales/categories

PSQ scales/sub-scales	Internal Consistency (Alpha)	Test-Retest (Inter-Class Correlation)
Peer support occurrence	0.57	0.85**
Peer support numbers	0.57	0.86**
Adult support occurrence	0.93	0.72**
Adult support numbers	0.93	0.75**
Domestic violence occurrence	0.60	0.86**
Domestic violence frequency	0.60	0.72**
Peer violence occurrence	N/A****	0.64**
Peer violence frequency	N/A***	0.65**
Teacher violence occurrence	N/A****	0.15
Teacher violence frequency	N/A***	0.45**
Community violence	0.51	0.68**
Sexual abuse occurrence	N/A****	0.99**
Sexual abuse number of acts	N/A****	0.71**
Sexual abuse frequency	N/A***	Scale/part scale has zero variance
Sexual abuse number of perpetrators	N/A****	0.71**
Family social support network	N/A***	0.82**
Parental nurturance	0.86	0.76**
Parental consistency in using CP	N/A***	0.69**
Parental dialogue in using CP	N/A***	0.62**
Parental fairness in using CP	N/A***	0.68**
Physical consequences of CP	N/A***	0.65**
Main perpetrator of CP	N/A***	0.70**
Time of day when using CP most	N/A***	0.69**
Reason for CP	N/A***	N/A*
Attitude to CP	0.80	0.67**

CP Corporal punishment

*This item required the child to write the reason for the most recent episode of corporal punishment. As this response would generally differ from week to week, computation of ICC would not be relevant.

**p<0.001

*** Only one/two item(s) for the construct

**** Too few responses to compute alpha

A majority of the PSQ scale/sub-scale/category's test-retest reliabilities met or exceeded the minimum acceptable criterion of an ICC of 0.7 [De Vaus, 1991]. The sub-scales/categories of Peer violence Occurrence category (ICC = 0.64), Teacher Violence Occurrence category (ICC = 0.15), Teacher Violence Frequency category (ICC = 0.45) and Parental Dialogue when using Corporal Punishment (ICC = 0.62) however were below this criterion. Discussions with experts on public health and mental health on the viability of retaining the two Teacher Violence categories in the PSQ led to their continued inclusion. It was hypothesized that these low test-retest reliabilities may be due to teacher violence being so frequent that children may be unable to remember its details or because it is accepted as normative. It was also hypothesized that in the punitive Sri Lankan school milieu in which the data was collected, children may have reported inconsistently due to the anxiety of being found out for reporting on their teachers. The internal consistency estimates of all but one (i.e. Community Violence sub-scale: alpha = 0.51) of the PSQ scales/sub-scales/categories met or exceeded the minimum acceptable criterion of a Cronbach's alpha of 0.6 [De Vaus, 1991].

The PSQ has shown promising psychometric properties for several of its scales/sub-scales/categories. These can be used with some confidence in research settings with 12-year-old Sinhala speaking government school children. As the few scales/sub-scales/categories that indicated reliability estimates lower than the acceptable criterion were retained in the PSQ, it is important to interpret results based on these with caution.

Procedure

Following the school principal's permission at each school, the instruments were administered to all children who were indicated as literate by the class teacher and who attended class that day. Children were informed of the nature of the study and that confidentiality of answers would be maintained. The administration of all three instruments took about one to one-and-half hours, and the instruments were administered in the same order for all children. The PSQ was administered first and once it was collected, the CTSPC and the PAQ was handed out. The first author administered the instruments and was available throughout to clarify any questions.

Data analysis

SPSS v10.0 [1998] was used for data collation and descriptive and inferential analysis. Structural Equation Modeling [LISREL 8.7: Joreskog & Sorbom, 2004], a statistical technique that analyses complex relationships among study variables, was applied to the data of the present study. There are a number of advantages in using SEM [Ullman, 1996]. For instance, when relationships are complex and multidimensional, SEM is the only analysis that allows complete and simultaneous tests of all the relationships. Furthermore, in SEM, when relationships among factors are examined, the relationships are free from measurement error because the error has been estimated and removed, leaving only the common variance. Additionally, SEM also allows the testing of mediated processes.

SEM based on maximum likelihood estimation was used to test the empirical validity of the proposed theoretical model (see Figure 1) and the estimated models of the present study. For SEM results to be interpreted reliably, several statistical assumptions need to be met [Ullman, 1996]. These include checking the data for missing information, multivariate normality, linearity, univariate and multivariate outliers, multicollinearity and singularity, adequacy of covariances, and checking the residuals of the analyses to ensure that they were small and centered around zero. To satisfy these assumptions, the original sample of 1319 was reduced to a sample of 1226 for SEM.

Given the scaling of the data [both ordinal and continuous], the computation of the correlation matrix included Pearson Moment, Polychoric, and Polyserial correlations as it was seen to be more appropriate than the covariance matrix [Joreskog & Sorbom, 1986]. Further, an asymptotic covariance matrix was also created that enabled an adjustment to the chi-square for non-normality - the Sartorra-Bentler Scaled Chi-Square based on Maximum Likelihood estimation techniques [Joreskog & Sorbom, 1986].

After the theoretical model was specified (see Figure 1) and then estimated, the strength of the model was examined [Ullman, 1996] by assessing how "good" the model was by the fit between the sample covariance matrix and the estimated population covariance matrix [Ullman, 1996]. One rough rule of thumb is that a good fitting model may be indicated when the ratio of the x^2 to the degrees of freedom is less than 2 [Ullman, 1996]. There are also other measures of model fit that have been proposed. For instance, Bentler-Bonnet Normed Fit Index [NFI: Bentler, 1989] evaluates the estimated model by comparing the x^2 value of the model to the x^2 value of the independence model. High values (greater than 0.9) are indicative of a good-fitting model. The Comparative Fit Index [CFI: Bentler, 1989] also assesses the fit relative to other models with values greater than 0.9 indicative of good-fitting models. Two widely used fit indices calculate a weighted proportion of variance in the sample covariance matrix accounted for by the estimated population covariance matrix. They are the Goodness of Fit Index (GFI) and Adjusted Goodness of Fit Index (AGFI) [Tanaka & Huba, 1989, cited in Tabachnick & Fidell, 1996]. GFI and AGFI values greater than 0.9 are indicative of good-fitting models. The Root Mean Square Residual (RMR) and the Standardized Root Mean Square Residual (SRMR) are the average differences between the sample variances and covariances and the estimated population variances and covariances. These have a range of 0 to 1. Good-fitting models have a small RMR [Ullman, 1996] and SRMR values less than 0.05 [Sorbom & Joreskog, 1982, cited in Tabachnick & Fidell, 1996]. The present study utilized all the above-indicated indices in determining the fit of the proposed models.

Results

Descriptive analyses

In the present sample of children, 70% had experienced at least one act of corporal punishment in the past year with an average of 12 such acts in that year. And, 37.8% children had experienced at least one act of physical abuse in the past year with an average of 11.6 such acts in that year.

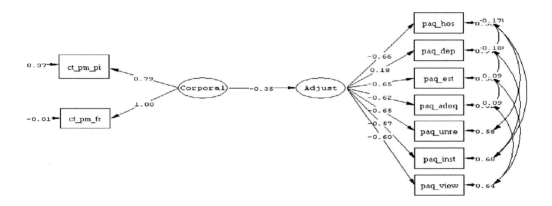

Figure 2. Diagram of model I (basic model), with the latent and measured variables and standardized path coefficients
(* $p < 0.05$)

Corporal Corporal Punishment
Adjust Psychological Maladjustment
ct_pm_pi Annual Prevalence of Corporal Punishment
ct_pm_fr Annual Frequency of Corporal Punishment
paq_hos Hostility and Aggression
paq_dep Dependency
paq_est Negative Self-Esteem
paq_adeq Negative Self-Adequacy
paq_unre Emotional Unresponsiveness
paq_inst Emotional Instability
paq_view Negative World View

Structural models

The basic model, that of the direct relationship between corporal punishment and psychological maladjustment is presented as Model I (see Figure 2). The theoretical model which tested the nature of association between corporal punishment and psychological maladjustment with the hypothesized mediators included is presented as Model II (see Figure 3). These mediators were the variables of children's experience of non-parent-to-child violence, children's support network, parent-child relationship and the children's attitude to corporal punishment. Following an iterative procedure where successive models were examined for their fit to the data, Model III (see Figure 4) was seen to be the best fit based on several indices of statistical fit (see Table 4) and theoretical relevance.

It was also hypothesized that physical abuse is an outcome of corporal punishment. Model IV (see Figure 5) tested this hypothesis in the context of the final model (i.e. model III).

Table 4. x^2 test values, fit indices and R^2 for structural equations, for all models

Model	\multicolumn{8}{c}{x^2 test values, fit indices and R^2}								
	x^2 (df)	x^2/df	GFI	AGFI	NFI	CFI	SRMR	R^2
Model I (basic model)	22.51 (18)	1.25	1.00	0.99	1.00	1.00	0.02	0.12
Model II (theoretical model)	673.07 (150)	4.49	0.95	0.93	0.94	0.95	0.07	0.50
Model III (final model)	137.91 (46)	3.00	0.98	0.97	0.98	0.99	0.04	0.26
Model IV (with physical abuse)	358.48 (91)	2.06	0.96	0.95	0.98	0.98	0.05	0.22 (0.34)

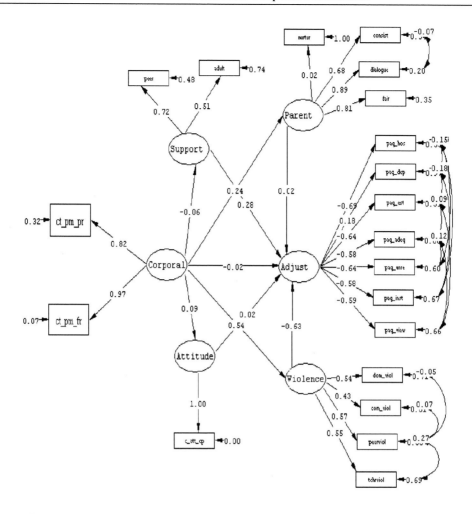

Figure 3. Diagram of model II (theoretical model), with the latent and measured variables and standardized path coefficients (*p <0.05; ** Standardized Indirect Effects of KSI on ETA)

Corporal = Corporal Punishment
paq_est = Negative Self-Esteem
peerviol = Peer Violence
Adjust = Psychological Maladjustment
aq_adeq = Negative Self-Adequacy
tchrviol = Teacher Violence
Support = Children's Support Network
paq_unres = Emotional Unresponsiveness
fair = Fairness in Using CP
Attitude = Children's Attitude to CP
paq_inst = Emotional Instability
dialogue = Dialogue in Using CP
Violence = Non-Parent-to-Child Violence

paq_view = Negative World View
consist = Consistency in Using CP
Parent = Parent-Child Relationship
peer = Peer Support
nurture = Nurturance
ct_pm_pi = Annual Prevalence of CP
adult = Adult Support
ct_pm_fr = Annual Frequency of CP
dom_viol = Domestic Violence
paq_hos = Hostility and Aggression
com_viol = Community Violence
paq_dep = Dependency
c_att_cp = Children's Attitude to CP

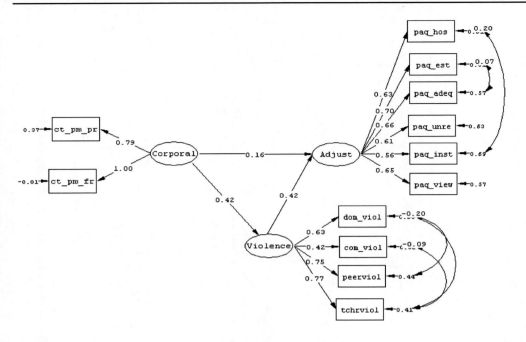

Figure 4. Diagram of model III (final model), with the latent and measured variables and standardized path coefficients
(*p <0.05; ** Standardized Indirect Effects of KSI on ETA)

Corporal Corporal Punishment
Adjust Psychological Maladjustment
Violence Non-Parent-to-Child Violence
Abuse Physical Abuse
ct_pm_pi Annual Prevalence of CP
ct_pm_fr Annual Frequency of CP
paq_hos Hostility and Aggression
paq_unres Emotional Unresponsiveness

dom_viol Domestic Violence
com_viol Community Violence
peerviol Peer Violence
tchrviol Teacher Violence
paq_view Negative World View
paq_inst Emotional Instability
paq_adeq Negative Self-Adequacy
paq_est Negative Self-Esteem

As can be seen from Figure 2, the basic model showed that increasing levels of corporal punishment were directly and moderately, but significantly, associated with a child's psychological maladjustment. The full theoretical model explored whether this association might be better represented through the mediation of select third variables (see Figure 3). However, the indices of fit for the full theoretical model indicated a poor overall fit to the data (see Table 4). Several post hoc model modifications [Ullman, 1996] were performed on the theoretical model in an attempt to develop a better fitting, more parsimonious model. Pathways were added based on the fit Indices and their theoretical sense. Pathways were deleted based on their significance across latent/indicator variables and theoretical appropriateness. Two indicator variables, with non-significant pathways with its latent variable - Dependency loading on to Psychological Maladjustment and Nurturance loading on to Parent-Child Relationship - were deleted at the first post hoc model modification. The consequent model showed that Corporal Punishment had a significant and direct association with Psychological Maladjustment and that Non-Parent-to-Child Violence significantly mediated this association. However, and based on the Baron and Kenny [1986] criteria, Parent-Child Relationship, Children's Support Network and Children's Attitude to Corporal Punishment were deemed to not mediate the association. Successive iterations of models were performed with non-significant pathways and latent and indicator variables being deleted to arrive at the final model (Model III: see Figure 4). This model showed that increasing levels of corporal punishment were moderately, but significantly and directly, associated with a children's psychological maladjustment. It also showed that non-parent-to-child violence acts as a significant mediator, impacting on the direct association between corporal punishment and psychological maladjustment. Table 5 presents the Intercorrelations among measured variables for all models tested.

Model IV (see Figure 5) showed that the experience of corporal punishment significantly predicted the occurrence of physical abuse. LISREL also suggested a pathway from Non-Parent-to-Child Violence to Physical Abuse and from Non-Parent-to-Child Violence to Hostility and ggression. Both these pathways were significant and theoretically plausible.

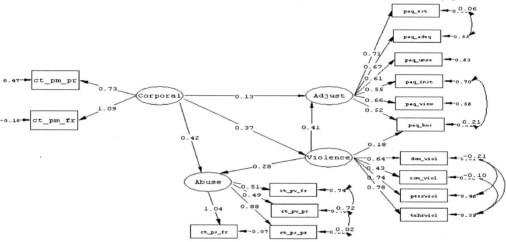

Figure 5. Diagram of Model IV (with Physical Abuse added as an outcome of corporal punishment), with the latent and measured variables and standardized path coefficients (*p <0.05; ** Standardized Indirect Effects of KSI on ETA)

Corporal   Corporal Punishment
Adjust   Psychological Maladjustment
Violence   Non-Parent-to-Child Violence
Abuse   Physical Abuse
ct_pm_pi   Annual Prevalence of CP
ct_pm_fr   Annual Frequency of CP
paq_hos   Hostility and Aggression
paq_est   Negative Self-Esteem
paq_adeq   Negative Self-Adequacy
paq_unres   Emotional Unresponsiveness
dom_viol   Domestic Violence
com_viol   Community Violence
peerviol   Peer Violence
tchrviol   Teacher
ct_ps_fr   Annual Frequency of Severe Physical Assault
ct_ps_pr   Annual Prevalence of Severe Physical Assault
ct_pv_fr   Annual Frequency of Very Severe Physical Assault
ct_pv_pr   Annual Prevalence of Very Severe Physical Assault
paq_inst   Emotional Instability
paq_view   Negative World View

Table 5. Intercorrelations among measured variables for all models

Variable	1	2	3	4	5	6	7	8	9	10	11	12	13	14	15	16	17	18	19
1. Domestic Violence																			
2. Community Violence	.24**																		
3. Peer Violence	.19**	.31**																	
4. Teacher Violence	.22**	.24**	.59**																
5. Peer Support	-.9**	-.12**	-.07*	-.07*															
6. Adult Support	.03	-.07*	-.03	-.01	.34**														
7. Nurturance	-.23**	-.16**	-.19**	-.19**	.12**	.11**													
8. Consistency in Using Corporal Punishment	.20**	.16**	.20**	.23**	-.05	-.03	-.15**												
9. Fairness in Using Corporal Punishment	.12**	.12**	.18**	.16**	.02	.02	.01	.73**											
10. Dialogue in Using Corporal Punishment	.11**	.13**	.17**	.15**	.01	.01	.01	.79**	.85**										
11. Attitude to Corporal Punishment	.07*	.07*	.02	-.02	-.04	-.02	.07*	.08**	.18**	.15**									
12. Hostility and Aggression	.29**	.23**	.28**	.26**	-.13**	-.09**	-.21**	.20**	.14**	.15**	.07*								
13. Dependency	-.07*	-.03	-.02	-.06*	.04	-.01	.12*	.01	.05	.07*	.07*	.14							

14. Negative Self-Esteem	.22**	.17**	.22**	.21**	-.12**	-.15**	-.25**	.12**	.05	-.04	.03	.42**	-.21**
15. Negative Self-Adequacy	.18**	.13**	.14**	.15**	-.16**	-.16**	-.21**	.09**	.05	-.05	.03	.4**	-.14**	.55**
16. Emotional Unresponsiveness	.17**	.12**	.22**	.18**	-.16**	-.17**	-.25**	.15**	.08	.07*	-.05	.34**	-.18**	.42**	.42**
17. Emotional Instability	.2**	.2**	.23**	.16**	-.11**	-.1**	-.18**	.18**	.11**	.13**	.06	.54**	.08**	.39**	.33**	.35**
18. Negative World View	.21**	.23**	.18**	.17**	-.16**	-.14**	-.23**	.14**	.06*	.08**	.01	.37**	-.11**	.47**	.45**	.4**	.33**
19. Prevalence of Corporal Punishment	.18**	.17**	.2**	.23**	-.07*	-.03	-.13**	.26**	.21**	.27**	.07*	.21**	.01	.17**	.16**	.18**	.17**	.13**
20. Frequency of Corporal Punishment	.18**	.19**	.23**	.24**	-.01	.01	-.17**	.19**	.14**	.13**	.06	.2**	-.05	.19**	.15**	.19**	.16**	.2**	.34**

N=1226
**p < 0.01, *p < 0.05

Discussion

An objective of the present study was to explore the nature of association between corporal punishment and psychological maladjustment of children. It also explored whether this association was mediated by select third variables. A further objective of the study was to explore the nature of association between corporal punishment and physical abuse of children. Sri Lanka is a signatory to the United Nation's Convention on the Rights of the Child [1989] which abides to protect children from all forms of physical and mental violence while in the care of parents and others. Despite this legal advancement and the public awareness of the negative outcomes of corporal punishment, the present study showed a high prevalence of parental corporal punishment in Sri Lanka. The frequency of such corporal punishment use (on average, 12 times annually) indicates that the use of corporal punishment is not a result of an isolated event triggered by an extreme circumstance, but rather a recurring pattern of the use of physical discipline by Sri Lankan parents. Ryan and Straus [cited in Straus, 1994] have shed some light to this apparent contradiction. They postulate that parents in societies which are rule-driven (as is Sri Lanka), as opposed to those which are more "loosely structured" emphasizing initiative and creativity, tend to rely more on physically forceful means for controlling their children. Further, cross-cultural comparative studies have shown that those societies high in conflict and warfare (again, as in Sri Lanka) tend to be high in the use of corporal punishment [Otterbein, 1974, cited in Straus, 1994]. Thus, the patriarchal social structure, the impact of its history of conflicts [Sivanayagam, 2005] in promoting a sense of normalization of violence, and the less strict child monitoring laws may be some of the factors contributing to the reported high prevalence of parental corporal punishment in the study.

In a similar study, Straus & Stewart [1999] reported a national annual prevalence of 50% for parental use of corporal punishment on 12-year-old Americans. The greater apparent use of corporal punishment by Sri Lankan parents may be due to the greater acceptance of its use in Sri Lanka as there is as yet no wide public debate on its potential negative outcomes unlike in the USA [e.g., Baumrind, 1996; Larzelere, 2000; Straus, 1994]. Another study using the Conflict Tactics Scale (an instrument similar to the CTPSC and by the same author) in two Asian countries - China and Korea - has reported annual prevalence figures of corporal punishment in two of its provinces as 42% and 9.4%, respectively [Kim et al., 2000]. In comparing these prevalence rates with that of the present study, it appears that Sri Lankan parents tend to use more punitive discipline than some of their Asian counterparts. However, it should be cautioned that, though these studies have all used the same or similar instruments, comparison of prevalence rates should be done with prudence as different definitions, study methods and age groups were employed [Creighton, 2004].

The study revealed that 37.8% of 12-year-olds had experienced some form of physical abuse in the past year. A similar study in the USA reported a national annual prevalence of 2.5% for physical abuse of 12- to 17-year-olds (Straus & Runyan, 1997). In Asia, a study on child physical abuse in China and Korea, revealed annual rates of 22.6% and 51.3%, respectively (Kim et al.,. 2000). The physical abuse prevalence rates are much higher in Korea, Sri Lanka and China than in the USA. Studies have shown that poverty (Frias-Armenta & McCloseky, 1998), lack of support and solidarity within a community

(Runyan, 1998), family policy related to child care arrangements (Krug *et al,.* 2002), strength of the social welfare system (Krug *et al.* 2002), social protection and strength of the criminal justice system (Krug *et al,.* 2002), and social conflicts and war (Krug *et al,.* 2002) are factors associated with parental stress and consequent physical abuse of their children. Thus, in Sri Lanka too, its issues with poverty (Department of Census & Statistics, 1997), dearth of family welfare policies, lack of social protection, and the longstanding ethnic conflict might lead to stress for its people. Such stress, combined with the cultural tolerance of violence in general (Belsky, 1984) and corporal punishment in particular (as evidenced by its high prevalence in this study) may account for the high rate of physical abuse (Gelles & Cornell, 1990) in Sri Lanka.

The frequency of physical abuse in this study was 11.6 for the past year. This means that those children who reported physical abuse had experienced it on average 11.6 times in the past year. This shows that physically abusive acts are not a result of an isolated event triggered by an extreme circumstance (as some tend to believe) but rather a recurring pattern of severe violence in the parent-child relationship. It is hypothesised that those parents who have repeatedly gone on to use physically abusive strategies in disciplinary encounters that started with corporal punishment, may tend to use physical abuse more often in the future because they are familiar with it and are desensitised by their own violence.

There is increasing evidence that corporal punishment is associated with a host of negative psychological outcomes for children [Gershoff, 2002], a finding corroborated in the present study. The final model (Model III: see Figure 4) that best captured the association between corporal punishment and psychological maladjustment, showed that increasing levels of such punishment were moderately but significantly associated with a children's psychological maladjustment and that Sri Lankan children's experience of non-parent-to-child violence (i.e., domestic, community, teacher and peer) impacted this relationship. Hence, experiencing corporal punishment, belonging to a violent community and/or witnessing domestic violence can exacerbate the levels of psychological maladjustment, a finding corroborated by previous research [Dietz, 2000; Hughes, 1998]. Being a recipient/witness of such violence has been associated with several psychological problems in the child [Gershoff, 2002; Straus, 1994]. Such psychological difficulties may lead to a deficit in coping skills predisposing such children to further violence by teachers and/or peers [Hughes, 1998; Silverman et al., 1994], leaving the vulnerable child in a vicious cycle of violence.

The SEM theoretical model (Model II: see Figure 3) and intermediate models revealed that children's favorable attitude towards corporal punishment did not have a significant mediating impact on the association between corporal punishment and psychological maladjustment. Thus, though the formation of children's favorable attitude towards corporal punishment was significantly associated with their experience of it, such an attitude may not buffer against its negative psychological impact - findings corroborated by previous research [Flynn, 1996; Rohner, Kean, & Cournoyer, 1991]. This finding appears to contradict the often heard saying that "I was spanked and I am OK". The experience of corporal punishment may have led to the formation of such a favorable attitude to corporal punishment, but though such persons believe that they are "OK", the present study indicates that they may not, in reality, be as "OK" as they might have been without such punishment [Kuczynski & Hilderbrant, 1997].

Although a healthy peer and adult support system has been shown to buffer the negative psychological outcomes of corporal punishment [Milner, Robertson, & Rogers, 1990], this was not confirmed in the present study. The SEM theoretical model and intermediate models indicated that a child's support system was significantly associated with greater psychological adjustment, but that it did not buffer the negative psychological outcomes of corporal punishment.

It was also hypothesized that a positive parent-child relationship would mediate the negative psychological outcomes of corporal punishment [Kuczynski & Hilderbrant, 1997]. Nurturant parenting, consistent use of corporal punishment, with dialogue, and the children's perceived fairness of such punishment was combined to reflect a positive parent-child relationship in this study. The non-significant parenting-nurturance pathway in the theoretical (and intermediate models) indicated that parental nurturance does not significantly buffer the negative outcomes of corporal punishment. This finding is supported by previous research [McCord, 1997b]. Thus, even though a child may perceive his/her parents as loving, if the parents use corporal punishment on him/her, it may still be associated with a negative psychological outcome.

The results also showed that Sri Lankan parent's use of corporal punishment was significantly associated with the children's rating of it being used consistently, fairly and with dialogue. It appears that Sri Lankan parents tend to use corporal punishment in a more instrumental manner than in an emotional manner, reflective of cultures with normative acceptance of corporal punishment [Grusec, Rudy, & Marhni, 1997]. However, the non-significant parenting-psychological maladjustment pathway in the theoretical (and intermediate models) indicates that such consistency, fairness and dialogue does not appear to buffer corporal punishment's negative psychological outcomes.

It was also hypothesized in this study that physical abuse would be an outcome of the increasing frequency and severity of corporal punishment use (Zigler & Hall, 1989). It was further hypothesized that any characteristics or processes in the child (Gershoff, 2002) would not mediate the association between corporal punishment and physical abuse. The results confirmed this hypothesis (Model IV: see Figure 5), supporting some previous research (Zigler & Hall, 1989) but contradicting others that view corporal punishment and physical abuse as distinct phenomenon (e.g., Strassberg *et al.,* 1994).

LISREL, in Model IV, suggested a significant pathway from Non-Parent-to-Child Violence to Physical Abuse. It is speculated that the negative psychological outcomes of non-parent-to-child violence (added to that of corporal punishment) may impede the development of a healthy personality in the child. This may make the child vulnerable to longer and more severe parental victimization leading to abusive levels. In fact, previous research has shown an association between physical abuse and domestic violence (Frias-Armenta & McCloskey, 1998) though its causality was unclear. This pathway opens up new research questions on when, why and for whom the use of corporal punishment (within the larger context of non-parent-to-child violence) leads to physical abuse.

LISREL, in Model IV, also suggested a significant pathway from Non-Parent-to-Child Violence to Hostility and Aggression. This indicates that Non-parent-to-child violence significantly predicts children's level of hostility and aggression. Each increase in non-parent-to-child violence is therefore associated with a corresponding increase in children's level of hostility and aggression. It may be that children who have either experienced or witnessed non-parent-to-child violence may consider aggression as legitimate (White & Straus, 1981) and attribute hostile intent to the behaviour of others (Dodge *et al.*, 1986). Therefore, they would be more likely to resort to aggression when in conflict with others. Such aggression may also be evident long-term. In fact, research has shown that the experience of non-parent-to-child violence increases an individual's likelihood of acting violently with an adult romantic partner (Straus & Yodanis, 1996). The suggestion of a pathway from non-parent-to-child violence to hostility and aggression also has another important implication. Some researchers have opined that children's aggressive tendencies may elicit forceful disciplinary methods from caregivers (Belsky, 1984). However, the present study findings suggest that it is the violence the children experiences/witnesses that may lead to their being aggressive, rather than the children's aggressive tendencies eliciting corporal punishment. However, a word of caution on this interpretation is that the data of the present study is based on a cross-sectional research design that does not allow for interpretation of causality. Hence, future research would need to have longitudinal studies that would explore this finding further.

A culturally-relative model evaluates the appropriateness of corporal punishment by the acceptance of it in a given culture [Krug, Dahlberg, Mercy, Zwi, & Lozano, 2002]. It deems that in cultures that widely accept corporal punishment, it could be considered an appropriate form of discipline and may lead to few negative outcomes [Larzelere et al., 1997]. However, the present study results suggest that it is not the wide acceptance of corporal punishment that may be considered in deciding its appropriateness, but rather its outcome for children. As is seen from the present study, even though Sri Lankan children accept corporal punishment, such acceptance does not appear to ameliorate its negative outcomes for them. These findings lend some support to the universal harm view which postulates that corporal punishment is associated with harm, despite the culture-based favorable attitude towards it [Straus, 1994]. These findings have implications for raising awareness among Sri Lankan parents on child-rearing in general and corporal punishment in particular as most Sri Lankans, even some professionals in child protection, accept corporal punishment as useful [De Silva, 2001] and preventing its use is considered by the pro-corporal punishment advocates as imposing "Western" ideas to Sri Lanka.

Conclusion

The validated CTSPC, PAQ and PSQ were used in a cross-sectional survey with a representative sample of 12-year-old Sinhala speaking government school children in the Colombo district. The study found the prevalence and frequency of corporal punishment and physical abuse among the study sample to be very high. Further, SEM revealed that the experience of corporal punishment was moderately but significantly and directly associated with psychological maladjustment and physical abuse of children. Moreover, the corporal punishment-psychological maladjustment association was significantly mediated by the children's experience of non-parent-to-child violence. The finding that corporal punishment is significantly associated with psychological maladjustment and physical abuse indicates that despite the belief of many Sri Lankans to the usefulness of corporal punishment [De Silva, 2001], it has negative repercussions. Therefore, one of the most important contributions of this study is that it can inform social policy-makers and designers of parent education programs that the use of aversive disciplinary techniques by Sri Lankan parents is very high and that these techniques are significantly associated with negative outcomes for the child.

The psychosocial correlates identified in this study elucidated some of the key determinants of the use of corporal punishment by Sri Lankan parents. The correlates so identified are consistent with research findings elsewhere in the world. Identification of such correlates unique to a particular culture is important [Larzelere et al., 1997] such that evidence-based culturally appropriate preventive programs might be formulated. Such prevention can be addressed at three levels of the problem at hand: primary, secondary and tertiary [Agathonos-Georgopoulou & Browne, 1997]. Based on the present study findings, primary prevention might include the elimination of cultural norms and media influences that legitimize and glorify violence. Secondary prevention might include identifying and working with families such as low socio-economic groups who are at high risk for violence. Tertiary prevention might include efforts to intervene and treat families identified as maltreating their children. Effectiveness of such treatment programs could be assessed by the use of the validated CTSPC and PAQ at pre- and post-therapy time intervals.

Despite the contributions of the present study, its limitations should also be acknowledged. One of the main considerations is the difficulty in generalizing the study findings beyond Sinhala speaking 12-year-olds attending government schools in the Colombo district. Also, this study relied solely on the children's report of the phenomenon of parental use of physical force. Children may not have reported all incidents of physical force experienced or witnessed by them due to memory lapse [English, 1998] particularly as the referent period in the CTSPC was the past year. Also, incidents such as domestic and/or community violence may have occurred when the child was not at home/community. Further, the interpretations of experiencing and witnessing physical force may differ from parents, to siblings, to the respondent child. Additionally, retrospective self-reports on experiencing and witnessing violence can be subject to distortion. For example, it is difficult to determine if reported incidents of corporal punishment were labeled as such at the time they occurred or if it was labeled subsequently upon reflection. Having multiple informants [Haj-Yahia & Ben-Arieh, 2000] may have averted some of these limitations.

Sri Lankan society places much value on the relationship between the nuclear family and the extended family. It is common that, other than biological parents, extended family such as grandparents, aunts, uncles and cousins assist in child rearing [i.e. multiple parenting: Haj-Yahia & Musleh, 2002]. Future research would benefit from determining the extent to which children experience corporal punishment at the hands of these multiple parents. Likewise, future research could also determine how these multiple caregivers might ease the biological parent's stress of child rearing such that the use of physical force might not be seen to be so necessary in disciplining.

The present study only explored a limited number of variables. Only two aspects of corporal punishment were studied whilst aspects such as its intensity were left unexplored. Furthermore, though this study addressed some deficits of previous research on parental use of corporal punishment [e.g., consistency of discipline: Straus & Mouradian, 1998], it did not control for other variables (e.g., poor supervision) that may influence the association between corporal punishment and its outcomes. Financial concerns, time constraints and the need to keep the study brief enough to ensure respondent interest were the main reasons for limiting the number of variables studied.

Cross-sectional design, unlike longitudinal or experimental design, does not offer itself to causal inferences [Paolucci & Violato, 2004]. It is important that the causal pathway between corporal punishment and its outcomes be established through research that is longitudinal. A goal for future research in this area in Sri Lanka is to establish a longitudinal design whereby such causal pathways may be clearly identified and investigated. Future studies based on a creative experimental design, within ethical boundaries [Cohen, 1996], would also make a major contribution to understanding the causal pathway between corporal punishment and its potential outcomes [Bauman, 1996].

References

Agathonos-Georgopoulou H., & Browne K. D. (1997). The prediction of child maltreatment in Greek families. *Child Abuse & Neglect; 21,* 721-735.

Ammerman, T. R., Hersen, M., Van Hasselt, V. B., Lubetsky, M. J., & Sieck, W. R. (1994). Maltreatment in psychiatrically hospitalised children and adolescent with developmental disabilities: prevalence and correlates. *Journal of the American Academy of Child and Adolescent Psychiatry, 33*: 567-576.

Asdigian, N. L., & Straus MA. (2001). *There was an old woman who lived in a shoe: number of children and corporal punishment.* http://pubpages.unh.edu/~mas2/. Accessed on 3rd November 2002.

Bank, L., Forgatch, M. S., Patterson, G. R., & Fetrow. R. A. (1993). Parenting practices of single mothers: mediators of negative contextual factors. *Journal of Marriage and the Family, 55,* 371-384.

Baron, R. M., & Kenny, D. A. (1986). The moderator-mediator variable distinction in social psychological research: conceptual, strategic, and statistical considerations. *Journal of Personality and Social Psychology, 51,* 1173-1182.

Bauman, L. J. (1996). Response. Assessing the causal effect of childhood corporal punishment on adult violent behavior: methodological challenges. *Pediatrics, 98,* 842-844.

Baumrind, D. (1996). A blanket injunction against disciplinary use of spanking is not warranted by the data. *Pediatrics, 98,* 28-31.

Baumrind, D. (1997). Necessary distinctions. Commentary on "Externalizing behavior problems by culture, context, and gender" by Deater-Deckard, K. & Dodge, K. *Psychological Inquiry, 7,* 176-229.

Belsky, J. (1984).The determinants of parenting: A process model. *Child Development, 55,* 83-96.
Bentler, P. M. (1989). Comparative indexes in structural models. Psychological Bulletin, 107, 238-246.
Biernat, M., & Wortman, C. (1991). Sharing of home responsibilities between professionally employed women and their husbands. *Journal of Personality and Social Psychology, 8,* 423-440.
Campbell, J. J., & Frabutt, J. M. (1999, 1999). *Familial antecedents of children's overt and relational aggression.* Poster presented at the biennial meeting of the Society for Research in Child Development, Albuquerque, NM.
Cohen, J. (1996). Response. How can generative theories of the effects of punishment be tested. *Pediatrics, 98,* 834-836.
Cohen, P., Brook, J. S., Cohen, J., Velez, N., & Garcia, M. (1990). Common and uncommon pathways to adolescent psychopathology and problem behavior. In L. Robins, & M. Rutter (Eds.), *Straight and devious pathways from childhood to adulthood* (pp. 242-258). Cambridge: Cambridge University Press.
Coie, J. D., & Dodge, K. A. (1998). Aggression and anti social behavior. In W. Damon (Series Ed.), & N. Eisenberg (Vol. Ed.). *Handbook of child psychology: Social, emotional, and personality development* (5th Ed. Vol. 3. pp. 779-862). New York: John Wiley & Sons.
Creighton, S. J. (2004). *Prevalence and incidence of child abuse: international comparisons.* UK: NSPCC Research Department.
Culp, R. E., Culp, A. M., Dengler, B., & Maisano, P. (1999). First-time young mothers living in rural communities use corporal punishment with their toddlers. *Journal of Community Psychiatry, 27,* 503-509.
Darling, N., & Steinberg, L. (1993). Parenting style as context: an integrative model. *Psychological Bulletin, 113,* 487-496.
Day, D. E., Peterson, G. W., & McCrackors, C. (1998). Predicting spanking of younger and older children by mothers and fathers. *Journal of Marriage and the Family, 60,* 79-94.
Deater-Deckard, K., & Dodge, K. A. (1997). Externalizing behavior problems and discipline revisited: nonlinear effects and variation by culture, context, and gender. *Psychological Inquiry, 8,* 161-175.
Deater-Deckard, K., Dodge, K. A., Bates, J. E., & Pettit, G. S. (1996). Physical discipline among African American and European American mothers: Links to children's externalizing behavior. *Developmental Psychology, 32,* 1065-1072.
Department of Census & Statistics. (1997). *Statistical abstract of the Democratic Socialist Republic of Sri Lanka.* Colombo, Sri Lanka: Ministry of Finance, Planning, Ethnic Affairs and National Integration.
De Silva, D. G. H. (2001). Child abuse in Sri Lanka. In B. Schwartz-Kenney, M. McCauley, & M. A. Epstein (Eds.), *Child abuse: A global view* (pp. 223-240). Westport: Greenwood Press.
De Silva, D. G. H., De Zoysa, P., Kannangara, N. (2000). *Corporal punishment of children. Is it really necessary?* Colombo, Sri Lanka: National Child Protection Authority.
De Vaus, D. A. (1991). *Surveys in social research.* Australia: Allen & Unwin Pty Ltd.

De Zoysa, P. (2005). Parental use of physical force towards school children in the Colombo district: prevalence, psychosocial correlates and psychological consequences. Unpublished doctoral dissertation. University of Colombo, Sri Lanka.

De Zoysa, P., Rajapakse, L., & Newcombe, P. (2003). *Cross-cultural validation of research instruments: Preliminary validation of the Personality Assessment Questionnaire in Sri Lanka*. Paper presented at the 59th annual conference of the Sri Lanka Association for the Advancement of Science, Colombo, Sri Lanka.

De Zoysa, P., Rajapakse, L., & Newcombe, P. (2005). Adaptation and validation of the parent-child conflict tactics scale for use in Sri Lanka. *The Ceylon Medical Journal, 50,* 11-14.

Dietz, T. L. (2000). Disciplining children: Characteristics associated with the use of corporal punishment. *Child Abuse & Neglect, 24,* 1529-1542.

DiLalla, L. F., & Gottesman, I. I. (2000). Biological and genetic contributions to violence - Widom's untold tale. Psychological Bulletin, 109, 125-129.

Dishion, T. J, & Patterson GR. (1999). Model building in developmental psychology: a pragmatic approach to understanding and intervention. *Journal of Clinical Child Psychology, 28,* 502-512.

Dix, T. (1992). Parenting on behalf of the child: empathic goals in the regulation of responsive parenting. In I. E. Sigel, A. McGillicuddy-Delisi, & J. J. Goodnow (Eds.), *Parental belief systems* (2nd Ed, pp. 319-346). Mahwah, NJ: Erlbaum.

Dodge, K. A., Pettit, G. S., McClaskey, C. L., & Brown, M. M. (1986). Social competence in children. Monographs of the Society for Research in Child Development, 51: serial no. 213.

Durrant, J. E., & Rose-Krasnor, L. (1995). *Corporal punishment. Research review and policy recommendations* (pp. 7-9). Canada: The Family Violence Prevention Division of Health Canada and the Department of Justice Canada.

English, D. J. (1998). *The extent and consequences of child maltreatment. The future of children. Protecting children from abuse and neglect*. http://www.futureofchildren.org

Farber, E. A., & Egeland, B. (1987). Invulnerability among abuse and neglected children. In E. J. Anthony, & B. J. Cohen (Eds). *The invulnerable Child* (pp. 253-288). New York: Guildford Press.

Flynn, C. P. (1996). Regional differences in spanking experiences and attitudes: A comparison of Northeastern and Southern college students. *Journal of Family Violence, 11,* 59-80.

Freidman, S. B, & Schonberg, S. K. (1996). The short- and long-term consequences of corporal punishment. *Pediatrics, 98,* 22-25.

Frias-Armenta, M., McCloskey, L. A. (1998). Determiners of harsh parenting in Mexico. *Journal of*
Abnormal Child Psychology, 26, 129-39

Fry, D. P. (1993). The intergenerational transmission of disciplinary practices and approaches to conflict. *Human Organization, 52,* 176-185.

Gelles, R. J., Cornell, C. P. (1990). Intimate violence in families. (2nd ed., pp. 24-69). Beverly Hills,
CA: Sage.

Gershoff, E. T. (2002). Corporal Punishment by parents and associated child behaviors and experiences: A macro-analysis and theoretical review. *Psychological Bulletin, 128,* 539-579.

Gershoff, E. T., Miller, P. C., & Holden, G. W. (1999). Parenting influences from the pulpit: religious affiliation as a determinant of parental corporal punishment. *Journal of Family Psychology, 13,* 307-320.

Greenfield, P. M., & Suzuki, L. K. (1998). Culture and human development: implications for parenting, education, pediatrics, and mental health. In W. Damon (Series Ed.), I. E. Sigel, & K. A. Renninger (Vol. Eds.). *Handbook of child Psychology: child psychology in practice* (5th Ed, Vol. 4, 1059-1090). New York: John Wiley.

Greven, P. (1991). *Spare the child: the religious roots of physical punishment and the psychological impact of physical abuse.* New York: Knopf.

Grusec, J. E. (1993). The internalization of altruistic dispositions: a cognitive analysis. In E. T. Higgins, D. N. Ruble, & W. W. Hartrup (Eds.), *Social cognition and social development* (pp. 275-293). New York: Cambridge University Press.

Grusec, J. E., & Goodnow, J. J. (1994). Impact of parental discipline methods on the child's internalisation of values: a reconceptualisation of current points of view. *Developmental Psychology, 30,* 2-5.

Grusec, J. E., Rudy, D., & Marhni, T. (1997). Parenting cognitions and child constructs: an overview and implications for children's internalization of values. In J. E. Grusec, & L. Kuczynski (Eds.), *Parenting and child internalisation of values: A handbook of contemporary theory* (pp. 259-282). New York: Wiley.

Gunnoe, M. L., & Mariner, C. L. (1997). Towards a developmental-contextual model of the effects of parental spanking on children's aggression. *Archives in Pediatric Adolescent Medicine, 151,* 768-775.

Haeuser, A. A. (1991, September). *Reaffirming physical punishment of child-rearing as one root of physical abuse.* Paper presented at the 9th National Conference on Child Abuse and Neglect, Colorado, Denver.

Haj-Yahia, M., & Ben-Arieh, A. (2000). The incidence of Arab adolescents exposure to violence in their families of origin and its socio-demogrpahic correlates. *Child Abuse and Neglect, 24,* 1299-1315.

Haj-Yahia, M., & Musleh, K. (2002). The incidence of adolescent maltreatment in Arab society and some of its psychological effects. *Journal of Family Issues, 33,* 1032-1064.

Hall, C. S., & Lindzey, G. (1991). *Theories of personality* (3rd Ed.) Delhi: Wiley Eastern Limited.

Hart, C. H., & Robinson, C. C. (1994). Comparative study of maternal and paternal disciplinary strategies. *Psychological Reports, 74,* 495-498.

Heyman, R. E., & Smith Slep, A. M. (2001). Risk factors for family violence: introduction to the special series. *Aggression and Violent Behaviour, 6,* 115-119.

Holden, G. W. (2002). Perspectives of the effects of corporal punishment: comment on Gershoff. *Psychological Bulletin, 128,* 590-595.

Holden, G. W., Coleman, S. M., & Schmidt, K. L. (1995). Why 3-year-old children get spanked: parent and child determinants as reported by college-educated mothers. *Merrill-Palmer Quarterly, 41,* 431-452.

Holden, G. W., Thompson, E. E., Zambarano, R. J., & Marshall, L. A. (1997). Child effects as a source of change in maternal attitudes toward corporal punishment. *Journal of Social and Personal Relationships, 14,* 481-490.

Houston, A. C. (1983). Sex-typing. In P. I. T. Mussen (Series Ed.), & E. M. Hetherington (Vol. Ed.). *Handbook of child psychology: socialisation, personality, and social development* (4th Ed, Vol. 4, pp. 384-467). New York: Wiley.

Howard, B. J. (1996). Advising parents on discipline: what works. *Pediatrics, 98,* 809-815.

Hughes, H. M. (1998). Psychosocial and behavioral correlates of family violence in child witnesses and victims. *American Journal of Orthopsychiatry, 58,* 77-90.

Joreskog, K. G, & Sorbom, D. (1986). *PRELIS: a preprocessor for LISREL.* Mooresville, IN: Scientific Software, Inc.

Joreskog, K. G., & Sorbom, D. (2004). *LISREL 8.7.* Lincolnwood, IL: Scientific Software International.

Kadushin, A., & Martin, J. A. (1999). *Child abuse. An international event. Educational, psychological and sociological inquiry.* New York: Columbia University Press.

Kempe, C. H. (1991). Preface. In J. Korbin (Ed.), *Child abuse and neglect. Cross-cultural perspectives.* Berkley, CA: University of California Press.

Krug, E. G., Dahlberg, L., Mercy, J. A., Zwi, A. B., & Lozano, R. (Eds.). (2002). *World report on violence and health.* Geneva: World Health Organisation.

Kim, D., Kim, K., Park, Y., Zhang, L. D., & Lu, M. K. (2000). Children's experience of violence in China and Korea: A trans-cultural study. *Child Abuse and Neglect, 24,* 1163-1173.

Kuczynski, L., & Hilderbrant, N. (1997). Models of conformity and resistance in socialisation theory. In J. E. Grusec, & L. Kuczynski (Eds.), *Parenting the internalisation of values: A handbook of contemporary theory* (pp. 227-256). New York: Wiley.

Lasky, M. R. (1993). Family genesis of aggression. *Psychiatric Annals, 23,* 494-499.

Larzelere, R. E. (1994). Should the use of corporal punishment by parents be considered child abuse? No. In M. A. Mason, & E. Gambrill (Eds.), *Debating children's lives: current controversies on children and adolescents* (pp. 202-209). Thousand Oaks, CA: Sage.

Larzelere, R. E. (1996). A review of the outcomes of parental use of nonabusive or customary physical punishment. *Pediatrics, 98,* 824-828.

Larzelere, R. E. (2000). Child outcomes of non abusive and customary physical punishment by parents: An updated literature review. *Clinical Child and Family Psychology Review, 3,* 199-221.

Larzelere, R. E. (2001). Combining love and limits in authoritative parenting. In J. C. Westman (Ed.), *Parenthood in America. Undervalued, underpaid and under siege* (pp. 81-89). Madison, WI: University of Wisconsin Press.

Larzelere, R. E., & Merenda, J. A. (1994). The effectiveness of parental discipline for toddler misbehavior at different levels of child distress. *Family Relations, 43,* 480-488.

Larzelere, R. E., Silver, C., & Polite, K. (1997). Nonabusive spanking: Parental liberty or child abuse? *Children's Legal Rights Journal, 17,* 7-17.

Lau, J. T. F., Liu, J. L. Y., Cheung, J. C. K., Yu, A., & Wong, C.K. (1999). Prevalence and correlates of physical abuse in Hong Kong Chinese adolescents: a population based approach. *Child Abuse and Neglect, 23,* 549-557.

Lepper, M. R. (1983). Social control processes and the internalisation of social values: An attributional perspective. In E. T. Higgins, D. N. Ruble, & W. W. Hartup (Eds.), *Social cognition and social development* (9th Ed., pp. 294-300). New York: Cambridge University Press.

Loeber, R., Dinkwater, M., Yim, Y., Anderson, S. J., Schmidt, L. L., & Crawford A. (2000). Stability of family interaction from ages 6 to 18. *Journal of Abnormal Child Psychology, 28,* 353-369.

Lyons, J. S., & Larzelere, R. E. (1996, August). *Where is the evidence that non-abusive corporal punishment increases aggression?* Poster Presentation at the XXVI International Congress of Psychology, Canada, Montreal.

Mahoney, A., Donnelly, W. O., Lewis, T., & Maynard, C. (2000). Mother and father self reports of corporal punishment and severe physical aggression toward clinic referred youth. *Journal of Clinical Child Psychology, 29,* 266-281.

Mason, C. A., Cauce, A. M, Gonzales, N., & Hiraga, Y. (1996). *Neither too sweet nor too sour: Problem peers, maternal control, and problem behavior in African American adolescents.* Thousand Oakes, CA: Sage.

Mausner, J. S., & Kramer, S. (1985). *Epidemiology: an introductory Text.* Philadelphia, PA: WB Saunders.

McCord, J. (1997a). On discipline. *Psychological Inquiry, 8,* 215-217.

McCord, J. (1997b). Some child-rearing antecedents of criminal behavior in adult men. *Journal of Personality and Social Psychology, 37,* 1477-1486.

McLoyd, V. C., Jayaratne, T. E., Ceballo, R., & Borquez, J. (1994). Unemployment and work interruption among African American single mothers. Effects on parenting and adolescents socioemotional functioning. *Child Development, 65,* 562-589.

Milner, J. S., Robertson, K. R, & Rogers, D. C. (1990). Childhood history of abuse and adult child abuse potential. *Journal of Family Violence, 3,* 15-34.

Moldrich, D. (1986). Somewhere a child is crying. Colombo: Ceylon Printers Ltd.

Mrazek, P. J., & Haggerty, R. J. (1994). *Reducing risks for disorders: frontliners for preventive intervention.* Washington DC: National Academy Press.

Narada Thera. (1972). *Dhammapada. Pali text and translation with stories in brief and notes.* Colombo: The Colombo Apothecaries' Co. Ltd.

Newsom, C., Flarell, J. E., & Rincover, A. (1983). The side effects of punishment. In S. Axelrod, & J. Apsche (Eds.), *The effects of punishment in human behavior* (pp. 285-316). New York: Academic Press.

O'Connor, T. G., Deater-Deckard, K., Fulker, D., Rutter, M., & Plomin, R. (1998). Genotype-environment correlation in late childhood and early adolescence: antisocial behavioural problems and coercive parenting. *Developmental Psychology, 34,* 970-981.

Paolucci, E. O., & Violato, C. (2004). A meta-analysis of published research on the cognitive and behavioural effects of corporal punishment. *The Journal of Psychology, 138,* 197-221.

Paquette, D., Bolte, C., Tucotte, G., Dubeau, D., & Bouchard, C. (2000). A new typology of fathering: defining and associated variables. *Infant and Child Development, 9,* 213-230.

Parke, R. D. (2002). Punishment revisited - science values and the right question: Comment on Gershoff, 2002. *Psychological Bulletin, 128,* 596-601.

Peisher, E. S. (1989). To spare or not to spare the rod: a cultural-historical view of child discipline. In J. Valsiner (Ed.), *Child development in cultural context* (pp. 111-141). Lewiston, NY: Hogrefe & Huber.

Peltoniemi, T. (1983). Child abuse and physical punishment of children in Finland. *Child Abuse and Neglect, 7,* 33-36.

Pinderhughes, E. E., Dodge, K. A., Bates, J. E., Pettit, G. S., & Zelli, A. (2000). Discipline responses: Influences of parent's socio-economic status, ethnicity, beliefs about parenting, stress and cognitive-emotional processes. *Journal of Family Psychology, 14,* 380-400.

Ritchie, J., & Ritchie, J. (1981). *Spare the rod.* Australia: Allen and Unwin.

Rodriguez, C. M., & Sutherland, D. (1999). Predictions of parents physical disciplinary practices. *Child Abuse and Neglect, 23,* 651-657.

Rohner, R. P. (1999). *Handbook for the study of parental acceptance and rejection.* USA: Rohner Research.

Rohner, R. P., Bourque, S. L., & Elordi, C. A. (1996). Childrens' perceptions of corporal punishment, caretaker acceptance, and psychological adjustment in a poor, biracial southern community. *Journal of Marriage and the Family, 58,* 842-852.

Rohner, R. P., Kean, K. J., & Cournoyer, D. E. (1991). Effects of corporal punishment, perceived caretaker warmth, and cultural beliefs on the psychological adjustment of children in St. Kitts, West Indies. *Journal of Marriage and the Family, 53,* 681-693.

Runyan, D. K. (1998). Children who prosper in unfavourable environments: the relationship to social

 capital. *Pediatrics, 110,* 12-18

Rutter, M., Giller, H., & Hagell, A. (1998). Emotional development: action, communication, and understanding. In W. Damon (Series Ed.), & N. Eisenberg (Vol. Ed.), *Handbook of Child Psychology: social, emotional, and personality development* (5th Ed., Vol. 3, pp. 237-309). New York: Wiley.

Save the Children. (2001). *Ending corporal punishment of children: making it happen.* Sweden: Save the Children.

Silverman, A. B., Reinherz, H. Z., & Gioconia, R. M. (1994). The long-term sequelae of child and adolescent abuse: a longitudinal community study. *Child Abuse and Neglect, 20,* 707-723.

Simons, R. L., Lin, K., & Gordon, L. R. (1998). Socialisation in the family of origin and male dating violence: a prospective study. *Journal of Marriage and the Family, 60,* 467-478.

Simons, R. L., Lorenz, F. O., Wu, C., Congeer, R. D. (1993). Social network and marital support as mediators and moderators of the impact of stress and depression on parental behavior. *Developmental Psychology, 29,* 368-381.

Simons, R. L., Whitbeck, L. B., Melby, J. N., & Wu, C. (1994). Economic pressure and harsh parenting. In R. D. Conger, & G. H. Elder Jr. (Eds.), *Families in troubled times: Adapting to change in rural America* (pp. 207-222). New York: Aldine de Gruyter.

Sivanayagam, S. (2005). *Sri Lanka: witness to history. A journalist's memoirs 1930-2004.* London: Sivayogam.

Smith, J. R., & Brooks-Gunn, J. (1997). Correlates and consequences of harsh discipline for young children. *Archives of Pediatric and Adolescent Medicine, 151,* 777-786.

SPSS. (1998). *For Windows® brief guide.* 10th Version. New Jersey: Prentice-Hall, Inc.

Stolley, K. S., & Szinovacz, M. (1997). Caregiving responsibilities and child spanking. *Journal of Family Violence, 12,* 99-112.

Strassberg, Z., Dodge, K. A., Pettit, G.S., & Bates, J. E. (1994). Spanking in the home and children's subsequent aggression towards kindergarten peers. *Development and Psychopathology, 6,* 445-61.

Straus, M. A. (1994). *Beating the devil out of them: Corporal punishment in American Families.* San Francisco: Jossey-Bass/Lexington Books.

Straus, M. A. (2000). Corporal punishment of children and adult depression and suicidal ideation. In J. MacCord (Ed.), *Coercion and punishment in long term perspective* (pp. 92-114). New York: Cambridge University Press.

Straus, M. A. (2001). The benefits of never spanking: new and more definitive evidence. In M. A. Straus (Ed.), *Beating the devil out of them: corporal punishment in American Families and its effects on children* (2nd Ed., pp. 193-217). New Brunswik, NJ: Transaction.

Straus, M. A, & Gimpel, H. S. (1992, August). *Corporal punishment by parents and economic achievement: a theoretical model and some preliminary empirical data.* Paper presented at the 1992 meeting of the American Sociological Association, Pennsylania, Pittsburgh.

Straus, M. A., Hamby, S. L., Finklehor, D., Moore, D. W., & Runyan, D. (1998). Identification of child maltreatment with the parent-child conflict tactics scales: Development and psychometric data for a national sample of American parents. *Child Abuse and Neglect, 22,* 249-270.

Straus, M. A., & Mathur, A. K. (1995, April). *Corporal punishment of adolescents and academic achievement.* Paper presented at the annual meeting of the Pacific Sociological Association, California, San Francisco.

Straus, M. A., & Mourdian, V. E. (1998). Impulsive corporal punishment by mothers and antisocial behaviors and impulsiveness in children. *Behavioral Sciences and the Law, 16,* 353-374.

Straus M. A., & Runyan, D. I. (1997). Physical abuse. In: Friedman, M., Stanford, B., Fisher, M.M., Schonberg, S.K., & Alderma,n E. M. eds. *Comprehensive Adolescent Health Care* (2nd Ed., PP. 723-28). St Louis, MO: Mosby-Year Book, inc.

Straus, M. A., & Smith, C. (1992). Family patterns and child abuse. In M. A. Straus, & R. S. Gelles (Eds.), *Physical violence in American families: risk factors and adaptations to violence in 8,145 families* (pp. 245-261). New Brunswick, NJ: Transaction.

Straus MA, Stewart J. H. (1999). Corporal punishment by American parents: National data on prevalence, chronicity, severity and duration, in relation to child and family characteristics. *Clinics of Child Family Psychology Review, 2,* 55-70.

Straus, M. A., Sugarman, D. B., & Giles-Sims, J. (1997). Spanking by parents and subsequent antisocial behavior of children. *Archives of Pediatric and Adolescent Medicine, 151,* 761-767.

Straus, M. A, & Yodanis, C. L. (1994). Physical abuse. In M. A. Straus (Ed.), *Beating the devil out of them: corporal punishment* (pp. 81-97). San Francisco, CA: Jossey-Bass/Lexington Books.

Swinford, S. P., De Maris, A., Cernkovich, S. A., & Giardano, P. C. (2000). Harsh physical discipline in childhood and violence in later romantic involvements: The mediating role of problem behaviors. *Journal of Marriage and the Family, 62,* 508-519.

Tabachnick, B. G., & Fidell, L. S. (1996). *Using multivariate statistics* (3rd Ed.). New York: Harper Collins.

Ten Bensel, R. W., Rheinberger, M. M., & Radbill, S. X. (1997). Children in a world of violence: the roots of child maltreatment. In R. E. Helfer, K. S. Kempe, & R. D. Krugman (Eds.), *The battered child.* (pp. 3-28). Chicago, IL: University of Chicago Press.

Ullman, J. B. (1996). Structural Equation Modeling. In B. G. Tabachnick, & L. S. Fidell (Eds.), *Using multivariate statistics* (3rd Ed., pp. 712-715). New York: HarperCollins.

United Nations Convention on the Right's of the Child. (1989). *Rights of the Child.* http://www.uncrc.info/:Convention. Accessed on 23rd August 2001.

Vander Zanden, J. W. (1997). *Human development.* New York: The McGraw-Hill Companies, Inc.

Whaley, A. L. (2000). Socio-cultural differences in the developmental consequences of the use of physical discipline during childhood for African Americans. *Cultural Diversity and Ethnic Minority Psychology, 6,* 5-12.

White, K. (1993). Where pediatricians stand on spanking. *Pediatric Management, September,* 11-15.

White, G.O, & Straus, M. A. (1981). The implications of family violence for rehabilitation strategies. In Martin, S. E., Sechrest, L. B., Redner, R., (Eds.), *New directions in the rehabilitation of criminal offenders* (pp. 255-288). Washington DC: National Academy Press.

Wilson, J. Q., & Herrnstein, R. J. (1985). *Crime and human nature.* New York: Simon & Schuster.

Wissow, L. S. (2001). Ethnicity, income, and parenting contexts of physical punishment in a national sample of families with young children. *Child Maltreatment, 6,* 118-129.

Xu, X., Tvng, Y., & Dunaway, R. G. (2000). Cultural, human and social capital as determinants of corporal punishment: toward an integrated theoretical model. *Journal of Interpersonal Violence, 15,* 603-630.

Yamamoto, M., Iwata, N., Tomoda, A., Tanaka, S., Fujimaki, K., & Kitamura, T. (1999). Child emotional and physical maltreatment psychopathology: a community study in Japan. *Journal of Community Psychology, 27,* 377-392.

Youssef, R. M., Attia, M. S., & Kamel, M. I. (1998). Children experiencing violence I: parental use of corporal punishment. *Child Abuse and Neglect, 22,* 959-973.

Zigler, E. L., & Hall, N. W. (1989). Physical child abuse in America: past, present and future. In D. Cicchetti, & V. Carlson (Eds.), *Child maltreatment. Theory and research on the causes and consequences of child abuse and neglect* (pp. 38-75). New York: Cambridge University Press.

Index

A

abdomen, 60, 70
abortion, 22
abuse, viii, 19, 20, 21, 22, 23, 24, 25, 26, 29, 30, 31, 32, 33, 34, 35, 36, 37, 38, 39, 40, 42
abusive parenting, viii, 19, 33
academic performance, 98, 104, 105
acceptance, 32, 39
access, 25, 74, 87, 92, 95
accidents, 76
accuracy, 3, 5, 16
achievement, 31, 102, 112, 127, 160
acid, 61
activation, 74
Adam Walsh Child Protection and Safety Act, ix, 81, 83
adaptation, 55, 56, 134, 135
addiction, xi, 116, 117, 118
adipose, 60
adipose tissue, 60
Adjusted Goodness of Fit Index (AGFI), 140, 142
adjustment, 45, 54, 103, 106, 108, 110, 111, 140, 150, 159
administration, 134, 136, 137, 139
adolescence, viii, 19, 20, 21, 22, 23, 24, 26, 31, 32, 33, 38, 42, 111, 158
adolescent female, 24
adolescent(s), viii, x, 19, 20, 21, 22, 23, 24, 25, 26, 31, 32, 33, 34, 35, 36, 37, 38, 39, 40, 41, 42, 46, 97, 99, 100, 101, 102, 104, 105, 106, 107, 109, 110, 111, 112, 156, 157, 158, 160
adrenal gland, 62, 68

adulthood, viii, 19, 20, 21, 22, 23, 24, 25, 26, 31, 33, 35, 38, 52, 103, 104, 105, 109, 127, 154
adult(s), x, xi, 3, 21, 27, 28, 29, 30, 31, 32, 34, 45, 91, 92, 99, 100, 111, 115, 116, 117, 118, 123, 126, 135
advertising, 46
affect, 23, 40
African American(s), 37, 154, 158, 161
age, vii, xi, 1, 2, 3, 4, 6, 8, 10, 11, 12, 15, 21, 24, 25, 34, 39, 45, 47, 49, 50, 65, 73, 82, 91, 100, 102, 104, 122, 124, 128, 133, 148
aggression, 100, 102, 103, 105, 126, 127, 132, 134, 135, 136, 151, 154, 156, 157, 158, 160
alcohol, viii, x, 38, 43, 103, 104, 106, 107, 108, 109, 115, 118, 119, 126
alcohol abuse, 38, 107, 108, 109
alcohol consumption, 38, 103
alcoholics, 110, 111, 112
alcoholism, 106, 107, 111
alienation, 105, 106, 107
alternatives, 133, 137
amendments, 83, 84
America Online, 91
American Civil Liberties Union, 90
American culture, 111
American Psychiatric Association, 56
American Psychological Association, 16
amino, 61
anemia, 68
anger, 102, 105, 109, 126, 129, 135
ankles, 67
annual rate, 148
anorexia, 99
antisocial behavior, 126, 127, 130, 158, 160, 161
anus, 60
anxiety, 41, 44, 46, 102, 104, 105, 126, 139

apoptosis, 74, 78
appraisals, 23, 40
arrest, 65, 126
Asia, 148
Asian, x, 48, 98, 106, 110, 111, 148
Asian American, 110
Asian countries, 148
asphyxia, 71, 72
aspiration, 71, 72
assault, 52, 55, 82, 84, 87, 134
assertiveness, 126
assessment, 17, 46, 107, 108
assignment, 94
assumptions, 47, 65, 117, 133, 140
attachment, 44, 103, 105
attention, vii, x, 1, 3, 7, 13, 15, 35, 44, 59, 75, 97, 98, 103, 115, 116, 117
attitudes, 39, 45, 60, 103, 105, 117, 125, 155, 157
Attorney General, 82
attribution, 44, 52, 53
auditory hallucinations, 98
Australia, 109, 121, 154, 159
authority, ix, 81
autopsy, 62, 65, 67, 69, 73, 79
availability, 92, 95, 107
avoidance, 52
awareness, xii, 45, 75, 122, 148, 151

B

behavior(s), xi, 4, 9, 14, 41, 47, 100, 102, 103, 104, 105, 110, 112, 115, 122, 123, 124, 126, 127, 129, 130, 131, 153, 154, 158, 159, 161
behavior of children, 161
behavioral change, 123
behavioral dispositions, 135
behavioral problems, 103, 123
behaviorists, 123
belief systems, 155
beliefs, viii, 3, 22, 37, 41, 43, 44, 45, 46, 53, 54, 103, 128, 159
benefits, 123, 125, 160
betrayal, 55
bias, 135, 137
binge drinking, 119
biological parents, 152
birth, 20, 21, 24, 25, 33, 37, 38, 39, 41
blame, 44, 45, 52, 53, 55, 56
blocks, 30, 50
blood, 68, 100

body, 20
body fat, 65, 74
body weight, 63, 64, 65, 74, 75
bonds, 109
bowel, 60
boys, 6, 101, 109
brain, 127
breast cancer, 92
breathing, 65
bronchus, 74
brothers, 70
buffer, 52, 130, 132, 149, 150
burn, 67

C

California, 91, 157, 160
caloric intake, 65
campaigns, 87, 116
Canada, 19, 20, 25, 33, 34, 36, 37, 40, 42, 101, 155, 158
Canadian, viii, 19, 40
cancer, 92
cardiac arrest, 65
caregivers, 151, 152
caretaker, vii, 76, 159
case study, 17, 40
cast, 71
categorization, 137
Catholic, 133
causal inference, 153
causal relationship, 52, 53
causality, 127, 150, 151
cell, 78
census, 42, 133, 149, 154
cerebral hemisphere, 69, 70
certainty, 70, 77
Chicago, 13, 42, 161
child abuse, viii, ix, 12, 16, 17, 19, 20, 21, 22, 23, 24, 25, 26, 27, 29, 30, 31, 32, 33, 34, 35, 36, 37, 38, 39, 40, 41, 42, 59, 60, 63, 74, 75, 76, 78, 79, 87, 110, 111, 112, 154, 157, 158, 160, 162
child development, 123
child maltreatment, vii, 16, 39, 40, 41, 42, 55, 102, 108, 110, 113, 153, 155, 160, 161
Child Online Protection Act (COPA), ix, 89, 90, 91, 92, 93
child poverty, 40
child protection, 83, 107, 125, 151
child rearing, 106, 152

Index

childbearing, 40, 41
childcare, 123, 124, 129
childhood, viii, x, 14, 17, 43, 50, 51, 52, 54, 55, 56, 57, 76, 97, 100, 101, 102, 103, 104, 105, 108, 109, 111, 112, 126, 127, 131, 153, 154, 158, 161
childhood sexual abuse (CSA), viii, 43, 44, 45, 46, 48, 51, 52, 53, 54, 56, 57, 97, 99, 100, 101, 102, 103, 104, 105, 106, 108, 109, 111, 112
childrearing, 31, 32, 34, 37
Children's Internet Protection Act (CIPA), ix, 89, 90, 92, 94
China, 148, 157
Chinese, 100, 112, 158
choroid, 60
cigarette smoking, 103
classes, 41, 82, 107
classroom, 4, 112, 134
cleaning, 98
clinical approach, 53
cluster analysis, 108
clusters, 49
codes, 83
coding, 7
cognition, 14, 56, 156, 158
cognitive ability, 127
cognitive development, 127
cognitive disorders, 47
cognitive performance, 127
cognitive processing, 52
cohesion, 107
cohort, 41
college students, x, 97, 112, 116, 117, 119, 155
colleges, 116, 117
colonization, 123
Columbia University, 157
commerce, 83, 84
common law, 26
common symptoms, 102
communication, 17, 91, 93, 94, 106, 126, 159
communication skills, 106
Communications Decency Act (CDA), ix, 89, 90, 91, 94
community, ix, x, xi, 27, 39, 46, 59, 76, 79, 86, 91, 103, 111, 115, 116, 118, 122, 123, 129, 131, 137, 148, 149, 152, 159, 161
Community, 19
comorbidity, 111
Comparative Fit Index (CFI), 140, 142
compassion, 123
compensation, 34

competence, vii, 1, 3, 13, 41, 103, 106, 155
complex, 33
complexity, 36, 105
compliance, 16, 81, 125
complications, 38, 101
components, 107
comprehension, 117
compulsive behavior, 104
computation, 138, 140
computers, 92
concentration, 99
concept, 40, 41, 42
conceptual model, viii, 43, 44, 45, 51, 52, 54
conceptualization, 55
concrete, 3
confidence, 53, 103, 126, 139
confidentiality, 139
conflict, 32, 98, 106, 132, 148, 149, 151, 155, 160
conflict resolution, 132
conformity, 157
confusion, 21, 22, 23, 24, 33, 35
Congress, ix, 89, 90, 91, 92, 93, 94, 158
consensus, 12, 100
consent, 47, 133
consequence, 38
conspiracy, 82
Constitution, 90
constraints, 133, 153
construction, 98
consumption, 38, 103
context, 37, 38
contexts, 37
contracture, 60, 61, 74
control, 4, 5, 6, 12, 27, 28, 30, 35, 36, 42, 44, 53, 84, 102, 103, 111, 122, 127, 129, 153, 158
control group, 53, 102
conviction, 82, 83, 85, 86, 101
cooking, 98
coping, 36
coping strategies, 36, 56
corporal punishment, xi, 121, 122, 123, 124, 125, 126, 127, 128, 129, 130, 131, 132, 133, 134, 137, 142, 145, 148, 149, 150, 151, 153
correlation(s), 23, 49, 50, 140, 158
correlational analysis, 51
cortex, 74
Costa Rica, 101
Court of Appeals, 91
covering, xi, 115
creatine, 68

creativity, 148
crime, ix, 2, 17, 59, 76, 83, 84, 86, 87, 90, 93
criminal acts, 105, 106, 107
criminal behavior, 126, 158
criminal justice system, 149
criminality, 125, 126, 131
criticism, 52
cross-sectional study, xi, 53, 121
CRS, ix, 81, 90, 91, 92, 94, 95
crying, 76, 158
CTSPC, xi, 121, 133, 134, 136, 137, 139, 151, 152
cues, 7
cultural beliefs, 159
cultural differences, 161
cultural factors, 110
cultural norms, 152
cultural perspective, 157
culture, 37, 123, 124, 125, 130, 132, 151, 152, 153, 154
cycles, 126

D

data analysis, 27
data collection, x, 97, 101
data gathering, 107
dating, 159
death, vii, 63, 64, 68, 69, 70, 71, 74, 75, 76, 84, 85, 105, 106
decision(s), ix, xi, 25, 89, 116, 118
decubitus ulcer, 74
deficiency, 73
deficit(s), xi, 64, 65, 74, 75, 78, 116, 117, 132, 149, 153
definition, x, 20, 90, 91, 97, 100, 101, 122
degrees of freedom, 140
dehydration, 74
delinquency, 82, 100
delinquent adolescents, 100
delinquent behavior, 110, 131
delirium, 47
delivery, 22
demand, 116
dementia, 47
demographics, 136
denial, x, 98
Denmark, 39, 110
density, 40
Department of Commerce, 93, 95
Department of Justice, 87, 91, 92, 155

depression, 41, 44, 46, 56, 98, 100, 102, 103, 104, 105, 106, 107, 126, 159, 160
depressive symptomatology, 126
deprivation, 40, 75, 78
designers, 152
desire, 103
destruction, 56
detection, 45, 77
detention, 84
developmental disabilities, 129, 153
developmental psychology, 155
developmental psychopathology, 55
deviant behaviour, 117
diagnostic criteria, 49
differences, 27, 40
differentiation, 25
dignity, 105
directives, 11
disability, 13
discipline, 34, 123, 124, 125, 126, 127, 129, 130, 134, 148, 151, 153, 154, 156, 157, 158, 159, 160, 161
disclosure, x, 2, 7, 45, 98, 107, 109
discontinuity, 113
discourse, 7
disorder, viii, 17, 43, 55, 56, 57, 73, 112
disposition, 127
dissatisfaction, 106
dissociation, 14, 44, 46, 98
distortions, 54, 56, 110
distress, 45, 49, 51, 102, 104, 126, 157
distribution, 25
District of Columbia, 82
diversity, 53
divorce, 34, 105, 106
dizziness, 99
DNA, 82, 83, 86
doctors, 60, 65
domestic chores, 98
domestic violence, 149, 150
Dominican Republic, 101
doors, 42
Dot Kids, ix, 89, 93
draft, 90
drug abuse, 103, 116, 119
drug addict, xi, 116, 118
drug addiction, xi, 116, 118
drug trafficking, 83
drug use, 100, 116, 117, 118
drugs, viii, x, xi, 43, 115, 116, 117, 118

drying, 60
DSM-IV, 47, 49
due process, 82
dura mater, 70
duration, viii, 43, 45, 47, 49, 50, 51, 74, 160
duties, 99

E

eating, 98, 103, 104
eating disorders, 103
economic status, 126, 128, 159
edema, 60, 61, 74
education, viii, 19, 22, 24, 26, 27, 28, 29, 31, 32, 35, 37, 38, 40, 41, 48, 53, 59, 78, 79, 92, 102, 108, 118, 125, 152, 156
educational attainment, 22, 24, 25, 27, 31, 32, 127
educators, 76
effective, 33, 36
electrodes, 66, 67
eligibility criteria, 46
emotional abuse, vii
emotional processes, 159
emotional state, 128
emotions, 3, 6
empathy, 24
empirical research, 20
employability, 23, 32
employment, viii, 19, 23, 24, 25, 26, 28, 29, 31, 32, 36, 37, 38
employment status, 24, 25, 26, 28, 31
empowerment, 92
energy, 73, 74
England, 4, 15
environment, x, xi, 33, 35, 38, 40, 41, 93, 105, 115, 116, 117, 118, 132, 158
epidemic, 59
epidemiology, 109
Erikson's theory, viii, 20, 24, 31, 35
estimating, 74, 75, 133
ethnic background, 47
ethnic groups, 122, 125, 126
ethnicity, 37, 159
etiology, 53, 126
Europe, 101
evening, 98
evidence, x, 2, 12, 13, 14, 21, 51, 73, 76, 77, 84, 97, 106, 107, 109, 123, 124, 125, 127, 149, 152, 158, 160
evil, 94

examinations, 48
exclusion, 54
excretion, 92
expectations, 24
experimental design, 153
explicit memory, 47
exploitation, vii, 83, 84, 85, 105
exposure, 6, 23, 32, 52, 95, 101, 106, 109, 130, 156
externalizing behavior, 103, 154
eyes, 24, 60

F

fabric, 124
factors, 41, 42
failure, vii, 60, 76, 83, 135
failure to thrive, 76
fairness, 131, 137, 138, 150
families, 23, 24, 25, 28, 33, 34, 37, 39, 40, 42
family, x, 6, 7, 25, 29, 33, 37, 42, 44, 54, 98, 99, 100, 101, 103, 104, 105, 106, 107, 108, 109, 110, 111, 112, 126, 128, 130, 132, 149, 152, 156, 157, 158, 159, 160, 161
family conflict, 106
family environment, 105, 106
family functioning, 54, 108, 112
family members, x, 6, 7, 98, 99, 100, 106, 107
family violence, 109, 156, 157, 161
fat, 60, 61, 65, 74
fear(s), 6, 100, 102, 107, 126, 134
feces, 60
federal criminal law, ix, 81, 84
federal funds, 92
federal government, 94
federal law, 81, 90
feedback, 4, 15
feelings, 32, 33, 36, 52, 98, 103, 104, 126, 130
feet, 60, 61, 74
females, xi, 5, 6, 24, 53, 99, 100, 101, 122
fetus, 38
Filipino, 111
filters, 91, 95
financial support, 105
Finland, 4, 129, 159
First Amendment, 90, 91, 94
flooding, 104
focus groups, 122
food, 63, 75
forensic, vii, 1, 3, 4, 5, 12, 15, 16, 60, 76, 78

formerly adolescent mothers (FAMs), viii, 19, 20, 21, 22, 24, 25, 26, 27, 28, 29, 30, 31, 32, 33, 34, 35, 36, 37, 38
fragmentation, 46
France, 103
free recall, 4, 11
freedom, 94, 117, 140
frequency, 25
friendship, 39
fulfillment, 33
functioning, 21, 32
funding, 92
funds, 83, 92

G

GAO, 95
gender, 101, 126, 128, 153, 154
Geneva, 157
genitourinary tract, 76
gestures, 3
girls, 6, 42, 62, 64, 67, 101, 111, 133
gland, 62, 68
glass, 23
glucocorticoids, 74, 78
glycogen, 61, 73
goals, 22, 23, 155
Goodness of Fit Index (GFI), 140, 142
government, xi, 60, 82, 86, 87, 90, 91, 94, 121, 132, 133, 139, 151, 152
Government Accountability Office (GAO), 95
Greece, 101
group therapy, 47
groups, x, 8, 9, 10, 11, 25, 26, 27, 28, 30, 32, 34, 97, 98, 102, 104, 122, 125, 126, 134, 136, 137, 148, 152
growth, 38, 64, 127
guidance, 11, 135
guidelines, vii, 1, 4, 12, 82
guiding principles, xii, 122
guilt, viii, 43, 45, 46, 47, 50, 51, 52, 53, 54, 104
guilty, 98, 99

H

hallucinations, 98
hands, 71, 76, 152
harassment, 6
harm, vii, 23, 95, 123, 125, 151
Harvard, 40, 110

hazards, 125
health, x, xi, 31, 38, 40, 41, 60, 76, 77, 78, 97, 99, 100, 105, 107, 108, 111, 116, 117, 118, 128, 139, 156, 157
health care, 77
health education, 108
health problems, 38
heart, 62, 67
helplessness, 126
hemisphere, 69, 70
hemoglobin, 70
hemorrhage, 65, 66, 69, 71
heroin, 116
high school, 22, 26, 27, 28, 31, 35, 48, 90, 98, 119
higher quality, 12
hip, 21, 60
Hispanic, 48
HIV, viii, 43, 47, 53
HIV infection, viii, 43
homogeneity, 53
homosexuality, 92
Hong Kong, 100, 112, 158
hospitalization, 99, 105, 106
host, 149
hostility, 104, 151
household income, 47, 48
households, 42
human behavior, 14, 158
human development, 156
human nature, 161
human subjects, 47
humiliation, 126
Hurricane Andrew, 14
hyperactivity, 102
hypothesis, 27, 28, 29, 30, 31, 32, 51, 126, 127, 142, 149, 150

I

iatrogenic, 118
identification, 7, 77, 82, 108, 109, 110, 130
identity, viii, 19, 21, 22, 23, 24, 25, 26, 27, 30, 31, 32, 33, 35, 38, 41, 42, 43, 45, 46, 49, 50, 51, 52, 53, 54, 55
illusion, 56
images, 95
imprisonment, 83, 84, 85, 86, 94, 105, 106
impulsive, 99
impulsiveness, 160
in situ, 123

incidence, 2, 38, 154, 156
inclusion, 35, 37, 47, 54, 139
income, 34, 37, 41, 47, 48, 161
independence, 140
independent variable, 30, 49, 52, 54
India, 122
indicators, 76, 130, 133
indices, 40, 140, 142, 144
individual characteristics, 112
industrialized countries, 59
industry, 92
infants, 39, 75, 127
infection, viii, 43
inferences, 153
influence, 23, 40
informed consent, 47
initiation, x, 115, 117
injury(ies), 20, 76, 122
insane, 99
insight, 53
instability, 136
instruments, xi, 76, 121, 133, 139, 148, 155
intellectual development, 133
intellectual disabilities, 3
intensity, 65, 116, 153
interaction(s), 15, 37, 44, 53, 103, 106, 117, 127, 130, 158
internal consistency, 48, 49, 134, 136, 137, 139
internal working models, 32
internalization, 125, 156
internalizing, 103
internet, ix, 83, 85, 89, 91, 92, 93, 94
Internet Corporation for Assigned Names and Numbers (ICANN), 93
interpersonal relationships, 98, 99
interpretation, 151
interval, 134, 136
intervention, vii, 19, 20, 31, 38, 45, 107, 108, 118, 119, 128, 155, 158
interview(s), vii, 1, 2, 3, 4, 5, 6, 7, 8, 9, 12, 13, 14, 15, 16, 17, 46, 47, 99, 101, 107, 122, 136
intestine, 60
investment, 36
involution, 74, 78
isolation, 52
Israel, 4, 105, 106, 112

J

Japan, ix, 59, 60, 63, 76, 78, 79, 161

jobs, 36
joints, 60, 61, 74
judiciary, 94
jurisdiction, 82
justice, 149
juvenile delinquency, 82
juveniles, 95

K

kidney, 62, 68
killing, 84
kinase, 68
kindergarten, 160
knowledge, viii, 19, 38, 41
Korea, 97, 99, 100, 105, 106, 107, 108, 110, 148, 157
Korean, x, 97, 98, 100, 101, 104, 105, 106, 107, 110

L

language, 16, 17, 122, 133
later life, 40, 56, 103
law enforcement, ix, 81, 87, 95
laws, ix, 82, 89, 90, 92, 123, 124, 148
lead, xi, 22, 23, 29, 52, 115, 125, 126, 127, 129, 132, 149, 151
learning, 13, 17, 105, 125
legislation, 89, 90, 94
lesions, 65, 66, 67
life experiences, 38
lifecycle, viii, 19
lifespan, 42
lifetime, viii, 19, 21, 133
likelihood, viii, 20, 21, 22, 24, 29, 30, 31, 32, 33, 34, 35, 38, 106, 127, 140, 151
limitation, 53
literature, viii, 19, 44, 51, 53, 56, 100, 109, 112, 123, 126, 130, 132, 157
liver, 61, 63, 73
living environment, 26
local community, 123
locus, 44
London, 15, 160
longitudinal study(ies), 23, 39, 54, 126, 127, 151
long-term impact, 55, 111
love, 135, 157
low risk, 117
lung, 62, 67
lying, 70, 74, 122

M

maiming, 84
males, 6, 99, 100, 101
malnutrition, 73, 74
maltreatment, vii, 16, 39, 40, 41, 42, 55, 76, 102, 108, 110, 111, 113, 153, 155, 156, 160, 161, 162
management, 17, 117
marital status, 26, 29, 30, 36, 37
marriage, 47
maternal control, 158
matrix, 140
mean, 22, 26, 27, 35
measurement, 116, 139
measures, viii, xi, 24, 43, 49, 54, 76, 121, 125, 140
media, 87, 110, 152
median, 133
mediation, 144
medical student, 76
membership, 35
memory, 2, 3, 7, 14, 15, 16, 17, 47, 100, 102, 152
memory processes, 7
men, 56, 100, 101, 109, 158
mental age, 3
mental disorder, 106
mental health, 128, 139, 156
mental illness, 102
mental retardation, 14, 15, 16, 17
meta-analysis, 110, 158
metabolism, 63, 64
Mexico, 155
military, 82
milk, 74
minors, ix, 89, 91, 92, 93, 94, 95
modeling, 126
models, 32, 37, 126, 133, 140, 142, 145, 146, 149, 150, 154
moderate activity, 63
moderators, 159
mood, 99, 135
morale, 52
morning, 68
motherhood, 20, 21, 22, 23, 24, 25, 27, 28, 30, 31, 35, 37, 38, 103
mothers, viii, 19, 20, 21, 22, 23, 24, 25, 26, 27, 28, 29, 30, 31, 32, 33, 34, 35, 36, 37, 38, 39, 40, 41, 103, 106, 135, 153, 154, 156, 158, 160
motivation, 17, 126
motives, 123
movement, 123

multidimensional, 139
multiple regression analysis, 49, 50, 54
multivariate, viii, 20, 26, 27, 133, 140, 161
multivariate statistics, 161
murder, 76, 84
muscles, 60
Muslim, 122, 133

N

narratives, 3, 16
nation, 110
National Child Abuse Registry, ix
National Research Council (NRC), 92
Native American, 48
Nebraska, 113
needs, 22, 33, 35, 36, 38
negative consequences, 44, 118
negative emotions, 6
negative outcomes, xii, 102, 122, 125, 131, 148, 150, 151, 152
negative relation, 21
neglect, vii, 39, 40, 41, 59, 60, 75, 76, 104, 105, 106, 109, 112, 155, 157, 162
Netherlands, 17
network, xi, 36, 41, 121, 132, 137, 138, 142, 159
neural connection, 127
neuropsychiatry, 14
New Jersey, 160
New York, 14, 15, 16, 17, 40, 42, 57, 90, 154, 155, 156, 157, 158, 159, 160, 161, 162
New Zealand, 129
newspapers, 46
nightmares, 99, 102, 104
non-clinical population, 101
normal development, 123
North America, 101, 111
Norway, 101
nuclear family, 152
nudity, 92
nurses, 41, 60, 79
nursing, 108
nurturance, 126, 130, 137, 138, 150
nutrition, 78

O

obedience, 127
obligation, ix, 59, 76
offenders, ix, 81, 82, 83, 84, 85, 86, 87

omission, 15
organ, 73
organization(s), 94, 116
orientation, x, 98
Ottawa, 40
outliers, 133, 140

P

Pacific, 38, 111, 160
pain, 6, 76, 122, 134
pairing, 129
parameter, 74
parental control, 129
parental support, 107
Parent-Child Conflict Tactic Scale, xi, 121, 133
parenthood, viii, 19, 22, 32, 41
parenting, viii, xii, 19, 22, 23, 24, 31, 32, 33, 36, 37, 39, 40, 41, 103, 106, 108, 109, 122, 123, 124, 126, 128, 130, 131, 132, 150, 152, 154, 155, 156, 157, 158, 159, 161
parents, xii, 21, 23, 39, 44, 60, 63, 64, 65, 70, 73, 74, 76, 77, 98, 99, 103, 106, 107, 117, 122, 123, 124, 125, 126, 127, 129, 130, 132, 133, 135, 136, 137, 148, 149, 150, 151, 152, 156, 157, 159, 160, 161
parole, 82
PAS stain, 63
passive, 105
pathogenic, 52
pathologist, 78
pathways, 131, 144, 145, 153, 154
pediatrician, 63, 75
peer relationship, 103
peer support, 137
peers, 3, 23, 132, 149, 158, 160
pelvis, 60, 61
penalties, 83, 84
perception(s), xii, 16, 22, 23, 26, 37, 52, 53, 122, 129, 135, 159
performance, 3, 98, 104, 105, 111, 127
perinatal, 39, 40
perpetration, viii, 19
personal, 2, 16, 47, 128
personal history, 128
personality, 21, 32, 42, 105, 128, 130, 135, 150, 154, 156, 157, 159
personality dimensions, 135
perspective, 24, 37, 38
philosophers, 123
phobic anxiety, 104

photographs, 82
physical abuse, vii, xi, 6, 8, 14, 20, 39, 60, 65, 71, 74, 76, 102, 112, 122, 126, 129, 133, 134, 141, 142, 145, 148, 149, 150, 151, 156, 158
physical activity, 63, 64, 75
physical aggression, 158
planning, 107, 108
Poland, x, 115, 116, 117
police, vii, 1, 2, 5, 6, 8, 11, 12, 16, 68, 70, 100, 116
policy makers, 2, 89
poor, 24, 31, 33, 36, 45, 76, 99, 100, 102, 103, 104, 106, 135, 144, 153, 159
population, viii, x, 21, 35, 38, 43, 53, 54, 79, 97, 100, 102, 106, 109, 122, 133, 140, 158
pornography, ix, 83, 84, 85, 86, 89, 90, 92, 94, 95
positive relationship, 20, 130
Post Traumatic Stress Disorder (PTSD), viii, 43, 44, 45, 46, 49, 50, 51, 52, 53, 54, 56, 57
posttraumatic stress, viii, 43, 55, 57, 102, 105, 112
potatoes, 6
poverty, 40, 148, 149
power, 37, 77
predicate, 84, 86
prediction, 24, 38, 41, 111, 153
pregnancy, 22, 23, 34, 37, 41
preschool children, 14, 15
preschoolers, 102
president, 116
pressure, 45, 159
prevention, vii, ix, xi, 19, 20, 31, 36, 38, 41, 59, 77, 81, 87, 108, 109, 111, 115, 116, 117, 118, 119, 152
preventive programs, 152
privacy, 25
probability, 127
problem behavior(s), 106, 154, 158, 161
problem-solving, 53
production, viii, 19, 85, 86
profit(s), 91, 118
program, xii, 14, 17, 36, 83, 87, 122, 133
promote, 90, 107, 124
prophylaxis, xi, 115, 116, 117, 118
protective factors, 102, 128
protein(s), 65, 73, 74
protocol(s), 4, 5, 12, 16
prudence, 148
psychiatric disorders, 109
psychiatric patients, x, 97
psychiatrists, 59, 123
psychoactive, x, xi, 115, 116, 117, 118, 119

psychological distress, 45, 51, 102, 104
psychological health, 118
psychological pain, 134
psychological problems, 103, 107, 132, 149
psychology, 15, 16, 40, 154, 155, 156, 157
psychometric properties, 49, 134, 135, 139
psychopathology, 38, 55, 56, 103, 105, 111, 154, 161
psychosis, 112
Psychosocial Questionnaire (PSQ), xi, 121, 136, 137, 138, 139, 151
psychosomatic, 98, 102, 112
psychotherapy, 47
psychoticism, 104
public awareness, 148
public education, 92
public health, x, 31, 41, 60, 76, 97, 108, 139
public opinion, xi, 116
public support, 76
punishment, xi, xii, 20, 24, 100, 121, 122, 123, 124, 125, 126, 127, 128, 129, 130, 131, 132, 133, 134, 137, 138, 141, 142, 144, 145, 148, 149, 150, 151, 152, 153, 154, 155, 156, 157, 158, 159, 160, 161

Q

quality control, 4, 5, 12
quality of life, 76
questioning, 13, 14
questionnaire(s), 25, 100, 104, 107, 130

R

race, 128
range, x, 44, 46, 47, 65, 68, 69, 83, 97, 100, 101, 103, 115, 123, 129, 140
rape, 57, 83, 109
ratings, 7, 112
reality, 74, 150
reasoning, 127, 129
recall, 2, 3, 4, 7, 11, 12, 14, 16
recall information, 3, 12
recognition, 7, 107
recovery, 55, 111
red blood cells, 68
reduction, 35, 36
reflection, 152
registry(ies), ix, 81
regression, viii, 19, 27, 29, 30, 44, 49, 50, 51, 54
regression analyses(is), viii, 19, 49, 50, 54

regulation, 49, 55, 155
regulations, 82
rehabilitation, 108, 161
rehabilitation program, 108
reinforcement, xi, 116
rejection, 105, 106, 159
relationship(s), viii, xi, 16, 19, 20, 21, 24, 27, 28, 29, 30, 31, 34, 35, 36, 39, 40, 41, 44, 47, 49, 50, 51, 52, 53, 55, 98, 99, 103, 106, 109, 110, 111, 112, 121, 126, 127, 130, 132, 137, 139, 142, 149, 150, 152, 159
relatives, 100
relevance, 125, 142
reliability, 13, 48, 49, 75, 134, 136, 137, 139
religion, 128
research design, 104, 151
reserves, 65, 74
residuals, 140
resilience, 44, 47, 54, 55, 110, 128
resistance, 157
resolution, 21, 25, 132
resources, xi, 5, 33, 52, 116, 118
respiratory, 71
response, 35
responsibility, 25, 31, 34
retardation, 14, 15, 16, 17
retention, 13, 102
rewards, 123
risk, vii, viii, ix, 2, 13, 19, 20, 21, 22, 23, 24, 26, 27, 29, 31, 33, 35, 36, 37, 38, 39, 40, 42, 43, 47, 49, 53, 55, 59, 76, 83, 95, 99, 102, 104, 105, 106, 107, 108, 111, 117, 128, 129, 152, 160
risk behaviors, 49
risk factor(s), 39, 47, 106, 107, 108, 128, 160
romantic involvements, 161
Root Mean Square Residual, 140
rural communities, 154

S

safety, ix, 45, 76, 81, 83, 86, 105, 107
sample, viii, xi, 8, 19, 21, 22, 24, 25, 41, 47, 48, 49, 53, 82, 100, 112, 122, 133, 140, 141, 151, 160, 161
sample variance, 140
sampling, xi, 122, 133
scaling, 140
schema, 56
schizophrenia, 47

Index

school, x, xi, 14, 22, 26, 27, 28, 31, 35, 48, 65, 75, 76, 82, 89, 90, 92, 98, 102, 103, 105, 106, 111, 119, 121, 123, 132, 133, 137, 139, 151, 152, 155
school performance, 111
science, 123, 159
sclera, 60
scores, 20, 45, 49, 50, 102
search, ix, 81, 91
search engine, 91
search terms, 91
searches, 83
secondary education, 27, 36
secondary prophylaxis, 117
security, 82
selection, 25
self, viii, 19, 22, 23, 24, 25, 26, 28, 29, 31, 32, 36, 37, 38, 39, 40, 41, 42
self worth, viii, 43, 51, 53
self-destruction, 56
self-efficacy, 55
self-esteem, viii, 19, 22, 23, 24, 25, 26, 28, 29, 31, 32, 36, 37, 38, 39, 41, 99, 100, 102, 103, 104, 105, 135, 136
self-image, 52
self-perceptions, 23, 52, 53
self-reports, 152
self-worth, 36, 45, 46, 50, 54
sensitivity, 23, 104
sentencing, ix, 81, 84
separation, 34
series, xi, 93, 115, 118, 124, 156
severity, 20, 45, 46, 52, 56, 133, 150, 160
sex, viii, ix, x, 2, 15, 41, 43, 50, 81, 82, 83, 84, 85, 86, 87, 92, 94, 97, 98
sex offenders, ix, 81, 84, 86, 87
sexual, 41
sexual abuse, vii, viii, x, 2, 5, 6, 8, 13, 14, 15, 16, 17, 43, 44, 45, 46, 47, 49, 51, 52, 54, 55, 56, 57, 76, 84, 85, 87, 97, 98, 99, 100, 101, 102, 103, 104, 105, 106, 107, 108, 109, 110, 111, 112, 113, 137
sexual activity(ies), 41, 84
sexual behavior, 47, 100, 102
sexual contact, 85, 91, 92
sexual experiences, 100
sexual harassment, 6
sexual intercourse, x, 97, 99, 100
sexual violence, 59, 106
sexually transmitted diseases, 76
shame, viii, x, 43, 45, 46, 47, 50, 51, 52, 53, 54, 55, 98

sharing, 95, 113
shock, 66, 68
shy, 98
sibling(s), 41, 99, 100, 107, 108, 152
side effects, 158
signs, ix, 59, 60, 76, 100, 128
sites, 91, 92, 93, 94, 95
situation, 31, 32
skills, 3, 17, 22, 36, 41, 53, 105, 106, 108, 117, 118, 132, 149
skin, 65, 66, 67
sleep disorders, 104
sleep disturbance, 99
small intestine, 60
smoke, 103, 112
smoking, 103, 109
social attitudes, 45, 60
social behavior, 126, 154
social capital, 161
social cognition, 56
social conflicts, 149
social context, 40, 110
social development, 156, 157, 158
social environment, 112
social factors, xi, 14, 41, 116, 117
social isolation, 52
social life, 106
social network, 41
social policy, xii, 122, 152
social problems, 99
social roles, 116
social security, 82
Social Services, ix, 59, 76
social structure, 148
social support, 26, 37, 41, 44, 52, 56, 102, 112, 138
social support network, 138
social welfare, 149
social withdrawal, 52, 100
social workers, 59
socialisation, 157
socialization, 105, 124
society, 35, 37, 105, 116, 124, 126, 152, 156
software, 82, 92, 95
solidarity, 148
somatization, 104
South Korea, 97, 99, 107, 110
Spain, 101
special education, 102
specialization, xi, 116
specificity, 56, 117

speech, 90, 92, 127
sperm, 92
spirituality, 44
SPSS, 139, 160
Sri Lanka, xi, xii, 121, 122, 123, 125, 132, 133, 134, 135, 136, 139, 148, 149, 150, 151, 152, 153, 154, 155, 160
stages, 26, 27, 36, 44
standard deviation, 8, 9, 10, 49
standards, ix, 52, 81, 91
starvation, 60, 75, 78
statistics, 41, 49, 137, 161
statute of limitations, 84
statutes, 84
stigma, 55
stigmatized, 52
stomach, 60, 70, 71, 72
strategies, 13, 36, 41, 52, 56, 105, 108, 112, 118, 122, 129, 133, 149, 156, 161
strength, 129, 140, 149
stress, viii, 33, 34, 43, 52, 53, 55, 56, 57, 74, 78, 102, 105, 112, 117, 132, 149, 152, 159
stressful events, 16
stressful life events, 102
stressors, 36, 104
students, x, xi, 76, 97, 100, 110, 112, 115, 116, 117, 118, 119, 155
subcutaneous tissue, 71
subgroups, 76
subpoena, 92
substance abuse, 39, 47, 102, 103, 105, 106, 112
substance use, 116
suffering, 74, 107
suicidal ideation, 99, 160
suicide, 68, 103, 126
suicide attempts, 103
summaries, 2
summer, 70
supervision, 4, 5, 11, 12, 13, 15, 89, 153
supervisors, 54
supply, 35
suppression, 126
Supreme Court, ix, 89, 90, 91, 92, 94
surveillance, 40, 42, 108
survivors, viii, 43, 44, 45, 46, 51, 52, 53, 54, 56, 57, 103, 105, 109, 110, 112
suspects, 6, 7, 17
Sweden, 1, 2, 4, 13, 159
swelling, 65, 66

symptom(s), viii, 43, 44, 45, 46, 49, 50, 51, 52, 53, 54, 55, 76, 98, 102, 104, 107, 128
syndrome, 78, 99
synthesis, 109, 110
systems, 87, 92, 155

T

tactics, 155, 160
teachers, 60, 76, 107, 123, 124, 125, 132, 135, 139, 149
technical assistance, 87
teens, 37
Telecommunications Act, 90
telephone, 101
temperament, 127, 128, 129
territory, 82
test scores, 102
test-retest reliability, 48, 49, 134
theory, viii, xi, 19, 21, 22, 23, 24, 26, 31, 35, 55, 105, 116, 117, 127, 156, 157
therapists, 54, 107
therapy, 47, 152
thinking, 52
threat, 25, 100
thymocytes, 74
thymus, 60, 67, 74
tibia, 71, 73
time, vii, ix, 1, 12, 13, 20, 21, 22, 25, 26, 32, 34, 36, 44, 45, 63, 65, 74, 75, 82, 89, 93, 102, 116, 117, 123, 124, 128, 132, 133, 134, 152, 153, 154
time constraints, 133, 153
tissue, 60
toddlers, 102, 154
Tokyo, 78, 79
trade, 27, 48
training, vii, 1, 2, 4, 5, 8, 10, 12, 13, 14, 15, 16, 17, 23, 76, 118
training programs, 4
transcripts, 5, 7
transformation, x, 56, 115
transition(s), 20, 24
translation, 158
transmission, 132, 155
trauma, 46, 51, 52, 53, 57, 102, 107, 108, 110
traumatic events, 2, 46, 53, 56
traumatic experiences, 14
treatment programs, viii, 43, 44, 152
trend, 101
trial, 91

Index

tribal, ix, 81, 82, 86, 87
trust, 45, 130
Type I error, 54
typology, 108, 111, 159

U

UK, 14, 16, 21, 154
underestimation, x, 97
undergraduate, 55, 76
unemployment, 23, 29, 32, 39, 40
uniform, ix, 81, 82
United Kingdom, 1, 21, 39
United Nations, 161
United States, 4, 20, 21, 32, 33, 34, 37, 40, 75, 82, 93, 101
univariate, 140
universities, 116, 117
university students, 100, 110
urine, 60
users, 91, 95, 117
utterances, 7

V

validation, viii, 43, 49, 134, 135, 137, 155
validity, 35, 49, 140
values, 105, 123, 124, 126, 134, 136, 140, 142, 156, 157, 158, 159
variability, 128
variable(s), viii, 19, 22, 24, 25, 26, 27, 28, 29, 30, 32, 33, 34, 35, 36, 37, 38, 44, 46, 49, 50, 51, 52, 53, 54, 111, 128, 130, 132, 136, 139, 141, 142, 143, 144, 146, 148, 153, 159
variance, viii, 30, 44, 50, 51, 52, 138, 140
variation, 6, 154
vehicles, 82
veterans, 56
victimization, x, 87, 97, 103, 105, 110, 112, 150
victims, x, 2, 4, 5, 6, 8, 11, 15, 16, 17, 46, 52, 53, 55, 56, 57, 60, 76, 78, 84, 98, 99, 100, 101, 102, 103, 104, 105, 106, 107, 108, 109, 112, 157
violence, xi, 25, 40, 59, 68, 83, 84, 104, 106, 108, 109, 110, 121, 122, 123, 126, 131, 132, 133, 136, 137, 138, 139, 142, 145, 148, 149, 150, 152, 155, 156, 157, 159, 160, 161
vocational training, 23
vulva, 60

W

war, 149
warrants, 82
Washington, 16, 41, 56, 158, 161
web, 42
websites, 92, 94, 95
weight gain, 63, 75
welfare, ix, 59, 60, 76, 149
welfare system, 149
West Indies, 159
Western countries, 100, 102, 105, 106, 107
Western Europe, 101
windows, 137
winter, 60
Wisconsin, 157
withdrawal, 52, 98, 100, 102
witnesses, 3, 13, 14, 16, 17, 151, 157
women, viii, 21, 25, 26, 27, 28, 30, 31, 32, 33, 34, 35, 36, 37, 38, 43, 46, 47, 48, 49, 54, 55, 56, 57, 100, 101, 103, 104, 108, 109, 112, 154
words, 30, 32, 33
workers, 14, 60, 76, 77, 107
World Health Organisation, 157
worldview, x, 98, 106
wrists, 67, 71, 74
writing, 91

Y

yes/no, vii, 1, 12, 137
yield, 84
young adults, xi, 111, 116, 118